# Garden Plots

# Garden Plots

Canadian Women Writers and Their Literary Gardens

SHELLEY BOYD

McGill-Queen's University Press

Montreal & Kingston • London • Ithaca

© McGill-Queen's University Press 2013
ISBN 978-0-7735-4126-9 (cloth)
ISBN 978-0-7735-4156-6 (paper)
ISBN 978-0-7735-8870-7 (ePDF)
ISBN 978-0-7735-8871-4 (ePUB)

Legal deposit second quarter 2013
Bibliothèque nationale du Québec

Printed in Canada on acid-free paper that is 100% ancient forest free (100% post-consumer recycled), processed chlorine free

This book has been published with the help of a grant from the Canadian Federation for the Humanities and Social Sciences, through the Awards to Scholarly Publications Program, using funds provided by the Social Sciences and Humanities Research Council of Canada.

McGill-Queen's University Press acknowledges the support of the Canada Council for the Arts for our publishing program. We also acknowledge the financial support of the Government of Canada through the Canada Book Fund for our publishing activities.

Library and Archives Canada Cataloguing in Publication

Boyd, Shelley, 1974- . Garden plots : Canadian women writers and their literary gardens / Shelley Boyd. Includes bibliographical references and index.
ISBN 978-0-7735-4126-9 (bound). – ISBN 978-0-7735-4156-6 (pbk.)
ISBN 978-0-7735-8870-7 (ePDF). – ISBN 978-0-7735-8871-4 (ePUB)
1. Canadian literature – Women authors – History and criticism. 2. Gardens in literature. I. Title.
PS8101.G37B69 2013    C810.9'364    C2013-900712-1

Book designed by Pata Macedo
Illustrations by Olavo Moe de Macedo Collins
Set in Minion Pro 11/14

For Mom and Dad, and my Saskatchewan roots

# Contents

# Illustrations

# Acknowledgments

This book was made possible through the guidance and support of many people. Foremost, I would like to thank Nathalie Cooke at McGill University for her insight and enthusiasm during the various stages of this research. I could not have asked for a better supervisor, colleague, and friend. It was my distinct privilege and pleasure to work with you. Thank you also to McGill-Queen's University Press for their diligence and creativity, and especially to Philip Cercone for his patience and skill. The two anonymous reviewers' comments proved invaluable in giving this "plot" direction and shape, as did Susan Glickman's fine pruning of the manuscript.

I would like to thank Catherine Hobbs, Lynn Lafontaine, Monique Ostiguay, Jean Matheson, and Helen Gillespie at Library and Archives Canada for their assistance with primary research in the Traill Family Collection and the Fonds Gabrielle Roy. Warm thanks are also due to Elizabeth Seitz at the University of Regina Library for her assistance with the Lorna Crozier archives. I acknowledge Library and Archives Canada for the materials reprinted from the Traill Family Collection and the Patrick Hamilton Ewing Collection of Moodie-Strickland-Vickers-Ewing Family Papers. I especially thank François Ricard for his kindness and generosity, as well as the (c) Fonds Gabrielle Roy for permission to reprint the Gabrielle Roy images and text. I also acknowledge the McGill University Rare Books and Special Collections for providing the illustration from Jane Loudon's *Instructions in Gardening for Ladies,* and Barb Hall for the poster of the SATCO theatre's production of *The Sex Lives of Vegetables.*

I am grateful to Lorna Crozier for permission to reprint archival material and excerpts from many garden poems published in *Inside Is the Sky, The Garden Going On Without Us, Everything Arrives at the Light, Apocrypha of Light,* and *A Saving Grace: The Collected Poems of Mrs. Bentley.* I also acknowledge Random House of Canada for granting copyright permission for the poems excerpted from *The Blue Hour of the Day* by Lorna Crozier. Copyright (c) 2007 Lorna Crozier. Reprinted by permission of McClelland and Stewart. I would like to thank Margaret Atwood and her publishers for permission for the following: portions of five poems from *The Journals of Susanna Moodie.* Reprinted by permission of Margaret Atwood. Available in the UK in *Eating Fire,* (c) 1998 O.W.Toad Ltd, published by Virago Press. Atwood, Margaret, *The Journals of Susanna Moodie,* Copyright 1970 (c) Oxford University Press Canada 2005. Reprinted by permission of the publisher. "Dream 1: The Bush Garden" and "The Double Voice" *The Journals of Susanna Moodie* by Margaret Atwood. Copyright (c) 1976 by Oxford University Press. Reprinted by permission of Houghton Mifflin Harcourt Publishing Company. All rights reserved. Finally, I acknowledge the permission to reprint excerpts from "Pumpkin: A Love Poem" from *Stone Hammer Poems 1960–1975* by Robert Kroetsch (Oolichan Books, 1975). Copyright (c) 1975 Robert Kroetsch. With permission of the author.

This book has been published with the help of a grant from the Canadian Federation for the Humanities and Social Sciences, through the Awards to Scholarly Publications Program, using funds provided by the Social Sciences and Humanities Research Council of Canada. The Department of English at McGill University, the McGill Institute for the Study of Canada, the *Groupe de recherche sur Gabrielle Roy* (in the French Language and Literature Department at McGill University), and the Max Bell Foundation provided generous financial support for this research, which I undertook during my doctoral studies and post-doctoral fellowship. Both the McGill Institute for the Study of Canada (under the direction of Antonia Maioni and William Straw) and the *Groupe de recherche sur Gabrielle Roy* (under the direction of François Ricard, Jane Everett, and Sophie Marcotte) provided energizing, collegial communities, and I am grateful to have been a member of their teams.

Some of my research has appeared in *English Studies in Canada* 32.4 (2006): 189–211, as "Domestic Gardening: Gabrielle Roy's Bower of Innocence in *Enchantment and Sorrow*"; in Françoise Le Jeune, and Charlotte Sturgess, eds., *Her Na-rra-tion, Women's Narratives of the Canadian Nation* (Nantes, Canadensis series 3, editions du CRINI, 2009): 71–87, as "Carol Shields and the Quest for Paradise in Canadian Suburbia"; and in *Essays on Canadian Writing* 84 (Fall 2009): 35–57, as "'Transplanted into Our Gardens': Susanna Moodie and Catharine Parr Traill."

The pursuit of this research was enriched through many friends, including Tricia Antonini, Lorna Hutchison, and Medrie Purdham, who served as constructive sounding-boards; and Stéphanie Roesler, who edited my translations of the French passages in chapter three. To my parents, Keith and Marilyn Boyd, thank you for your endless support and encouragement that made this garden possible.

# Garden Plots

# Garden Plots

Gardening, reading about gardening, and writing about gardening
are all one; no one can garden alone
Elizabeth Lawrence
(quoted in Elliott, *The Quotable Gardener* 18)

The garden has long maintained a curious, archetypal presence in the field of Canadian literature. With Northrop Frye's 1971 publication *The Bush Garden: Essays on the Canadian Imagination*, the "bush garden" quickly became emblematic of a distinctly Canadian literary imagination and its struggle for an authentic, national expression befitting the environment. Frye admitted in the preface that he had "pilfered" this garden image "from Margaret Atwood's *Journals of Susanna Moodie*, a book unusually rich in suggestive phrases defining a Canadian sensibility" (x). In Atwood's famous poem, "Dream 1: The Bush Garden," the Upper Canadian pioneer writer, Susanna Moodie, finds herself in her re-imagined (and failed) backwoods garden, "sold, deserted and / gone to seed" (34). This highly literary terrain encapsulates an oppositional struggle between nature (the unruly wilderness) and civilization (the orderly garden) that Frye believed was "organic" to Canadian writers' sensibilities (219).[1] Ironically, Frye was not so interested in examining the garden, even as he used its image to promote a wilderness myth structured by "a physical or psychological 'frontier'" (225).

Frye's influence soon manifested itself in the works of other critics who echoed his assertion: the wilderness was of primary significance to the Canadian imagination. When Atwood produced her own thematic interpretation of Canadian literature in *Survival* (1972), for instance, the extreme challenges of the wilderness remained at the forefront, but "Nature the Divine Mother," she acknowledged, rarely makes an appearance in the Canadian experience and is "not much help with the vegetable garden" (51). Eventually, this line of criticism met with critics' derision. In 1983, Frank Davey's pivotal denouncement in his essay "Surviving the Paraphrase" urged Canadian literary scholars to pursue rigourous study of the formal aspects of texts. And in 1999, John Moss argued that the "bush garden of Canadian letters" systematized the canon according to national traits, "obscuring rather than enhancing the luminescence of individual works" (23). Nonetheless, the bush garden remains a formative symbol of the early promotion and conceptualization of the Canadian canon, even though this archetype has very little to do with a close investigation of garden terrain, its possible functions, its many forms, or its significance.

While the bush garden archetype lingers in Canadian literary history, the second topic of garden-related discussion that has circulated continuously since the 1960s concerns an idealized paradise. In *The Gay]Grey Moose*, D.M.R. Bentley suggests that John Milton's *Paradise Lost* has profoundly shaped many Canadian texts, particularly those of the settlement period: "Milton's epic is the quintessential English poem of transplantation and adaptation. As it opens, Satan and his followers are faced with the task of assessing, exploring, and accommodating themselves to an environment that must have appeared to many unhappy exiles and emigrants to Canada to resemble their new home in its extremes of heat and cold, its gloomy sublimity, and its overall unpleasantness" (123).[2] By playing such a prominent role in the writing of the "new world," the paradise archetype is a central part of Canadian literature's early mythology and remains a pervasive theme, finding new expressions across different periods and contexts.[3]

Although the versatility of this garden myth appeals to a range of Canadian writers, it also readily traverses national traditions. By way of comparison, American literature scholar Annette Kolodny examines paradisal visions of the American western frontier. In these fictional narratives, male writers frequently create a solitary Adam "intent on possessing a virgin continent," while women writers generate fantasies in which "the garden implie[s] home and community, not privatized erotic mastery" (xiii). In contrast, with respect to the many "Adam" and "Eve" figures who populate Canadian literature, critics perceive clear idiosyncrasies relating to the difficult construction of a national imagination. In Bentley's view, Canada's "Adam" poets did not always experience "an entirely happy fit between words and things" (*The Gay]Grey* 124). Similarly, in *Butterfly on Rock* D.G. Jones describes a model of a troubled Adam: the exiled, sleeping, and dreaming Adam of Canadian literature who longs for a yet-unrealized new world order (15). Alternatively, Robert Kroetsch suggests in his essay "No Name Is My Name" that Canada's "Eden" was discovered in a second-hand fashion encumbered by other literary traditions: "It may well be that Canadian writing owes its first debt to the model of Eve ... Eve is created into the world after Adam has been created – and after the naming has been done. The Canadian writer in English must speak a new culture not with new names but with an abundance of names inherited from Britain and the United States" (50–1).[4] Taking Kroetsch's "model of Eve" a step further, I reconsider how early Canadian women authors and their contemporary counterparts function as veritable writing "Eves," not necessarily hampered in their expression by other cultural influences, but rather, innovative in their experimentations with form and their inscriptions of gendered experiences, daily life, and especially domestic surroundings.

With such emphasis on archetypal gardens with respect to the environment on a large scale (the wilderness "bush garden," or the "paradise" of the new world), the garden as a relatively more immediate terrain is often overlooked, effaced, or viewed as inconsequential in terms of writers' strategies and social critiques. Consequently, my interest lies in depictions of private domestic gardens as tended by individual gardeners. By the term domestic garden, I mean gardens that are immediate (proximate to the home), modest in scale, and tended for both practical and aesthetic reasons. These gardens play a vital role in the work and expression that take place within daily living and include a number of different kinds of gardens, such as kitchen gardens, flower gardens, and suburban lawns. This study's foregrounding of the domestic garden within the context of Canadian literary studies emulates a shift in focus onto vernacular landscapes that garden historians have long been promoting. In "The Postmodernization of Landscape," Dianne Harris notes, "Until quite recently, most landscape history focused on the elites and elite culture; this seemed almost inevitable, since archives are structured and preserved by wealthy and powerful members of societies, and elaborate gardens tend to be preserved longer than the ordinary yards of average folk" (438). With the development of this "'new garden history,'" Harris urges critics to embrace "a broader context and us[e] a wider and more questioning range of documents and sources" (438).

In the context of Canadian garden history, this approach can be seen in such studies as Carol Martin's *A History of Canadian Gardening* or Eileen Woodhead's *Early Canadian Gardening: An 1827 Nursery Catalogue*. Both employ a range of documents (photographs, drawings and paintings, anecdotes, or commercial catalogues) in order to tell the multifaceted, evolving story of everyday gardening in Canada. By way of complementing this kind of historical analysis of material gardens, my study looks to extend the potential sources and locations of Canada's gardening culture by revealing that gardens exist not simply in the actual landscape but also in the Canadian literary imagination. These literary gardens represent diverse expressions, deeply informative of writers' socio-temporal and especially gendered contexts. The fact that many of these terrains have been either ignored or over-written by early conceptualizations of the wilderness suggests that women writers, through their individual and inter-related contributions, need reassessment as inventive shapers of the Canadian literary tradition.

In response to popular archetypes, my project brings alternative uses of the garden as theme, trope, and setting into the fold of garden-related criticism. Specifically, my strategy is to cross-fertilize literary criticism with garden history and theory in order to generate a further appreciation of the role that gardens play in literature and their formal textual effects. The affinity between gardening and writing is something garden historians and theorists as well as authors have promoted for centuries. For example, John Dixon Hunt reflects in his essay "*Paragone* in Paradise: Translating the Garden" that a garden frequently "invokes words – in its inscriptions, its nomination of temples and fountains – as well as demands verbal formulations to recount our experience of it" (55). Furthermore, when it comes to the practicalities of research,

Hunt argues, "literary critics and art historians … have been most busy in the garden" because of the "fragility of gardens" and the fact that they are "largely studied through the written or graphic records of them" (56). Writing compensates for an actual garden's transitory nature, but the relationship between writing and gardening extends to the theorizing of how these comparable arts function. Many scholars reference Horace Walpole (1717–97) who famously wrote, "Poetry, Painting, and Gardening … will forever by men of Taste be deemed Three Sisters, or the *Three New Graces* who dress and adorn Nature" (in Hunt and Willis 11).[5] This statement operates as an extension of *Ars Poetica*: Horace's insistence on the relationship between the arts of poetry and painting. In Walpole's view, writers, visual artists, and gardeners all hold a deep appreciation for the artistic arrangements, effects, and meaning of their respective media.

Gardens invite interpretation, as do works of literature, and landscape critics urge us to "read" gardens as kinds of texts. As Charles W. Moore, William J. Mitchell, and William Turnbull write in *The Poetics of Gardens,* "Gardens are rhetorical landscapes. They are made of the same materials as all the rest, just as the rhetorician's words are those given by language, but they are composed to instruct and move and delight (Cicero's definitions of the rhetorician's duties). We can read gardens for content, and we can analyze the devices of structure and figure and trope by means of which they achieve their effects" (49).[6] Because the garden functions as a kind of readable "text," it follows that not only plants thrive within it, but also the thorny issues of class, gender, religion, and politics – those values and ideologies pertaining to the social context in and from which the garden takes its form. A Canadian example of this kind of rhetorical analysis of actual gardens can be seen in Edwinna von Baeyer's *Rhetoric and Roses: A History of Canadian Gardening* (1984) in which she argues that "twentieth-century garden promoters created rather public [garden] refuges, noisy with rhetoric" (176). Von Baeyer points to the Canadian Pacific Railway station gardens that were cultivated during the early decades of the twentieth century as a means of social persuasion. These green-spaces demonstrated the fertility of the western prairies in the hope of attracting settlers and investment (14). Walpole's famous statement about the three "sister arts" speaks, of course, to the social values of his own eighteenth-century English milieu in which the most notable practitioners of these three arts were men, particularly when it came to the profession of garden designer. Meanwhile the three sister arts are personified as women, and the acts of dressing and adorning are directed at an equally personified and feminized "Nature" who requires arrangement and embellishment. Nature as property is controlled by male authority, just as the three feminine figures of poetry, painting, and gardening are directed by male artists.[7]

While such comparisons between writing, rhetoric, and garden design serve to illuminate the shared manner in which different art forms operate, they also invite further crossings between disciplinary boundaries. One significant path of inquiry comes from Hunt's discussion in *Greater Perfections: The Practice of Garden Theory* of a symbolic "arithmetic of 'three natures'" that developed in the mid-sixteenth century and is "meant to indicate ... that a territory can be viewed in the light of how it has or has not been treated in space and in time" (35). Hunt points to two Italian writers, Bartolomeo Taegio and Jacopo Bonfadio, who independently but at around the same time (1559 and 1541, respectively), created the term *terza natura* or "third nature" in reference to Italian villa gardens so as to place the garden "in a scale or hierarchy of human intervention into the physical world: gardens became more sophisticated, more deliberate, and more complex in their mixture of culture and nature than agricultural land" (34).[8] This conceptualization of the garden was both an allusion to and an extension of Cicero's *De natura deorum*, in which human manipulations, such as the diversion of rivers and the irrigation of fields, create a "second nature within the world of nature" in which human society comfortably situates itself and derives benefit (Cicero 102–3). To clarify this "arithmetic" of nature, one must remember that first nature, or the wilderness, according to Hunt, is "unmediated, untouched, and primal, in reality or imagination," which in Cicero's understanding is "both the raw materials of human industry and the territory of the gods" (*Greater* 58, 34).[9] First nature is followed by second nature: the socio-cultural landscape, or "places where humans have made over the environment for the purposes of survival and habitation, where labor and productivity dominate and where the traces of that work are everywhere visible" (*Greater* 59). To these physical manipulations of the landscape, I would add that the human imagination and its conventional ways of perceiving further constitute what is "second nature" by enabling us to familiarize ourselves and function within a shared socio-cultural environment. The phrase "second nature," in my view, not only signifies a numerical categorization but also connotes what is habitual, familiar, or "second nature" in day-to-day life. Finally, third nature, according to Hunt, refers to gardens as concentrated "human interventions" in the world of first and second nature by involving "specific intention"; these interventions include "some relative elaboration of formal ingredients above functional needs; some conjunction of metaphysical experience with physical forms, specifically some aesthetic endeavor – the wish or need to make a site beautiful" (*Greater* 62). Hunt sees this model as "a sliding scale of cultural intervention in the natural world" and there can be "interpenetration or porousness" between the three territories (*Greater* 63, 64). What sets the third nature of the garden apart from the other natures, however, is that it is "best considered as existing in terms of the other two" and "is always engaged in a dialogue" with them (*Greater* 71).

The "third nature" of a garden provides, therefore, a significant interpretive lens as much as it presents a potentially pleasurable, ideally manipulated kind of space. According to Hunt in "*Paragone in Paradise*," the garden is a mimetic art by virtue of being "related to the other two [natures] – by its representation of them" (60–1). These representations can be both literal and figurative by operating, for instance, as a miniature model of landscape features beyond its boundaries (60), or by standing in as a figurative expression "of the owner's position in the world" in keeping with Thomas Fuller's famous adage "'As is the gardener, so is the garden'" (62). In *The Meaning of Gardens: Idea, Place, and Action*, professors of landscape architecture Mark Francis and Randolph T. Hester similarly proclaim the mimetic aspects of gardens in their description of them as analogues of the human subject: "Gardens are mirrors of ourselves, reflections of sensual and personal experience. By making gardens, using or admiring them, and dreaming about them, we create our own idealized order of nature and culture" (2). Through a garden we look to understand the situation and experience of the human subject within his or her surroundings and acquire a renewed perspective of what we consider to be the norm. Social and cultural values imbue a garden, making it truly an art of milieu and a space of heightened expression. As Hunt states in *Gardens and the Picturesque*, "Each phase of garden art is culturally specific, determined by ... ideas and events few of which are explicitly horticultural or architectural: they may be political, social, economic, religious" (9). The garden takes root in the larger context of "second nature" and potentially departs from it as a space of critical and creative reflection. In other words, through its proximate yet distinct perspective, the third nature of the garden reveals, questions, and potentially transforms what is habitual and familiar (our "second nature" experience and perceptions of daily life), as well as mediates our relationship with the supposedly less known, the "first nature" of the wilderness.

When emphasizing the culturally expressive and critical properties of a third nature, garden theorists consistently ground their models in the materiality of their subject. At its most fundamental level, a garden operates as both a physical and conceptual space of the in-between, combining both nature and culture, the given and the constructed environment. These two categories are not, of course, diametrically opposed, as Hunt's model of three natures "actively discourages the belief that nature is normative rather than culturally constructed" (*Greater* 51). There are, however, undeniable forces of nature readily encountered in the garden. In his study of place, Edward Casey highlights the inherent paradox, indirectly touching on the relational art of the garden with respect to the model of three natures: "Even if I am not yet in the wilderness in a garden I am in the presence of things that live and grow, often according to their own schedule" (154).

But how does this concept of the garden as a third nature, realized in both a material and cultural sense, apply to gardens composed not through plants, but through words? Just as Hunt asserts that the third nature of an actual garden is inextricably tied to its larger context of second nature, literary gardens uphold this same principle. Gardens depicted in literature – through both their form and content – are reflective of the socio-physical environments and time frames both in and of which authors write. For instance, the box lawns of twentieth-century Canadian suburbia that Carol Shields describes in her novels (chapter four) could not appear in the nineteenth-century backwoods kitchen garden as related by Susanna Moodie and Catharine Parr Traill (chapter one). In addition to the socio-physical context inherently tied to a garden's depiction, literary traditions also form a significant part of a textual garden. Hence, while the popular nineteenth-century trope of the "cultivated" woman influences Traill's writing of the garden, Robert Kroetsch's twentieth-century, post-modern reinterpretation of Traill brings a radically different vision to bear on this pioneer garden and its presentation of gender (chapter two). A literary garden has, therefore, different contexts at play: the socio-cultural and physical framework depicted in the text, and the larger milieus, including the literary, in which a text is originally produced and later circulates.

Herein lies an important distinction between an actual garden and a literary garden: while garden theorists understand gardens as situated, cultural artifacts, literary gardens are extremely portable. In *What Gardens Mean*, Stephanie Ross defines real gardens as unique works of art because they cannot "be notated, moved, forged or replicated because they are ever-changing and because they are site specific" (19). Ross' conclusions draw upon some of Mara Miller's assertions in *The Garden as an Art* where she suggests definitive qualities of gardens are a lack of consistency (because of their ephemeral nature; 76), and spatial location, since "differences in microclimate, in soil composition, in drainage make it difficult to reproduce a given garden somewhere else ... while differences in surrounding buildings or vistas contribute distinctive backgrounds that are integral to our overall impression of the garden" (75–6). In contrast to the materiality and temporality of a garden, a literary garden travels across time and space, and while this suggests a certain level of permanence, it is important to reiterate that gardens in literature can also, in effect, "change" when alternative interpretations – which can be in the form of criticism or creative works – engage with them.

In addition to being a context-specific art by virtue of being tied to the social, cultural, and literary milieus (but not absolutely to the physical locale), a literary garden also has the potential to function as a third nature on multiple levels. Actual gardens offer concentrated, artistic expressions of the human subject's relationship to, and experience in, the larger cultural landscape of second nature. A literary garden may similarly be endowed with this exceptional status, serving as an interpretive lens through which central concerns of a text as a whole may be reflected in a heightened manner and, therefore, more readily perceived and experienced on the part of a character, a reader, or both. A garden setting (as a literary version of third nature) can disclose and diverge from the larger socio-cultural landscape, or "second nature," depicted in the text, particularly if the garden in question is a differentiated zone where expression is imperative to its form and function. However, this third nature role extends well beyond the frameworks of individual texts. Because literary gardens are portable (as opposed to actual gardens that are site-specific), they enter into different temporal contexts. In doing so, literary gardens have the capacity to operate on multiple levels simultaneously, both in the text and at the level of the text, in effect allowing the garden to serve as a model for the writing itself. This figurative capacity means they extend their third nature role to reveal not only changing socio-cultural contexts of literary production in Canada but also popular modes of interpretation, or "second nature" ways of reading Canadian literature, at various points in time. In this way, literary gardens (at all levels) are important documents of cultural and artistic work across time and space, particularly in terms of the different expressions they facilitate and the responses they evoke depending on the writers' and readers' motivations and altering contexts.

When garden scholars point to the inter-relationship between gardening and writing, they inevitably promote the unique nature of the garden, foreseeing limitations in a purely textual version. According to Anna-Teresa Tymieniecka, the garden is a profoundly personal, tangible art form "manifesting in the world ... our inward dispositions that *no words can express*" (15, emphasis added). Hunt similarly argues, "Words do not cope well if at all with celebrating the formal effects of gardens, the mix of vegetation and built items, the passage of light, and the visual effects of seasons" (*Greater* 171). Inevitably, one cannot physically smell or touch a flower through a poem or short story; I believe, however, that authors can and do draw upon the formal and conceptual aspects of gardens to shape their writing. In response to theorists who describe actual gardens as rhetorical, material "texts" open to interpretation, I suggest that the inverse is possible: text-as-garden. In this way, many of the formal aspects of real gardens transform into textual features and effects in literary works, such as spatial frames, figurative language, dramatic staging, and other devices.

One way of representing this complex intersection between writing and gardening is through the concept of a "plot." The *Oxford English Dictionary* defines "plot" as a "fairly small piece of ground" cultivated in a particular locale and circumstance. With respect to garden work, the verb "to plot" also means "To draw or make a plan of (something to be laid out, constructed, or made)."[10] Alternatively, in its literary sense according to M.H. Abrams' *Glossary of Literary Terms*, "plot" refers to how "events and actions ... are rendered and ordered toward achieving particular artistic and emotional effects" (224). These events and actions are the means by which characters "exhibit their moral and dispositional qualities," suggesting that "[p]lot and character are ... interdependent critical concepts" (224). In the context of this interdisciplinary study therefore, the use of the term "plot" emphasizes the *strategic writing of place* as a means of both situating and constructing characters in texts engaged with social, cultural, and physical circumstances: in other words, that which is depicted as "second nature" with respect to a particular period and locale. Within the individual "plots" featured in this study, the writers contribute through both literal and figurative means, using garden settings, horticultural metaphors, and textual reinterpretations of actual gardens' formal features and processes (such as their role as informal theatrical venues or their ever-changing material nature). The relationship between gardening and writing is made explicit by the authors in this study, and their strategies contribute to a heightened, critical means of expression: a differentiated garden "plot" (or literary equivalent of third nature) that operates strategically within the larger frameworks of their texts and serves as a model for the texts themselves. Ultimately, my tracing of these literary gardens across different periods of Canadian literature includes their reconfigurations by other writers and critics within dramatically altered contexts. The portability and dynamism of these "plots" are precisely what contribute to a long tradition of garden writing in Canada.

By way of narrowing my study, I have chosen to focus on five Canadian women authors and how they employ garden "plots" in their preoccupation with women's experiences, relationships to the domestic, and changing gender roles during periods of social upheaval or ideological transition. This emphasis on women serves to illuminate their significant yet oftentimes overlooked contributions to the Canadian literary tradition as innovators of form and story-telling. In the past, many of these literary gardens were either dismissed or overwritten by critics who promoted the wilderness (first nature) as the distinctive way of conceptualizing the Canadian imagination during the rise of cultural nationalism following the Second World War. A shift in focus onto an alternative kind of spatial and landscape-related narrative reveals, however, the diverse challenges many women writers (from settler to contemporary periods) encounter when giving voice to gendered experiences and situating their domestic garden plots within a larger literary field. The writers in my study include Susanna Moodie (1803–85) and Catharine Parr Traill (1802–99), who describe their experiences as female settlers in Upper Canada during the nineteenth century; Gabrielle Roy (1909–83), who tells of her own experience as an aspiring writer just prior to the Second World War; Carol Shields (1935–2003), who traces the social conventions shaping women's lives throughout the twentieth century from a feminist perspective born out of the 1960s and 1970s; and finally Lorna Crozier (1948– ), who interrogates inherited myths, conventional uses of language, and social taboos through her feminist, postmodern poetic vision. These writers are by no means representative of particular time periods but rather are highly informative because of their recurring use of the garden throughout their writing careers (as opposed to producing only a single garden-related work).

While Moodie, Traill, Roy, Shields, and Crozier present a fairly uniform group with respect to class and race, they create rich variety through their diverse use of genre (pioneer sketches, household manual, children's fiction, autobiography, short stories, novels, and poetry) and their nuanced negotiations of domestic and gender ideals across time and space. By using women writers in my examination of the garden "plot," I contribute to what Harris sees as a "proliferation of gender studies relating to landscape topics" because of "the traditional figuration of nature-as-female and the garden as a feminine domain" (438).[11] What is important to remember here is the fact that the garden is not simply a place of "nature" (and its cultural construction) but of heightened, and consciously applied, artifice. This study argues that the domestic garden is a gendered construct and a socio-cultural ideal that these five Canadian writers perpetuate, negotiate, celebrate, or subvert. Moreover, the "plots" of their texts significantly posit women as active, even strategic contributors to larger cultural landscapes in which their gardens as third natures are situated. According to Francis and Hester, actual gardens do not serve merely as private retreats but rather as part of the "collective experience," providing "the unique opportunity for people visually to participate in others' private space. As part of this larger landscape, the garden communicates personal values to nearby residents and passersby. In turn, neighbors and visitors attach value to the private worlds of others" (14). In a comparable way, Casey argues that gardens "are at the threshold between a series of things," be it physical domains, concepts, or notions of stasis and change; gardens are "liminal" because *the place itself is a boundary*" (155). The garden "plots" in this literary study take advantage of this mediating, in-between aspect. All five writers reveal that supposedly private, domestic space is inextricably connected to meaningful and readily visible redefinitions of social, gendered conventions – a premise that is, not surprisingly, central to the theoretical underpinnings of architectural and garden historians.[12] In the end, the "third nature" aspects of garden plots force a reassessment of early conceptualizations of Canadian literature, the varied spaces and configurations of our literary landscapes, and, perhaps most importantly, women writers' contributions to our collective culture.

This book is organized chronologically and by writer so as to highlight both the context-specific quality of literary gardens and the different preoccupations of their authors with respect to gender across time and space. Chapters one and two examine the writings of Susanna Moodie and Catharine Parr Traill, and provide an introductory framework for the remaining chapters by approaching literary gardens in a dual sense: both within the text as literal green-spaces (chapter one), and as figurative models for writing (chapter two). Moodie and Traill are significant literary foremothers; their reflections on nineteenth-century British landscape aesthetics and garden ideals signal a prominent arrival of the garden topos and trope in English Canadian literary history and criticism. Because thematic and archetypal readings of Moodie and Traill have held such sway, chapter one undertakes the necessary task of separating their own gardens (as described in their published and private writing) from well-known lines of twentieth-century literary criticism. This chapter brings, therefore, the material garden back into view by determining the content and structure of Moodie's and Traill's actual kitchen gardens and placing them within the history of the English cottage garden and those of wilderness-settlers. As composite terrains, these actual backwoods gardens are examples of palimpsestic landscapes with diverse environmental, social, and cultural factors at play and in complex relation.

Chapter two extends and departs from chapter one by examining how gardens figure in and influence Moodie's and Traill's writing. Considering the language of the garden that was popular in nineteenth-century discourse concerning "cultivated" English women of refined socio-economic backgrounds, I suggest that Moodie and Traill adapted this traditional rhetoric to reflect their experiences as "transplanted" middle-class women who are "hardened-off" in their new environments and related roles as pioneers. In addition to their revision of horticultural metaphors, Moodie and Traill also use the garden as "plot," a significant spatial and ideological narrative frame that situates their characters and personae in order to express the shifting gender domains of female immigrants in Upper Canada. In turn, these innovative plots are the sources of inspiration behind the twentieth-century palimpsestic poetry of Robert Kroetsch and Margaret Atwood. The resulting pioneer garden palimpsests reveal the specific mandates of these contemporary writers as they generate their own respective visions of the Canadian imagination: one somewhat crowded by the presence of literary predecessors, and the other deeply informed by the wilderness.

Chapter three moves away from transplanted domestic plots of the nineteenth century and toward twentieth-century narratives of uprooting and tentative independence through Gabrielle Roy's journey of self-discovery. In her autobiography *Enchantment and Sorrow* (1984) and her short story (or novella) "Garden in the Wind" (1975), Roy fashions domestic-styled bowers from actual gardens she encountered during decisive moments in the early decades of her career, thereby mediating her own ambivalence as an artist coming to her vocation and having to leave behind familial responsibilities. Roy elucidates some of the particular challenges women artists face in the cultural, linguistic and even geographical isolation of a relatively young country. In her non-fiction and fiction, the bower is ultimately a site of reassurance during the difficult transition towards a more public engagement with the modern world.

If Roy depicts conflicted departures away from domesticity for her female artists, Carol Shields uses her fiction to offer a significant return to and examination of the domestic as an essential, abiding component of her characters' lives. Chapter four examines, in particular, Shields' relocating of the paradise myth (as a national literary trope) out of the proverbial wilderness and into the "plots" of everyday, middle-class lives. Her feminist mandate stems directly from critical discussions of women's domestic-situated roles in such works as Betty Friedan's *The Feminine Mystique* (1963). In constructing a range of superficial and genuine forms of "paradisal" fulfillment in *The Box Garden* (1977) and *The Stone Diaries* (1993), Shields interrogates assumptions about what ideally constitutes the domestic, using the garden to gauge the confluence between public expectations and private desires. To achieve this aim, she especially explores the performative aspects of domestic lives and settings by drawing upon the garden's formal capacity for staging "scenes."

Whereas the writers in the first four chapters subscribe to the domestic garden as an ideal in terms of its familiarity and comfort, poet Lorna Crozier turns to the garden for its defamiliarizing, or "denaturalizing," capacity. Over the course of her career, Crozier has increasingly modeled her writing practice of feminist re-vision (as inspired by American writer Adrienne Rich) in terms of the garden's interrelated functions as both product and process: its third nature role. This chapter effectively closes where this study began by turning to Crozier's creation of another pioneer garden palimpsest through her feminist re-writing of Sinclair Ross' 1941 novel *As For Me and My House* in her book *A Saving Grace: The Collected Poem of Mrs. Bentley* (1996). In this way, the final chapter highlights the intersections of gardening and writing through its focus on the dynamic "nature" of Canada's literary gardens being subject to change and regeneration as they travel across time and space and into the hands of other writers.

Ultimately, all five chapters work together to demonstrate that writing that is profoundly inspired by and modeled after the garden is a mode of expression in which both form and content are inextricably combined. The literary gardens that I trace reflect critically on the shifting historical and artistic milieus of and in which these authors write, and in that regard, operate as salient examples of a third nature at work within the larger Canadian literary tradition. Only by reading these "plots" attentively, will we discover that the heightened, critical expression of Canada's gardening culture takes place not just within the soil, but among the pages of our stories, our poetry, and our criticism.

CHAPTER ONE

# "[T]ransplanted into our gardens": Susanna Moodie, Catharine Parr Traill, and the Backwoods Kitchen Garden

In the spring of 1839, Susanna Moodie, a middle-class British emigrant, found herself living alone in the backwoods of Upper Canada, her husband John employed by the militia to pay the family's financial debts. Writing a wedding anniversary letter to her absent husband, Moodie recounted how there were court writs against their cattle and how the children were "rather ragged and bare" without proper clothing (*Letters of Love and Duty* 140). Despite the desperate situation, she included an imperative request of her own: "You must send me a pair of Indian Rubber shoes, to garden in for I am without" (*Letters of Love and Duty* 141). Having also emigrated in 1832, Moodie's sister Catharine Parr Traill shared the sentiment: a garden was indispensable. In Traill's pioneer manual, *The Canadian Settler's Guide* (1855),[1] readers learn practical gardening tips before they are educated in the essential task of making bread.[2] Traill promoted gardening among the public and, at the same time, took personal advantage of these publishing opportunities, as she reveals in an 1882 letter addressed to her son William: "I get some things from Vick of Rochester and write for his Illustrated Magazine and he sends me seeds – for my pay – I have sent him $15 – subscriptions for his Magazine since last May" (*I Bless You in My Heart* 224). Paid in seeds for her writing, Traill bestows tremendous material value on the garden. While both sisters view these terrains as vital to their daily lives, critics largely ignore this aspect of their domestic environs even when the scholarship focuses on landscape and landscape aesthetics.³ The majority of critics tend to discuss Moodie's and Traill's physical and intellectual processing of the environment on a grand scale, but an argument can also be made for the centrality of the garden to the sisters' expression of the female emigrant experience.

As actual sites described in their writing, Moodie's and Traill's gardens follow complex trajectories, revealing their changing aesthetics as they negotiate between themselves and their immediate surroundings. Combining British gardening theory, horticultural pragmatics, and the wilderness-settler environment, their gardens serve as layered reflections of the Strickland sisters' own physical and cultural transplanting to Upper Canada. In this regard, they are material, palimpsestic landscapes. *The Oxford English Dictionary* defines "palimpsest" as "Paper, parchment or other writing material designed to be reusable after any writing on it has been erased," but the term also has figurative applications in that it can be "a thing likened to such a writing surface ... a multilayered record."⁴ Among scholars of landscape architecture, cultural geography, and archaeology, the palimpsest is a popular conceptual model for understanding the layered production of space over time. Meto J. Vroom's *Lexicon of Garden and Landscape Architecture*, for instance, includes a brief definition of "palimpsest" under the entry "layer overlay" where "the physical, the biotic, and the human" components of landscapes are highlighted (187), with a palimpsest occurring "where former and new patterns are simultaneously visible" (188). Likewise, in his study of American cultural landscapes, geographer Richard H. Schein argues that the palimpsest "analogy ... provides the possibility for erasure and overwriting and the co-existence of several different scripts, implying not just different historical eras, but several historical and contemporary actors as well" (662). The landscape as a continual process of co-existent "actors" (both human and non-human) is further qualified by archaeologist Geoff Bailey who distinguishes between a "true palimpsest," where "all traces of earlier activity have been removed except the most recent" (203), and a "cumulative palimpsest," where "successive ... layers of activity ... remain superimposed one upon the other without loss of evidence, but are so re-worked and mixed together that it is difficult or impossible to separate them out into their original constituents" (204). As context-specific creations where British culture is visibly mixed in with the wilderness-settler environment of Upper Canada, Moodie's and Traill's backwoods gardens fall into this latter category. Their very success was contingent upon their ability to work within cumulative garden palimpsests where different "actors" – plant species (native or imported), landscape features, environmental conditions, themselves, or other individuals – were at play in complex, interrelated ways.

## The Garden in the Canadian Literary Landscape

In scholarship on Moodie and Traill, the garden has often been the target of harsh assessments, as domestic terrain represents, for many critics, an inadequate means of responding to the Upper Canadian landscape. This line of criticism is undoubtedly shaped by Margaret Atwood's gothic vision in her poetry collection *The Journals of Susanna*

*Moodie* (1970), a text which is, itself, a literary version of a palimpsest in its re-writing of Moodie's original *Roughing It in the Bush*. In Atwood's poem "Dream 1: The Bush Garden," Moodie's pioneer garden is a veritable nightmare where animalistic plants resist a productive harvest. Moodie's hands come "away red and wet" after picking strawberries and she declares, "I should have known / anything planted here / would come up blood" (34). Here, a deathly wilderness vision overrides pioneer terrain, and this provocative depiction of Moodie's garden has proved such a formidable layer in the "palimpsest of meaning" – what Bailey defines as "the succession of meanings acquired by a particular object" (208) – that other layers of Moodie's original text have been obscured from view. As Susan Johnston acknowledges, "So powerful is Atwood's reconstruction that not only most interpretations of *The Journals of Susanna Moodie*, but many independent discussions of *Roughing It in the Bush* as well, have succumbed to its lure" (28). One result is the conflation of Moodie's and even Traill's actual gardens of the nineteenth century (as described in the sisters' writing) with Atwood's contemporary image and its combative associations.

With Atwood's Moodie persona imposing a structure upon the wilderness and ultimately failing, the bush garden becomes the symbol for all that Northrop Frye believes is intrinsic to the Canadian literary imagination. His own model of the "garrison mentality" encapsulates Canadian society's polarization against the wilderness, which is perceived as a "huge, unthinking, menacing, and formidable physical setting" (225). In this battle against nature, Moodie is a soldiering force, "a British army of occupation in herself, a one-woman garrison" (237). In contrast, Traill exhibits "a somewhat selective approach to the subject [of nature] reminiscent of Miss Muffet" (244). While Frye renders Moodie masculine, he posits Traill's domestic-centred literary response as mere nursery-rhyme musings, inconsequential to

Canadian culture. The irony here is that while Frye disengages Canadian literature from the British tradition through his organic model of writers being "rooted" in their environment (i), he systematically denies Moodie and Traill those responses that stem not merely from their British origins, but from their Upper Canadian setting as material palimpsests formed in and through composite layers.

Eventually, Frye's thematic interpretations lose ground when critics turn instead to the language of landscape and its social, aesthetic, and political codes. Even in these studies, however, which tend to favour the larger landscape, Moodie's and Traill's gardens continue to be either overlooked or over-written. Susan Glickman's *The Picturesque and the Sublime* contends that eighteenth-century aesthetic conventions, rather than a fear of the wilderness, inform Moodie's response to the landscape of Upper Canada.[5] For Glickman, Moodie's Romantic aesthetics and sensibility prompt her to interpret the scenery in particular ways and in specific circumstances: "But as apprehension of the sublime is acknowledged to occur in moments of private meditation, and not of intense activity, it is hardly surprising that when [Moodie] represents herself as hard at work on her farm, we get little or no natural description" (62). While Glickman dispels garrison-minded interpretations, she persists in examining Moodie in relation to the most dominant setting – the wilderness or distant prospect – and in the process overlooks the immediate, personal foreground of this pioneer woman. According to Glickman, Moodie's farm "simply forms the *background* to labour. A half-starved nursing mother, digging potatoes, has little occasion for transcendent communion with nature!" (62, emphasis added).

If scholars emphasize Moodie's preoccupation with the larger landscape, conversely they deem Traill as too confined by the domestic. Marian Fowler contends that Traill creates a woman's version of a garrison against the wilderness through her scientific, orderly response to nature and her rigid home environment. Traill's "tight, bright little domestic circle" (Fowler 81) is responsible for her defective response to the wilderness, which is a failure to open herself to the awe-inspiring sublime. Echoing Fowler, Gaile McGregor argues that Traill's predominant image of the backwoods is that of the "cheerful, and homely kitchen-garden" (42). Here, Traill wills the wilderness into something safe, useable, and recognizable. For the most part, critics suggest that the garden is an indisputable means of dominating (or completely effacing) the wilderness and remaining safely polarized against the environment. The sublime, the picturesque, and even the garrison mentality are aesthetic and psychological ways of processing the wilderness, but the actual garden, unfortunately, is relegated to the insignificant, the banal.

Literary scholars' conscious or inadvertent dismissals of Moodie's and Traill's gardens are hardly surprising when viewed through the lens of English garden history that typically favours male-dominated, expansive, picturesque landscape parks of the eighteenth and nineteenth centuries, and elides more modest-scale gardens of the period.[6] Taking issue with these historical studies, Susan Groag Bell argues that women are virtually invisible in so far as they were active cottage and villa gardeners. The English landscape garden's purpose was, in part, to display the male landowner's aesthetic taste and his "wealth and political power" (472), a fact that not only highlights men's privileged relationship but also points indirectly to women's marginalized role as observers in this particular period of garden history.[7] Bell argues that articles, diaries, and letters make evident that women's "flower gardens blossomed throughout the century even as the celebrated innovation of the landscape park was being shaped under male authority" (479). Dorothy Wordsworth serves as one example of a woman revealing herself (in her *Grasmere Journals*, 1800–03) to be an active, daily cottage gardener. She communes with nature, plants lemon-thyme "by moonlight" (8), and listens to Coleridge read "Christabel" until 3:30 a.m. in the "still, clear moonshine of the garden" (19). Wordsworth describes herself as a learned gardener who has "read Mr Knight's Landscape" (14), the didactic poem by English landscape designer Richard Payne Knight.[8] Moreover, she boasts that her cottage garden attracts the attention of the more affluent seekers of picturesque nature: "A coroneted Landau went by when we were sitting upon the sodded wall. The ladies (evidently Tourists) turned an eye of interest upon our little garden & cottage" (9). Wordsworth's cottage garden is not on the grand scale of a landscape park, but it is a vital part of her Romantic sensibility and picturesque aesthetics.

As female members of the middle class, Moodie and Traill naturally partake in this culture. In accord with Bell's argument, Moodie's private letters convey a keen artistic interest in the treatment of terrain immediately surrounding the home, as opposed to a grand prospect: "I never tried to draw a landscape in my life, but I will send you two flower sketches, one of our *Wild Marsh Iris*, the other is a Rose that grew at my Cottage door" (*Letters of a Lifetime* 253). Another letter illuminates her life-time, sentimental involvement with flowers as a result of her childhood at Reydon Hall and her conspicuously feminized gardening activity: "I always recall our large gardens at home, with a sad regret, and the want of flowers is to me a sad privation, very hard to be borne ... In my old house, which was of stone every window was full of flowers, and I tended them with a mother's care" (*Letters of a Lifetime* 248). Unfortunately, literary scholars' dismissal of Moodie's and Traill's gardens in favour of the larger landscape results in an under-appreciation of the fact that gardens (even the most modest) form some of the most complex sites of human interaction with, and understanding of, the natural and social world. A case in point is Glickman's statement that nature on Moodie's farm "simply forms the *background* to labour" (62, emphasis added), which underestimates the significance of these terrains, especially because Moodie and Traill frequently located their gardens prominently in their front yards for personal and public display, as Traill reveals during her first spring in the backwoods: "I am anxiously looking forward to the spring, that I may get a garden laid out in front of the house; as I mean to cultivate some of the native fruits and flowers" (*Backwoods* 103).[9] A shift in critical focus reveals, therefore, that Moodie and Traill formulated garden ideals and perceptions according to particular socio-cultural and environmental criteria; their private and published writings impart these.

One feminist line of scholarship provides a constructive means of re-situating Moodie, Traill, and their gardens when it comes to their interactions with the environment. Helen Buss and Heather Murray shed light on female pioneers and how their experiences and writing of the wilderness differ significantly from those of their male counterparts. Setting aside the garrison mentality as a masculine construct, both critics argue that women assume an intimate, intermediary role between feminized nature (with which women identify) and culture (in which women participate). Buss suggests that women display a gendered connection to the land, as opposed to fear and dominance, through related creative activities such as child-rearing or writing and painting about the environment.[10] Buss does not include gardening in her list, but it certainly falls within her category. Alternatively, Murray argues for a landscape continuum, and her concept of the "pseudo-wilderness" specifically lends itself to an analysis of Moodie's and Traill's gardens. According to Murray, the "pseudo-wilderness" is a marginal, middle ground between nature and culture (75) and includes a range of locales: the backwoods, a farm, or a camp. Through such spaces, women are able to negotiate their surroundings, socio-cultural values, and gender roles. In the context of Buss' and Murray's revised models, Moodie's and Traill's gardens become pervasive interspaces of creativity: in and through them they realize a productive marginality as they reshape their understanding of women's place and daily work by accommodating the demands and realities of pioneer life. These terrains can no longer be dismissed as mere potato patches but rather must be re-evaluated as highly relevant, expressive backwoods gardens.[11] As material palimpsests, they are intricate composites of native flora and fauna, imported seeds, transplanted British aesthetics, pioneer pragmatics, and the sisters' own personal tastes and visions. In their capacity as third natures, therefore, Moodie's and Traill's backwoods gardens offer critical reflections of ongoing, direct engagement with both the first nature of the wilderness and the second nature of daily work and habitation.

### The English Cottage Garden Tradition

When Moodie and Traill began turning the soil in Upper Canada, their backwoods gardens were planted primarily with vegetables and fruit in order to supply the basic needs of their families. The backwoods kitchen garden represented both continuity with, and radical departures from, the cottage garden tradition and its incorporation of picturesque aesthetics and the thrifty practice of food cultivation. In their discussion of the growth of England's middle class from 1780 to 1850, Leonore Davidoff and Catherine Hall observe that gardening increased in popularity as more families purchased country or suburban homes with modest gardens. Consequently, the aesthetics of the landscape garden were in need of adaptation: "John Loudon …

and other nineteenth-century experts argued that a miniature version was within the means of all. But the broad sweep of grass and trees, the lack of ornamentation and muted colours recommended by Capability Brown or Humphrey Repton needed modification for middle-class taste" (370). The features of grand estates, particularly the lawn and "naturally" arranged plantings, were re-imagined in meaningful and tangible ways within the varied property dimensions of the middle class. These country villas and cottage gardens became highly idealized green-spaces, suggestive of the owners' social, cultural, and economic aspirations.[12] Whether belonging to an illustrious villa or a well-tended and romanticized cottage, these gardens contained a mixture of plantings that both beautified and provided sustenance. For the middle class, the cottage garden included flowers, vegetables, and often small livestock.[13] They were typically enclosed (through the construction of a fence, wall, or boundary of vegetation) and enclosing (by surrounding the home). In this way, they created an ideal domestic haven. Unlike the elite status of the landscape garden that was designed by a professional, tended by hired gardeners, and enjoyed through tours about the park, the English cottage garden meant direct involvement in picturesque aesthetics for the masses and reflected their propertied status, albeit within the limitations of a middle-class income.

A mercantile, middle-class family, the Stricklands did not possess a grand estate typical of the aristocracy's landscape parks but their comfortable stone home with expansive property was at the more illustrious end of the spectrum of cottage and villa gardens. In *Sketches from Nature; or, Hints to Juvenile Naturalists* (1830), Traill recounts the surroundings in which Reydon Hall was situated: "some pretty wild, woody lanes ... skirted the park and grounds of a nobleman, whose land lay contiguous to our own estate" (134). The adornment of this home and its grounds through all things green constituted a major component of Moodie's and Traill's understanding of cottage or villa gardening. The patriarch of the family, Thomas Strickland, was particularly attuned to aesthetic concerns, as is made apparent in Traill's description of an ordinary root-house: "This root-house ... was a shed in a secluded part of the garden ... and which papa had taken in hand to beautify, and render a very pretty and ornamental object, by planting ... ivy on either side of the door-way, which he had turned into a gothic arch" (5–6). Reydon Hall's presentation was, above all, that of picturesque beauty, even when it entailed a practical side. Traill recalls that at the age of seven, she was responsible for "cutting the decayed flowers of the purple thrift ... for which [she] was to receive ... the important sum of threepence" to pay for food for her pet animals, such as her rabbits (1). In *Narratives of Nature, and History Book for Young Naturalists* (1831), she describes in detail the seasonal gardening tasks that she and her siblings were "hired" to complete under their father's direction:

> In the spring there were borders to weed or seedlings to transplant, and tobacco plants to top. In the summer there was fruit to gather for home-made wine, for which we received one penny per peck; ripe seeds to collect ... with many other vegetables and pot-herbs; for all which a regular agreement was entered into, and a bargain made as to the price, before we commenced operations.
>
> In the winter season, when working in the garden was not practicable, we earned a little weekly stipend by cutting the leaves of the tobacco which had been cured in the autumn. (134)

Practical but not hard physical labour was essential to the Strickland children's outdoor education, and in this context, industry and thriftiness would always be related to the picturesque.

While the country-house and garden of Reydon Hall were at the centre of the Strickland family's private life, the fact remains that the cottage garden, for all its benign domestic associations, operated effectively as both a process and product of imperialism. Karen Sayer explains that "the history of gardening, even quintessentially English cottage gardening, is immutably bound up with the history of trade and the growth of empire" (43). The cottage garden's facility for colonization and appropriation operated both at home and abroad. In England, some of the "most popular plants were originally imports … thereby demonstrating the power of the English garden to take in, naturalise, and domesticate what was once essentially 'alien' to it" (43). Not surprisingly in *The Backwoods of Canada,* Traill identifies native plants in the Canadian backwoods as either carefully tended exotics or "naturalized" species that inhabit the cottage gardens back home in England: "Our [Canadian] woods and clearings are now full of beautiful flowers … You will recognize among them many of the cherished pets of our gardens and green-houses, which are here flung carelessly from Nature's lavish hand among our woods and wilds" (167). While English gardeners cherished these "pets" (or alien plant species), immigrants abroad, according to Sayer, used the cottage garden to appropriate and transform unfamiliar environments: "the imposition of a country garden on a native landscape worked as visible demonstration of the civilizing impact of the English" (43).

In keeping with this imperialistic view of gardening, Traill, during her early career in England as an author of children's literature, laid the groundwork for practical-minded aesthetics in preparation for emigration, with the ultimate objective of recreating a typically

English cottage garden in the "new world." Although she had not yet emigrated and had only learned about Upper Canada second-hand through her brother Samuel Strickland (who emigrated in 1825), in *The Young Emigrants; or, Pictures of Canada Calculated to Amuse and Instruct the Minds of Youth* (1826), Traill promotes sensible, colonial gardening. In that story the son, Richard Clarence, gathers hardy vegetable and flower seeds prior to his departure from England (26); as for his sister Agnes, the "flower-borders in the garden are to be [her] peculiar charge" in order to recreate the family's English "Roselands" home in Upper Canada (113).[14] The Clarence family's backwoods garden replicates the picturesque features of its English original with "verdant grass" planted in front of the house, floral ornamentation, and a fence of twisted osiers (113). By "improving" (112) the grounds in this fashion, the family appropriates the wilderness environment – an imperial act on a domestic scale best demonstrated by Agnes, who spends her time tending "several parterres of beautiful native flowers, besides those plants which [she] brought from Roselands" (150).

For young readers in England, Traill purposely creates an inspirational story of the Clarence family's emigration: their ostensibly English idyll recreated in the backwoods captures the imagination through its domestic comfort on unfamiliar ground. Outside the realm of children's fiction, however, the success of this transplanted garden would be improbable within the time-frame of the Clarences' first year of settlement. Following Traill's emigration six years after the publication of *The Young Emigrants,* she relates how her naïve expectations are quashed upon arriving in the colony when a long-time settler informs her that she must revise her timeline for creating a picturesque home: "Matters are not carried on quite so easily here as at home … At the end of five years you may begin to talk of these pretty improvements and elegancies, and you will then be able to see a little what you are about" (*Backwoods* 57). Upon Traill's first inspection, most of Upper Canada appears undesirable, particularly when she judges its modest dwellings by picturesque standards: "But, in my opinion, much less is done with the romantic situation than might be effected if good taste were exercised in the buildings, and on the disposal of the ground. How lovely would such a spot be rendered in England or Scotland. Nature here has done all, and man but little, excepting sticking up some ugly wooden cottages, as mean as they are tasteless" (*Backwoods* 19). Traill's comments belie her middle-class perspective as the "mean," "tasteless" cottages do not conform to that which she is accustomed: the picturesque grounds of Reydon Hall. These humble domains rank far below their lower-class English counterparts: "In Britain even the peasant has taste enough to plant a few roses or honeysuckles about his door or his casement, and there is the little bit of garden enclosed and neatly kept; but here no such attempt is made to ornament the cottages" (*Backwoods* 29–30). In nineteenth-century England, for the middle class, the cottage garden meant the pleasures of country-living through the benefits of fresh food and green ornamentation; for the lower classes, it meant largely subsistence. Sayer explains that the most humble "historically consisted of a small plot of land, normally, though not always attached to the labourer's house, mostly used for growing vegetables, fruit and herbs and sometimes for keeping" small farm animals (38). The "productive labourer's garden [did not] necessarily lac[k] flowery interest," but for the most part, "this small plot of land primarily had to provide the … family with additional food, or a surplus, to help them spin out their wages" (38). Traill appears aware of these class disparities when she comments on gardening practices and plant preferences.[15] What she fails to account for, however, in her initial viewing of Upper Canada, is that gardening is now situated in a radically new context. Decorative gardening is not popular because it is impractical.

Moodie's and Traill's experiences at Reydon Hall certainly prove foundational to their daily tending of the backwoods kitchen garden. While these sisters may have been fairly prepared as gardeners in this regard, their oftentimes unrealistic expectations confirm the necessity for adaptation. As an art of milieu inherently tied to first and second natures, gardens reflect the socio-physical contexts in and of which they are formed; therefore, ideals and aesthetics, particularly those derived from other historical and geographical contexts, must undergo what John Dixon Hunt describes in *Gardens and the Picturesque* as a process of cultural and material translation. To illustrate his premise, Hunt points to England during the eighteenth century and the interest at that time in ancient Rome and Classical art: "But a country like England had its own indigenous architectural forms, let alone its own distinct landscapes where (it could be argued) neoclassical buildings did not necessarily sit too happily ... So when writers or architects translated the classical languages of their models, they were obliged at least to address the question of how [these] would function in England and in English" (10). Artistically and physically dynamic forms, gardens require reinterpretation within new settings through the use of local materials and the layering of new signification. In terms of the Upper Canadian situation, Moodie's and Traill's cottage garden ideals undergo profound translation in order to accommodate timely settlement, provide sustenance, and grow successfully within the surrounding wilderness-settler environment. Out of necessity, this process results in backwoods kitchen gardens, context-specific creations composed of strange flora and growing within different physical and social conditions.

If gardening was familiar, however, while turning the soil Moodie and Traill soon realize they are working within an unknown environment. The first and second natures of the Upper Canada are predominant features of, and agents within, the sisters' palimpsestic gardens. During her first spring in the backwoods, Traill acknowledges her predicament. Although her "vegetable seeds are in the ground," she has been told that "[she and her husband] have been premature; there being ten chances to one but the young plants will be cut off by the late frosts" (*Backwoods* 122). Traill does not yet understand the planting seasons of her new climate, but even more startling is her recognition that her backwoods garden does not reflect her accustomed English aesthetic: "Our garden at present has nothing to boast of, being merely a spot of ground enclosed with a rough unsightly fence of split rails to keep the cattle from destroying the vegetables. Another spring, I hope to have a nice fence and a portion of the ground devoted to flowers. This spring there is so much pressing work to be done on the land in clearing for the crops, that I do not like to urge my claims on behalf of a pretty garden" (*Backwoods* 122). The urgency of clearing the wilderness, rather than planting flowers, points to the significantly altered context. The need for subsistence and the clearing of land are key factors, and her desire for progress hinges upon the philosophy of the "four stages theory" of civilization's development. As Wanda Ruth Campbell discusses in the context of early Canadian settlement writing, the four stages theory suggests that society progresses from the hunting-gathering stage, to the pastoral, to agricultural, and ultimately to the commercial, but "[o]nly with the arrival of the agricultural stage [can] sufficient leisure be found to cultivate the more sophisticated activities of science and art" (9–10). In the Strickland sisters' view, their desire to "improve" the wilderness through horticulture legitimizes their ownership of the land that the Native communities have seemingly "neglected." The process of appropriation is not, however, a simple task of effacing and overwriting the wilderness with English gardening ideals, but rather a complex, ongoing translation, where the varied components of these palimpsestic backwoods gardens are mutually informative and constitutive.

With a pressing pioneer need for practicality and the ultimate objective of establishing an agricultural society, the Strickland sisters develop their backwoods kitchen gardens via numerous acts of concession. Traill laments her lack of flowers in 1832, yet *The Canadian Settler's Guide* of 1855 reveals an evident shift in how she views things, subsistence now being a primary objective. In the *Guide*, edible plants and vegetables receive the majority of Traill's attention. Rather than focusing on what gardeners may desire, Traill instructs her readers on what is indispensable: "Rhubarbs should always find a place in your garden; a cool, shady place and rich soil is best: throw on the bed in the Fall a good supply of long dung … A bed of Carraways should also find a place in your garden; it is always useful, and the seeds sell well, besides being valuable as a cattle medicine" (49). The phrases "should always find," "it is always useful," and "is essential" indicate a garden designed to meet a settler's basic needs and to contribute to the farm's economy. The backwoods kitchen garden is first and foremost utility-based, providing a variety of foods for the table, everything from beans, corn, and broccoli, to hops and watermelons. Cabbage is particularly important to Traill, as she not only mentions her "cabbage plot" but also boasts how her Conical cabbage and Portugal ivory-stemmed varieties "caused quite a sensation among the country gardeners," with the new seeds being from "the Chiswick gardens" (52).[16] Staples include carrots and potatoes, and different varieties are sown in the garden (versus the fields) offering sustenance long before the larger crops are ready for harvest (51, 123). Traill also urges the planting of a bed of pot-herbs for culinary seasonings and instructs female settlers to bring their own seeds, as these are not easily accessible in the colony (49). The fact that Traill outlines the garden's contents so extensively indicates that her understanding has moved well beyond the concept of middle-class thrift that was part of her original English tradition. What Traill now experiences as second nature – her world of daily habitation – has radically altered, and so too, by extension, has the third nature of her domestic garden.

Whereas England's more well-to-do cottage gardeners focused ostensibly on aesthetic delights and supplementing the family's diet, the backwoods settlers viewed their gardens as the hub of their daily domestic economy. In the theory of three natures, Hunt reminds us that this model is a "sliding scale" of different and, in the case of the garden, inter-connected modes of engagement with the environment, and Traill's backwoods kitchen garden, as a third nature, closely integrates its expression with quotidian (or second nature) concerns (*Greater* 63). According to *The Canadian Settler's Guide*, the garden is one of the "most necessary appendages to a farm-house" because it "produces as large an amount of valuable crop as any part of a farm" (58). The garden sustains the family and even provides a means of goods-exchange with the local Chippewa Natives, as Traill recounts in *Forest and Other Gleanings*: "The squaws came frequently to get pork and flour from me, and garden vegetables, in exchange for fish, venison, or baskets … They are fond of … any vegetable; sometimes they will follow me into the garden, and beg 'onion,' or 'herb,' to put in soup: potatoes they never refuse" (150).[17] Unfortunately, this also facilitated exploitation, as Moodie recalls, in *Roughing It in the Bush*, one female settler who unfairly traded a single turnip for a china bowl that was owned by a pregnant Native woman, who "had never seen a turnip before" (317).

For settlers, the overall economic advantage of the backwoods kitchen garden lies in its productive management of the domestic-farm environment. Cattle are less likely to wander into the woods if they are regularly fed tasty garden treats, such as a "few refuse potatoes" or "the leaves of the garden vegetables daily in use" (Traill, *Backwoods* 185). The kitchen garden also recycles domestic waste. When discussing squash and cucumbers, for instance, Traill instructs readers to make a "good hot-bed" by "piling the weeds and rubbish, dried leaves and stalks of vegetables, and covering the mound with several inches of fine mould" (*Canadian Settler's* 131). Through composting, this island bed[18] is an example of what Catherine Alexander identifies as regenerative, outdoor domestic space by having "a transformative element vis-a-vis the house, purifying the unclean" (865). Household waste is fruitfully re-integrated with the outdoor environment, providing, in turn, "good, rich, mould" and excellent produce (*Canadian Settler's* 131). The multi-faceted economic role of the backwoods kitchen garden elevates women's work and de-marginalizes their terrain, a transition that, in Traill's estimation, many husbands and wives initially resist.

In *The Canadian Settler's Guide*, Traill relates that settlers do not always privilege the backwoods kitchen garden even though it is vital to a family's welfare. Clearing the land seems to be, particularly in the minds of male settlers, more pressing and worthy of their intensive labour: "In Canada where the heavy labour of felling trees and cultivating the ground falls to the lot of men, who have for some years enough to do to clear ground to support the family and raise means towards paying instalments [*sic*] on the land, little leisure is left for the garden and orchard ... [which are] either totally neglected or left to the management of women and children. That there is a miserable want of foresight in this, there can be no doubt" (57–8). While there is no "leisure" left to tend the supposedly superfluous third nature of the garden during the work of settlement, this outmoded understanding of the garden and of a gendered hierarchy of labour is incongruous with the economic value Traill emphatically places on the garden throughout her manual. Traill's choice in diction further suggests that she intuits apprehension on the part of female emigrants who more than likely perceive utility gardening as unrefined and unbecoming. The word "leisure" mollifies such worries in upholding the value and flattering nature of the manual work: "In the early years of our infant settlement ... all the ladies worked in their gardens, raised their own vegetables, and flowers, and reared the fruit trees ... They felt this work as no disgrace to them, but took pride and pleasure in the success of their labours" (59). In her *Guide* Traill describes an appealing scenario for the British public, but in a private letter she addresses to Frances Stewart, during the spring of 1853, the intensity and time-consuming aspects of the work are readily apparent: "The girls have been very busy working in their gardens. The boys ploughing and sowing. [Thomas] Traill has been helping in digging and tomorrow all that can will be out in the garden planting early potatoes" (78). In the day-to-day reality of the backwoods, the garden is a site not of leisure, but of constant toil.

The manner in which Traill describes the backwoods kitchen garden suggests that a formidable translation is ongoing within the garden itself and within her writing as she introduces would-be and new emigrants to a decidedly different style of cultivation. This process of reinterpretation does not mean a rejection of English gardening culture; on the contrary, original ideals often (but not always) maintain predominance in this imperialistic project. When Traill describes alternative practices of the Native peoples and their harvesting of Indian rice, for instance, she admits that "it affords a great quantity of food," yet persists in upholding English norms of cultivation in keeping with most settlers: "The gathering of wild rice is a tedious process, and one rarely practised [sic] by the settlers, whose time can be more profitably employed on their farms" (*Canadian Settler's* 106). The fact remains, however, that the Upper Canadian society and environment are not conducive to the kind of gardening to which Traill is accustomed, and the instructions in her *Guide* reflect the real challenge of making the unfamiliar relatable. At one point, Traill compares a device used in vegetable plots in the backwoods to a "ha-ha,"[19] a sunken fence used in English landscape parks to demarcate in a visually unobtrusive way the boundaries of a wealthy landowner's property: "There is a plan that I have seen recommended in horticultural books for growing cucumbers: this is on a frame of stick, placed close together, slanting like the pickets of a ha-ha fence" (*Canadian Settler's* 132). While the two structures are similar in appearance, Traill's miniature version of a "ha-ha" is situated in a radically altered context and used for vegetable cultivation. The shift away from a specifically English gardening culture is undeniable, particularly because the resources needed to support and promote gardening are sometimes difficult to procure in the colony. In *The Backwoods of Canada*, Traill urges new emigrants to bring a "selection of good garden-seeds, as those you buy at the stores are sad trash" (128–9), and in her *Guide* recommends subscribing to *The Horticulturalist*, a monthly magazine from the United States, as "so few plain practical gardening-books have as yet been published in Canada, devoted to vegetable and fruit culture, suited expressly for the climate and soil of Canada" (81). The circumstances of the colony as well as the drastic change in environment pose a challenge, and Traill senses that gardening knowledge, preferences, and expectations are in need of re-evaluation. To be sure, her handwritten revisions to *The Canadian Settler's Guide* (circa 1880) demonstrate a gardener who, in the subsequent twenty-five years, continues to learn and reinterpret. Where the published *Guide* informs readers to plant beans any time in May, she provides in her revisions an additional note in the margins: "not earlier than 10 or 20 of May" (*Canadian Settler's* Revisions). Reconfiguring her practices for the backwoods and for her readers, Traill reveals through her texts and editing an ongoing process of adjustment that is genuinely reflective of her understanding of the garden as a dynamic art of milieu: a material palimpsest that brings different times and actors (environmental, social, and cultural) into relation.

## Practical Aesthetics in the Backwoods

The practical backwoods kitchen garden may be indispensable, yet for Traill, who grew up surrounded by picturesque uses of greenery, the aesthetic acquires an equally pivotal role in allowing women to cultivate a sense of home and belonging in the backwoods. In *The Backwoods of Canada*, she mentions a number of aesthetic features that are typical of backwoods gardens, suggesting that a distinctive style is gradually being established, a fact with which Canadian garden historians concur.[20] Traill refers to the adornment of the front stoup through scarlet creeper and hop-vines (103), and also suggests transplanting young seedlings if trees are desired near the home (145). Flowers are, of course, central to Traill's aesthetic, as she admires the fact that scarlet columbine, one of her "favourite flowers," can be found "near every dwelling" (176). In Upper Canada, flowers may not be in abundance during the initial stages of settlement, but they eventually become a treasured part of these green-spaces. Moodie certainly values flowers, as is made evident by the fact that a pressed cutting of campanula with the note "taken from Aunt Moodie's house in Belleville" is part of the Traill Family Collection in the National Archives in Ottawa (Figure 1.1). Moodie's and Traill's backwoods gardens are mixtures of plants from England and native species such as the Canadian wild rose, branching white wood violet (*Viola canadensis*), and Indian grass (*Hierochloa borealis*) – which Traill has had "in [her] garden for many, many years" (*Studies of Plant Life* 214). The English cottage garden was known for incorporating both native and imported plant species, and now in Upper Canada, the backwoods garden similarly promotes diverse cultivation for a changing, composite, aesthetic appeal.

Commenting on Traill's interest in gardening and adornment, Elizabeth Thompson argues, "The tensions between the picturesque and the mundane, between the beautiful and the practical, between a long-range perspective and a closer scrutiny, and between the ideal world and the real world dominate all aspects of Traill's backwoods writing" (40). According to Thompson, Traill uneasily confronts these tensions by "justif[ying] her beautification projects with a practical dimension," such as the time Traill lists the aesthetic attributes on one hand, and the practical benefits on the other, when giving advice on the construction of a verandah (49). In the context of Hunt positing gardens as an art of milieu, however, Traill tends toward hybridiza-tion, rather than remaining strictly grounded in dualisms and oppo-sition. Hers is not a frivolous justification of aesthetics because she recognizes, and rightly so, that home is not purely about pragmatics; it should ideally involve a profound emotional connection. In this regard, Traill integrates aesthetic desires with issues of practical-ity as she takes into account the emotional needs and well-being of female settlers. In *The Canadian Settler's Guide*, the aesthetic becomes

FIGURE 1.1
Dried campanula (blue bells) from Susanna Moodie's garden in Belleville, Ontario

essential rather than superfluous, then, just as that which is practical necessarily acquires an aesthetic quality:

> I am the more particular in pointing out to you how you may improve the outside of your dwelling, because the log-house is rough and unsightly; and I know well that your comfort and cheerfulness of mind will be increased by the care you are led to bestow upon your new home in endeavouring to ornament it and render it more agreeable to the eye ... I write from my own experience. I too have felt all the painful regrets incidental to a long separation from my native land and my beloved early home. I have experienced all that you who read this book can ever feel, and perhaps far more than you will ever have cause for feeling. (16)

Traill's utmost concern is with the women, the primary gardeners. In the passage quoted above, the usually optimistic Traill briefly alludes to "painful regrets" that resulted from her separation from England and hints at her own trials as a female emigrant. Traill's warning speaks directly to the importance of creating an aesthetically pleasing, garden-embowered home if women want to feel genuine attachment to the new settlement.

A backwoods garden embellishes the home, demands difficult labour, and facilitates increased economic prosperity – all of which are essential factors in enabling women pioneers to create a sense of purpose and belonging. John Ruskin contends in his famous essay "Of Queens' Gardens" (1865) that women beautify the world around them through their delicate nurturing of others, as the "path of a good woman is indeed strewn with flowers; but they rise up behind her steps, not before them" (91). In the backwoods of Upper Canada, however,

Traill implies that the ornamentation of the garden serves a somewhat different and more urgent function: to naturalize, via a woman's own agency and volition, that which is initially perceived to be alien and unfamiliar: "How much pleasanter is the aspect of a house surrounded by a garden, nicely weeded and kept, than the desolate chip-yard, unrelieved by any green tree or flower ... What cheerful feelings can such a barren spot excite; what home affections can it nourish in the heart of the emigrant wife? Even though she may have to labour to rear it with her own hands, let her plant a garden" (*Canadian Settler's* 55–6). The cultivation of a backwoods garden serves not simply to naturalize the domestic feminine role, as the flower garden does for the English woman in Ruskin's essay, but rather to sustain – physically, mentally, and emotionally – the enduring emigrant wife who, in her new role, comes to appreciate the difficult labour of "her own hands" as an integral part of her transplanted garden aesthetic.

Traill's avid interest in gardening makes this domestic terrain readily visible in her writing. While gardening is less prominent in Moodie's texts, it nonetheless reflects, in its hybridized form, the reality of a less ornamental, more labour-intensive environment than that to which this educated British woman is accustomed. Moodie's cultivation is primarily related to supporting her family and to facilitating an all-important emotional connection to an unfamiliar home. In contrast to Atwood's pioneer persona, the actual Moodie appears in *Roughing It in the Bush* to enjoy early success as a gardener: "We had commenced gardening, too, and my vegetables did great credit to my skill and care; and, when once the warm weather sets in, the rapid advance of vegetation in Canada is astonishing" (180). The text offers a glimpse of some of the contents, including potatoes, peas, melons, and cucumbers; flowers are not, however, mentioned during these early years. After a three-year sojourn in the bush, Moodie's garden is not a site of leisure and beauty, but rather difficult adaptation: "I loved ... my own dear little garden, with its rugged snake-fence which I had helped Jenny to place with my own hands, and which I had assisted the faithful woman in cultivating for the last three years, where I had so often braved the tormenting mosquitoes, black flies, and intense heat, to provide vegetables for the use of the family" (507–8). Expressing her newly formed attachment to the backwoods, Moodie attributes tender, diminutive affection to her "dear little garden" which she learns to work successfully under difficult conditions. This backwoods garden is created in the elements, through the "torment" of insects and intense summer heat. The zig-zagging snake fence made of split rails requires heavy lifting and assembly – no easy task, as Moodie emphasizes that she helped to build it with her "own hands." Precisely because of the labour involved and its undeniable utilitarian value, the backwoods kitchen garden generates in Moodie a sense of accomplishment, that "comfort and cheerfulness of mind" to which Traill refers in her *Guide* when discussing the importance of gardening for pioneer women (16). During John Moodie's absence from home, Moodie relies on her garden for her family's welfare after the crop fails: "We [Moodie and her servant Jenny] therefore confined our attention to the garden, which, as usual, was very productive, and with milk, fresh butter, and eggs, supplied the simple wants of our family" (495). The vegetable plot demands intense manual labour, and this change in circumstance leads to Moodie's re-evaluation of basic features of her environment in one of the more famous passages of *Roughing It in the Bush:* "I have contemplated a well-hoed ridge of potatoes on that bush farm, with as much delight as in years long past I had experienced in examining a fine painting in some well-appointed drawing-room" (375). This vegetable garden is not as picturesque as the garden of her original home in England, yet Moodie has come to appreciate a pragmatic-minded aesthetic that is hard-won and necessarily part of her larger physical and cultural landscape.

In addition to involving female settlers economically, aesthetically, emotionally, and physically in the formation of their homes, backwoods kitchen gardening further counters the emigrant experience of displacement through the creation of social and geographic networks. Seed and plant exchanges are essential means for not only maintaining familial and cultural associations with England, but also fostering new communities within the colony. The Traill Family Collection at the National Archives contains seeds sent in tiny folded paper sleeves hand-labeled as "feathered columbine" and "mixed violets yellow and white"; an explanatory note attached reads, "found in envelope from Agnes Strickland and Granddaughter of Tom's sent to CPT in '96" (Figure 1.2). In a letter to Frances Stewart, Thomas Traill mentions receiving seeds from an esteemed source abroad: "We also got a box of most valuable garden seeds from Mr. Bridges out of Lord Kinnaird's garden in the Casse of Gowrie. Sowing them has occupied me and the girls fully and they have a very nice flower garden" (Traill Family Collection). These exchanges contribute to the flowery content of the palimpsestic backwoods garden and recreate, to a degree, English traditions and tastes.

Most significantly, though, plants and seeds are tangible, growing expressions of human sentiment and bridge the emotional and geographical separation from England. Poignantly demonstrating this point is a cutting of grasses (in the National Archives) taken from the grave of Agnes Strickland in England and sent to her sisters in Canada as a token of remembrance (Figure 1.3). In addition to these trans-Atlantic offerings, an indispensable network of gardeners forms within Upper Canada through Traill's correspondence. A letter addressed to Ellen Dunlop (dated 1860) reveals that plant-sharing and

FIGURE 1.2
Violet and columbine seeds with accompanying handwritten notes

the fostering of extensive social ties work in tandem: "This reminds me my dear about the seeds – give them to any of *your friends they are all mine too*; if it be not too late for sowing should there be more than you need to use, or keep them yourself for another year they will I think grow as they were new last fall … I shall beg from you my dear when you can give it a sweet violet and a slip of scarlet geranium if any of these we stuck in the boxes last year have struck. I know that you will spare me a small one for Kate" (146). During the next two decades, Traill dispenses gardening advice to both friends and family,

FIGURE 1.3
Bundle of grass with note: "Grass from the grave of my ever dear Agnes Strickland (gathered in memorial and sent to me by kind friend) 1899"

setting aside plants for her daughter Annie Atwood to decorate her newly renovated home, and mailing apple pips to her son William to experiment with in the less forgiving climate of his western prairie garden.[21] In these private letters that share green-thumb wisdom, Traill demonstrates the daily, lifelong significance of gardening, an activity that is profoundly intertwined with her tending of relationships. In this regard, Traill's domestic kitchen garden operates within a larger network of spatial and cultural relationships that is at once local, inter-regional, and inter-continental.

Although maintaining connections with their original English home is an intrinsic part of their gardening practice, Moodie and Traill continually demonstrate their emerging awareness that gardens are context-specific creations. In her analysis of Atwood's and Margaret Laurence's recreations of Moodie and Traill in *The Journals of Susanna Moodie* and *The Diviners* (1974), respectively, Fiona Sparrow argues that gardens should be "suited to their localities" (34), a fact that, she believes, sometimes eluded the pioneering Strickland sisters. Sparrow concludes, "People should take changes of soil and climate into account when they order their lives and their gardens. The real Susanna Moodie no less than Atwood's recreation of her found this hard to do" (35). Critics' and contemporary writers' tendencies to present Moodie and Traill as either failed or domineering gardeners posits these women as maladaptive in their confrontation with the wilderness. When it comes to Laurence's famous characterization in *The Diviners*, her Traill is extremely industrious and meticulous: "C.P.T. out of bed, fully awake, bare feet on the sliver-hazardous floorboards – no, take that one again. Feet on the homemade hooked rug. Breakfast cooked for the multitude. Out to feed the chickens, stopping briefly on the way back to pull fourteen armloads of weeds out of the vegetable garden and perhaps prune the odd apple tree in passing" (108).

Laurence's formidable backwoods domestic diva resonates with McGregor's assertion that the actual Traill enacts a strict "domestication strategy" by ignoring that which is "alien" or "threatening" in her environment, and instead concentrating exclusively on what can be "controlled, manipulated, used" (41). Traill's creative, palimpsestic gardening practice tells, however, an altogether different story. In the summer of 1834, as recounted in *The Backwoods of Canada*, Traill chooses not to maintain her garden path despite the sudden, unplanned presence of a plant: "Last week I noticed a succulent plant that made its appearance on a dry sandy path in my garden; it seems to me a variety of the hour-blowing mesembryanthium. It has increased so rapidly that it already covers a large space; the branches converging from the center and sending forth shoots from every joint" (169). Traill has been informed that this plant is "troublesome" (169), and it grows rapidly and inconveniently in the middle of her garden path. She neither labels the plant a "weed" nor makes any attempt to remove or eliminate it. Instead, she observes its structure and gathers seeds in order to understand its prolific growth. When Traill discovers this unfamiliar, unruly plant growing in her garden, readers witness her encountering the wilderness, albeit on a smaller scale than that of the sublime, panoramic vision for which McGregor and other critics argue. In this palimpsestic garden, the wilderness is an agent (in the form of a plant) capable of altering this composite terrain. In response, Traill acts not simply out of tolerance but of fascination, as the unknown plant thrives in her garden, a situation that contrasts directly with the more manicured garden aesthetics she depicts in stories set in England, or that critics, such as Atwood in *Survival*, describe as the settler norm: "fenced plots of ground with edible plants inside and weeds outside" (120).[22]

As a gardener of accommodation, not domination, Traill acclimatizes her skills and aesthetic vision to respond to the physical realities of her circumstances. For example, Traill must incorporate tree stumps, a feature that does not adhere to her original English ideal and mars the flow of the terrain. In *The Canadian Settler's Guide*, she recommends using these remnants of the forest as a type of trellis: "The wild vine planted at the foot of some dead and unsightly tree, will cover it with its luxuriant growth, and convert that which would otherwise have been an unseemly object into one of great ornament"

(15). Heavy stones prove equally difficult to dispense with in the back-woods kitchen garden, and Traill advises that they "must either remain a blot on the fair features of the garden plot, or be rolled away by the strong arm of the men, aided by the lever" (55). She encourages their incorporation through a number of strategies: using them to build the lower portion of the garden fence, creating "the effect of rockwork"; constructing a seat from blocks of granite and limestone; or arrang-ing the stones as a planter in which to grow wild cucumbers, orange gourds, and wild clematis (55).[23] Traill desires a "natural" cottage gar-den appearance, but her objective can only be achieved by accepting the mixed components of her environment. Both the features of the forest and the evidence of its destruction and appropriation remain ever-present within her palimpsest.

Likewise championing adaptability when it comes to backwoods gardening within a composite context, Moodie pushes herself to re-evaluate the hierarchy of the "cultivated" versus the "wild" when it comes to plant categories and garden boundaries. In *Roughing It in the Bush*, Moodie demonstrates her willingness to reflect on the less "cultured" features of her environment when she famously gathers dandelions during the potato harvest: "Few of our colonists are acquainted with the many uses to which this neglected but most valuable plant may be applied ... the time will come when this hardy weed, with its golden flowers and curious seed-vessels, which form a constant plaything to the little children ... will be transplanted into our gardens, and tended with due care. The dandelion ... makes an excellent salad, quite equal to endive, and is more hardy and requires less care" (377). Within the span of a few words, the dandelion alters from being a "neglected," unknown plant and "hardy weed" to being an array of "golden flowers" capable of exciting the interest of children. Providing advice on transplanting, she elevates the dandelion through its inclusion in the garden; yet her estimation is not because it is cultivated, but rather because this plant requires "*less* care" (emphasis added). Similar to endive, the dandelion is hardier, growing readily both within and beyond the garden, and it is the plant's natural abundance and prolific growth – in other words, its "wildness" – that Moodie clearly appreciates when she urges a shift in settlers' arbitrary categorization of plants and weeds. Moodie's questioning of the prescribed status of weeds, as determined by British cultural norms, is perhaps made further evident by her paintings and sketches that feature a range of plants, from highly revered roses to ubiquitous dandelions (Figure 1.4). Traill similarly has watercolours attributed to her that feature common, unidentified plants labelled by the National Archives as "Weeds" (Figure 1.5).

The acceptance of the unfamiliar and the rejection of insularity are especially evident in Traill's renovations to her garden fence. During her first spring in 1833, Traill writes in *The Backwoods of Canada* that her garden is surrounded by a split rail fence (122), which is in subsequent years replaced by a wattled fence of "two half circular wings [that] sweep off from the entrance to each side of the house," a structure that, in her view, is "much more picturesque ... than those ... of split timber" (224). She writes, "Along this little enclosure I have begun planting a sort of flowery hedge with some of the native shrubs that abound in our woods and lake-shores" (224). Her garden renovations do not end here, however, as she reveals in *The Canadian Settler's Guide* that she finally replaces the wattled fence, which only lasts three years, with a fence made entirely of transplanted wild plants: "I collected wild gooseberry bushes, currants, bush honey suckles, hawthorns, wild cherry and plum trees ... and planted them within side [sic] my fence, to make a living fence, when the other should have decayed" (59). She boasts, "It was the admiration of all my neighbours,

FIGURE 1.4
Watercolour of "Dandelions" by Susanna Moodie, ca. 1870

FIGURE 1.5
Watercolour of a "Weed" by Catharine Parr Traill, ca. 1894

and many came to look at 'Mrs. Traill's fence'" (59). Thomas Traill and John Moodie name their settlements Westove and Melsetter respectively, after their original family estates in Scotland, in the hope of reclaiming their socio-economic status, but Traill acquires a more profound association with the territory because of her own labour and creativity in designing this "living fence." In effect, she recomposes her material garden palimpsest by planting atop and around existing structures. These adjustments provoke an alternative naming of the space as it becomes a new formulation of a garden always in process. An enclosed garden implies a plot of ground garrisoned off from a threatening wilderness, and at first glance, the two half-circular wings of Traill's fence comply with Fowler's interpretation of a tight domestic circle. However, by continually modifying the enclosure and creating a paradoxical living fence more permanent than decaying rails yet ever-changing in its spontaneous growth, Traill demonstrates a dynamic garden aesthetic that is anything but insular. The organic fence is reminiscent of English hedgerows and plays into Traill's desire for a picturesque, cottage-style garden translated into her Upper Canada setting. Constructed from transplanted native plants, this bush fence incorporates the backwoods kitchen garden into the larger environment through an ambiguous boundary and sustainable form.

Moodie and Traill are gardeners who accommodate out of both necessity and desire, making their backwoods kitchen gardens extensive, context-specific translations of their original English cottage garden ideals. In the Upper Canadian environment, picturesque terrain is not a straightforward option; Moodie and Traill must adjust to the realities of backwoods kitchen gardens that initially lack flowers and are cultivated foremost for basic needs. That which is unfamiliar becomes the norm, forming the central components of these terrains, including the growth and destruction of native vegetation, the sisters' daily experiences and needs, and the proximity of the "cultivated" and the "wild." It is precisely by accounting for this new world setting that Moodie and Traill demonstrate that their gardens are far more attuned to, and necessarily a part of, both the Upper Canadian wilderness and the settler landscape than previously argued by critics. Their kitchen gardens operate as critical interspaces of third nature: that is, concentrated expressions of imperialism's impact on the socio-physical environment of the backwoods, and the subsequent translation of English gardening norms and visions for a new context. In these material palimpsests, there is an ongoing composition of terrain where more than just a single pioneer gardener is an agent of change.

In contrast, the violent nature of Atwood's bush garden constructs a maladaptive persona of Moodie, one whose original perceptions are utterly displaced and useless. In "Dream 1: The Bush Garden," the result is an image of dejection: Moodie standing in a failed garden "gone to seed" where both plant and settler "come up blood" (34). Atwood's disassembling bush garden and Frye's organic model of Canadian literature minimize the importance of English garden aesthetics in their efforts to promote a distinct imagination "rooted in Canada" and reflective of a "vegetable … imagination" that is synonymous with the wilderness (Frye i). Placing Moodie and Traill in the context of garden history and theory leads to a somewhat different conclusion. It is precisely through their transplanting and translation of tradition and experience that the sisters come to adapt to, and know, their new country. Instead of feeling "broken / in upon by branches, roots, tendrils, the dark" as the settlers do in Atwood's poem "The Planters" (17), the Strickland sisters help to create and experience a relatively open blend of wild vegetation, backwoods necessity, and adapted picturesque aesthetics. Their backwoods kitchen gardens stem directly from this intricate, palimpsestic mixture.

CHAPTER TWO

# When Authors Are Gardeners:
## Susanna Moodie's and Catharine Parr Traill's Figurative "Plots"

If Susanna Moodie and Catharine Parr Traill succeeded as back-woods kitchen gardeners because of their adaptability, they also revised their understanding and use of the garden as transplanted writers. Traill's *Cot and Cradle Stories* (1895), published during the later years of her career, makes the relationship between writing and gardening unequivocal. The story "The Five Little Gardeners" compares how each Strickland sister gardens according to how she lives and, in relevant cases, writes. Thus a ten-year-old Agnes Strickland plants an orderly garden, and in the editor's note, Mary Agnes FitzGibbon (a grand-niece of Traill)[1] writes, "Agnes revealed her character in the methodical plan of her garden. Authoress of the Royal biographies, many poems, historical tales and several novels, she accomplished an enormous amount of work" (60). In contrast to Agnes, four-year-old Katie (Catharine) chooses wild flowers from the meadows for her childhood home, foreshadowing "the valuable work she had done in bringing our Canadian *flora* to the knowledge of the world" (61). The youngest sister Susie (Susanna) "[gets] an old trowel from the garden-house, and [sets] to work to dig a great hole in the ground" with Katie assisting her in making the hole "bigger and deeper" (59). In her concluding note, FitzGibbon theorizes why Susie digs, rather than plants, through a figurative connection with Moodie's writing: "Susie, who was possessed of the greatest of all gifts, the priceless gift of true genius, was ever questioning the reason of things, ever digging deep into the well of the knowledge of life, ever seeking for the treasure of truth, and finding it in increasing beauty and wealth in the Book of Life. Generous, enthusiastic, a brilliant conversationalist, a true poet, and a graphic writer, Canadian literature owes much to her influence and her pen" (61). FitzGibbon's comparison between the adults' accomplishments as authors and their childish careers as gardeners may seem whimsical, but the relationship between gardening and Moodie's and Traill's writerly strategies is surprisingly persuasive.

The sisters' immersion in popular British horticulture – including their seasonal gardening as girls (see chapter one), study of botany, and plant-related artistic activities – means that garden settings and metaphors are prominent formal features they associate with women's (and children's) education, social grace, and physical beauty. In transporting this discourse to Upper Canada and subsequently encountering actual backwoods gardens incongruent with the refined and refining British ideals, however, they revise their language in order to capture the emigration experience. The unfamiliar, liminal space of their backwoods gardens precipitates an adjustment of their vision and considerable negotiation of their domestic-centred understandings of femininity. Moodie and Traill use their garden rhetoric to craft both their desire for gender and class continuity as British-born women and their experience of change and adaptation as Upper Canadian pioneers. The metaphors at the centre of this paradoxical situation are those of "cultivation," "transplanting," and the related process of "hardening-off": activities they undertake in actual gardens and apply figuratively to their own circumstances and characters.

Further departures from their original discursive context lead to a second remarkable literary application of the garden in both Moodie's and Traill's works: the ideological, spatially sensitive narratives, or garden "plots," of the female immigrant experience. The term "plot" is especially well suited to the actual kitchen gardens and related stories tended by the Strickland sisters as opposed to a nineteenth-century landscape park designed on a grand scale by a professional. With the garden's figurative applications being so popular during the nineteenth century, Moodie's and Traill's "plots" readily function as a topos, or commonplace: a complex, recurring integration of space, meaning, and event. According to Mieke Bal, a topos entails "well-known, stereotypical combinations: declarations of love by moonlight on a balcony, high-flown reveries on a mountain-top, a rendezvous in an inn, ghostly appearances among ruins" (96). For the sisters, the "garden plot" as topos means that events and behaviours that take place within the garden regularly position their characters both spatially and ideologically, foregrounding "cultivated" natures and, alternatively, social transgressions. These do not become stereotypical, however, because Moodie and Traill demonstrate their ingenuity and adaptability as literary pioneers. They reveal an affinity in their position as writers (and siblings) of a shared historical-cultural milieu, while also highlighting their distinctive sensibilities and preoccupations. Intensely personal creations, Moodie's garden plots feature interactions between individuals of different socio-economic classes and showcase profoundly disruptive behaviour, including murder. In contrast, Traill's garden plots, while similarly concerned with impropriety, resist delving into the more troubling aspects of human nature. Her writing impresses upon readers, both young and old, pragmatic lessons. Ultimately, the temporally and spatially contained, context-specific aspect of a garden "plot" (in both a narrative and garden sense) makes it an especially pertinent conceptual model for considering Moodie's independently crafted, brief sketches (as opposed to the entire trajectory) of *Roughing It in the Bush*, as well as Traill's short narratives interspersed throughout her children's fiction and domestic manual.

## *Women and the Language of "Cultivation"*

In nineteenth-century England, a close relationship between women and gardens finds its expression in both public texts and private journals. One such exemplary work, Jane Loudon's *Instructions in Gardening for Ladies* (1840), promotes gardening for the female members of the refined classes by reducing the unseemliness of dirt and easing the rigours of outdoor manual labour. Married to the famous designer John Claudius Loudon in 1830, Jane Loudon assisted her husband with the writing and editing of his works on gardening; at the same time, she pursued her own career, producing such works as *Instructions in Gardening for Ladies* and *Lady's Magazine of Gardening* (Simo 2). In mediating gendered tensions that result from daily chores such as weeding and digging, Loudon's texts employ a rhetoric that promotes the kind of refinement and beauty desired by the garden's female custodians. According to Loudon, gardening is a suitably delicate activity as long as the proper provisions are taken, such as the use of leather gloves, an iron "tramp" to strengthen women's shoes, and a "lady's spade" that is "sufficiently slender for a lady's hand to grasp" (9). The illustration on the title page of Loudon's manual depicts a mother and child delicately at ease, poised, rather than hard at work, in the flower-embowered garden (Figure 2.1). With the inclusion of slender tools suited to tiny hands and feet, this scene is especially becoming to young ladies, as the woman adorned with flowers in her dress pockets and hair appears to be as cultivated as her garden. While Loudon promotes refinement, she recognizes that not all types of gardening are proper forms of recreation for "cultivated" women. Kitchen gardens are obviously not considered picturesque, as Loudon suggests that "there should always be a convenient, and, if possible, partially concealed, road for servants to bring in vegetables" (137). Furthermore, with vegetable gardening being delegated to the domestic help because it is labour-intensive and utilitarian, Loudon anticipates that women of refinement may have some misgivings: "Whatever the doubts may be entertained as to the practicability of a lady attending to the culture of culinary vegetables and fruit-trees, none can exist respecting her management of the flower-garden, as that is pre-eminently a woman's department" (244).

Another well-known private gardener of the nineteenth-century who reveals similar apprehensions is Dorothy Wordsworth. Recording the daily activity of the garden, Wordsworth uses the genre of the journal and the kind of self-reflection it affords to express her assumptions with respect to class and the feminine disposition. Although she admits to weeding (a laborious gardening activity), she most often mentions her flower gardening and distances herself from the less ladylike tasks, attributing these to her hired help: "I worked in the garden & planted flowers ... Sate [sic] under the trees after dinner till tea time. John Fisher stuck the peas, Molly weeded & washed" (7). One of the most telling passages that points to Wordsworth's belief in her delicate nature and inability to perform arduous work is when she purchases some flowers and must transport them home: "Went to the

FIGURE 2.1

Title page illustration from Jane Loudon's
*Instructions in Gardening for Ladies*, 1840

Blind man's for plants. I got such a load that I was obliged to leave my Basket in the Road & send Molly for it" (6).

The nineteenth-century class and gender distinctions expressed through the garden in Loudon's manual and Wordsworth's journal are equally clear in the writings of the Strickland sisters. The backwoods makes additional physical demands, but even the adaptable Moodie has her limits. In *Roughing It in the Bush*, she reveals her refined relationship to garden labour when she delineates her work versus that of her servant: "I dropped [potatoes] into the earth, while Jenny covered them up with the hoe. Our garden was well dug and plentifully manured, the old woman [Jenny] bringing the manure, which had lain for several years at the barn door, down to the plot, in a large Indian basket placed upon a hand-sleigh" (444). Some chores undermine the desired refinement that Loudon, Wordsworth, and even Moodie usually attribute to gardening, and there is a pressing need expressed in both public and private texts to maintain a sense of decorum.

Tellingly, nineteenth-century rhetoric surrounding the delicate female cultivator is not limited to actual gardening, as the garden pervades women's culture in general as well as the figurative language relating to women's social roles and education. Women had to appear as "cultivated" – that is, educated, beautiful, and full of social grace – as the gardens they explored, but did not necessarily labour intensely within. In her discussion of eighteenth- and nineteenth-century ideals of femininity, former *Harrowsmith* editor Jennifer Bennett notes that women immersed themselves in plants and all things plant-related in order to cultivate a kind of "floral" femininity. According to Bennett, women "dressed in flowers, talked about flowers and fashioned flowers from all kinds of materials. Crocheting flowers from wool, making skeletonized or phantom flowers from calcium chloride, tending wardian cases, and using Lady Mary Wortley Montagu's floral code to communicate secret messages of affection were all activities women participated in as means of expressing their desirable feminine nature and social status (95–100). They were even named for flowers: Daphnes, Hazels, Camellias, Irises ... and Violets occupied Victorian cradles. Older names such as Rose and Flora experienced revivals" (93). Moodie and Traill are clear proponents of this popular plant-related feminine culture. In *Roughing It in the Bush,* Moodie paints botanicals (181) and "mak[es] acquaintance with every wild flower" (163). With her avid botanical and gardening interests, Traill creates an herbarium, tends ferns in her wardian case, fashions table mats by weaving together Indian grasses (*Pearls* 65, 133), and assembles notepaper (Figure 2.2) depicting scenery through her arrangement of natural materials.

FIGURE 2.2
A hand-made botanical card sent from Catharine Parr Traill to her grand-daughter Evelyne Muchall with the message, "For Dear Evelyne with Grandmother's very affectionate love and best wishes. Dec. 22 1888."

Moodie and Traill steadfastly believe in the garden as educator, a belief that carries over to their rhetoric of "cultivation" and their various characterizations of women and young children. According to Moodie in *Roughing It in the Bush*, the women of Upper Canada boast erroneously of their refined natures because, in contrast to Moodie's and Traill's own sophistication, these physically attractive yet poorly educated, lower-class female emigrants need to be "improved by *cultivation*" (218, emphasis added). These women are in need of "a little mental culture," and they remind Moodie of neglected gardens: "choice flowers half buried in weeds" (218). Such figurative language as it relates to class, education, and gender is typical of the advice found in nineteenth-century conduct books. Jacqueline Labbe points to Hannah More (1745–1833), a conservative-minded educator who worked to maintain proper gendered spheres for men and women, as an example of an author who was inspired by this rhetoric. Supporting her argument with examples from More's conduct books, Labbe contends that More believes women must first "[submit] to being gardened" – to being properly educated and supervised by their mothers – before "those women may 'garden,' may exercise discretion and perception" (45).[2] In the essay "Of Queens' Gardens," John Ruskin presents a comparable organic model of girlhood, arguing that while a boy is "chisel[ed] … into shape" (83) until he becomes a man who is "*always* hardened" (77) by society, a girl "grows as a flower does" (83), naturally and delicately in her male-prescribed, male-protected familial domain. Part of this "natural" growth involves turning young girls loose in the library to cultivate their minds (84).

Moodie and Traill certainly reveal their acquiescence to this rhetoric and to the garden as the site of learning when depicting children's developing intellects and characters. In Traill's children's book *Little Downy; or, The History of a Field-Mouse* (1822), Mrs Clifford instructs her young son, Alfred, in empathy through the middle-class setting of the family garden and the embedded narrative of Downy, the garden-dwelling mouse. The frontispiece (Figure 2.3) visually situates the teaching of this moral lesson from within the home, while the prominent window in the background provides a portal to the larger outside world: the rolling English hills in the distance, and the formal flower beds and garden – the differentiated third nature of concentrated human intervention – that surround this cultivated and "cultivating" home. While Alfred is educated through a story about the garden, young girls in Traill's texts are almost always learning directly in the garden. In *Pearls and Pebbles* (1894), Traill praises the experience of her own childhood; she and her sisters tended a woodland garden, developing in tandem their Romantic sensibilities and gender roles: "A hollow in the bank was fashioned into a grotto, which we lined with moss and decorated with dry striped snailshells and bright stones. Our garden tools were of the rudest – our trowel a rusty iron ladle, our spade a broken-bladed carving knife, and we daily watered the flowers from a battered tin teapot and a leaky japanned mug" (7). This grotto is in keeping with fashionable gardening activities, as Yvonne Cuthbertson notes that during the Romantic period "well-to-do ladies spent many hours decorating them with vast amounts and varieties of seashells" (78). Furthermore, the sisters partake in suitably delicate work by using well-worn kitchen utensils, not cumbersome garden tools. Their choice of implements is decidedly domestic-minded, and Traill writes in her *Narratives of Nature* (1831) that the sisters even furnished their "sylvan dwellings" (128) because the grottos "were intended to represent the country-houses and villas of [their] rag dolls or [their] paper dolls" (129).

Moodie similarly commends gardening in "Rachel Wilde, or, Trifles from the Burthen of a Life" (1848) in which the wayward Rachel

FIGURE 2.3

Illustrated title page from *Little Downy; or, The History of a Field-Mouse: A Moral Tale*, by Catharine Parr Traill, 1822

"Wilde" and her sister Dorothea are charged with the household responsibility of tending the flower borders, a task that leaves the girls "innocently employed" and with "joy in their eyes, and health in their cheeks" (101). In his introduction to the CSSL edition of *Voyages: Short Narratives of Susanna Moodie*, John Thurston acknowledges that "Moodie's account of the lives of the Wilde children in 'Rachel Wilde' accords with accounts of the early lives of the Stricklands. All the daughters except Jane are represented: Susanna as the eponymous heroine, Catharine as Dorothea" (x). In the story, Rachel learns the dangerous consequences of vanity when she and her sister Dorothea hang signs of poetry around the stems of their flowers: "crushed beneath the weight of flattery, which bowed their simple beauties to the earth; and which like the human flowers to whom the same treatment is applied, sadly marred their native charms" (103). Here, the garden trumps poetry as the more esteemed educator, as the potential excesses of poetic language are cause for concern. In his introduction, Thurston concurs that Thomas Strickland "controlled [his daughters'] reading" and enforced a "ban on merely ornamental or entertaining literature" (x), so it comes as no surprise that the "natural" home environment appears the best milieu for the cultivation of modest, gendered propriety. This advice carries over to texts set in Upper Canada when Moodie advises that nature is vital to the proper rearing of children. In *Life in the Clearings versus the Bush* (1853), she warns mothers against party-going for young girls: "parties operate like a forcing bed upon young plants, with this difference, that they bring to maturity the seeds of evil, instead of those of goodness and virtue, and that a child accustomed to the heated atmosphere of pleasure, is not likely in maturer years to enjoy the pure air and domestic avocations of home ... The garden or the green field is the best place for children"

(328–9). Social gatherings beyond the safe confines of home are artificial in nature, acting as "forcing beds" that foster corrupted growth – an excessive love of finery and vanity that prevents young girls from appreciating the "pure air" of their domestic environs and related gender roles.[3]

Such discourse demonstrates a clear political purpose: to naturalize paradigms of domestic femininity and family life. In his study of the garden in Victorian literature, Michael Waters concurs that the garden routinely upholds women's married position as the iconic Angel in the House. Constructions of women within gardens serve "to beautify, sanctify, and naturalize" (241) women's domestic role: the women exhibit "an 'instinctive' love of gardens and a 'native' affinity with the plants they nurture" (242). In doing so, a woman frequently serves as "ornamental icon or spectacle" (245) in the garden, in other words, an object of the gaze of a "privileged male observer" (245). This cultural icon of naturalized domesticity is most visible in "Of Queens' Gardens" in which Ruskin informs his female readers to "be no more housewives, but queens" of their domains through their maternal nurturing and sweet ordering (88). A "cultivated" young woman becomes a prospective wife through her self-regulation and usefulness. This model of housewifery is made explicit in Traill's "The Five Little Gardeners" when the second eldest sister, Sara, plants a practical yet sensual garden filled with herbs and flowers. Seeing the girl's work, the old gardener declares with a laugh, "Well, Miss Sara, you'll make a rare good housewife for some good husband one of these days" (57).

Moodie and Traill delineate marriageable femininity for readers of all ages, yet both writers also deviate from this discursive tradition. The old gardener in "The Five Little Gardeners" speculates about Sarah's domestic apprenticeship in the garden, but as we saw in the introduction to this chapter, FitzGibbon's footnote about the relationship between writing and gardening provides a conspicuous counterpoint. Traill's depiction of innocent childhood labour foretells not simply naturalized housewifery, but other expressive, intellectual pursuits, with the garden serving as a portal to female-directed creativity and agency in the literary realm. According to Dianne Harris, nineteenth-century American and British women writers embraced the garden manual as a means of expressing self-empowerment when faced with curtailed political, economic, and social freedoms. Garden manuals "provided a forum and safe outlet for the cultivation of what feminist historians have called a 'woman's culture,' a culture that nurtured independence and power" ("Cultivating Power" 113).[4] Women elevated and disseminated their own sources of knowledge about plants, while also subtly and even explicitly promoting social reforms. In her survey of these manuals, Harris detects a validation of women's agency within the private sphere and the institution of marriage through a number of pronounced desires, such as the desire for property ownership, financial independence (through the selling of garden produce and access to garden professions), freedom from familial responsibilities, and a far-reaching social exchange among women. These incentives hold true for *The Canadian Settler's Guide* with its pragmatic instruction for women pioneers to be active members of the settlement process via the backwoods kitchen garden (see chapter one). Traill's manual, as well as Moodie's garden writing, performs an additional function, however, by nurturing not just socioeconomic reforms for women, but also a modified literary culture. Their garden-related texts express a realization of the tangible impact of the backwoods on gender and class paradigms and their need, as writers, to generate appropriate figurative language and innovative treatments of character and narrative to convey these changes.

## The Settler Experience of "Transplanting" and "Hardening-Off"

When it comes to life in the backwoods, the hard work of milking cows, fighting house fires, and ploughing fields is incongruent with the "queenly" (to use Ruskin's phrase) tasks of beautifying and tending a home. Moodie and Traill must re-examine their understanding of femininity as they adapt their language to alternative stories of women's "education" and experiences that arise, not through moral instruction or reading, but rather through daily toil and the unrefined circumstances of a mixed, "uncultured" society. In the Upper Canadian texts, readers find a range of female figures serving as different models of cultivated femininity depending on the context. At one end of this spectrum are Moodie's original English notions of "cultivation" as portrayed in *Flora Lyndsay; or, Passages in an Eventful Life* (1854), a fictional autobiography that traces the Moodies' decision and preparation to emigrate. The aptly named protagonist, a middle-class woman and writer unaccustomed to difficult manual labour, captures this traditional femininity through her cultured status and physically fragile constitution. While the name "Flora" derives from a sensual Roman goddess of flowers, Bennett notes that "by the Victorian era, she had become a sort of comfortable great-aunt figure, and her name was given to countless baby girls. Flora's extended reign brought her – her revels and erotica left behind – into an age when she was considered decorative but useless" (26).[5] In keeping with these associations, Moodie's Flora appears entirely unsuited for life in the backwoods, suggesting that definitions of gendered refinement are necessarily context specific. When Captain Kitson enters Flora's pretty English cottage and asks her to confirm the rumours of her imminent emigration, he exposes her comfortable routine, naïve character, and drastically ill-prepared state for her new life across the

Atlantic: "'A fine settler's wife you will make; nervous and delicate, half the time confined to your bed with some complaint or other. And then, when you are well, the whole blessed day is wasted in reading and writing, and coddling up the baby. I tell you that sort of business will not answer in a rough country like Canada'" (15). Flora's delicacy is an intrinsic part of her identity as an educated, middle-class woman who remains primarily indoors. Cultivated for a certain lifestyle, Flora needs a revised education for life in Upper Canada.

If Flora sits at one end of the spectrum, at the other is the back-woods-educated, youthful pioneer Catharine Maxwell from Traill's *Canadian Crusoes: A Tale of the Rice Lake Plains* (1852), published twenty years after Traill's emigration. Unlike the soon-to-be emigrating Flora, the Canadian-born Catharine knows nothing "of book-learning beyond a little reading" and lacks "mental cultivation" (6). Catharine's alternative "cultivation" is evident, however, through her "well-regulated mind" (6) and her ability to create a garden-like shelter when lost in the woods:

Catharine had selected a pretty, cool shady recess, a natural bower, under the overhanging growth... Some large blocks of water-worn stone formed convenient seats and a natural table, on which the little maiden arranged the forest fare... The strawberries, set out in little pottles made with the shining leaves of the oak, ingeniously pinned together by Catharine with the long spurs of the hawthorn, were voted delicious, and the pure water most refreshing, that they drank... from a large mussel-shell which Catharine had picked up among the weeds and pebbles on the beach. (27)

While Catharine Maxwell lacks the typical attributes of a cultivated

English woman, she is, nonetheless, as Andrew O'Malley astutely notes, "an agent of domestic reform" who "clearly demonstrates the colonizing power of domesticity" (83). In his analysis of Traill's text as a robinsonade, O'Malley argues that Catharine's backwoods home-making re-creates a European, middle-class lifestyle, as she even mothers (and colonizes) the Native character Indiana, tames animals, and successfully builds a settler culture (79–83).

With this array of "cultivated" female figures occupying their texts, Moodie and Traill consequently revise their figurative language of the garden. Specifically, the terms "transplanting" and "hardening-off" form a necessary extension of this class- and gender-conscious discourse so as to reflect the dramatic change in context. According to the *Oxford English Dictionary*, "transplanting" denotes a crossing of boundaries and spaces as the verb means "[t]o remove (a plant) from one place or soil and plant it in another."[6] Central to the success of this process is a period of "hardening-off," which entails the movement of plants from one set of conditions to a harsher set, as plants are rendered "hardy, robust, or capable of endurance" by "inur[ing] plants to cold by gradually reducing the temperature of a hot-bed or forcing-house by increasing the time of exposure to wind and sunlight."[7] Traill outlines hardening-off in detail in *The Canadian Settler's Guide* when instructing her readers on how to acclimatize wild plants accustomed to the woods to grow successfully within the garden: "The reason why the native plants often fail to grow and thrive when removed to the garden, arises from the change in the soil and situation: to remove a plant from deep shade and light rich soil, to sunshine and common earth, without any attention to their previous habits, is hardly reasonable. A fine leaf mould, water, and shelter should be afforded til [sic] the tender stranger has become inured to its change of soil and position" (77). Both transplanting and hardening-off are integral to

Moodie's and Traill's gardening, and not surprisingly, these processes acquire additional dimensions in their texts to account for the social and physical repercussions of newly arrived emigrants' exposure to the backwoods experience.

According to *The Canadian Settler's Guide,* each female emigrant is first transplanted and then hardened-off: an all-encompassing adaptation with respect to skills, habits, attitude, and physical appearance. This formative experience applies to all female settlers of divergent backgrounds: the wives of officers, gentlemen, labourers, or mechanics. Even those settlers "enured from childhood to toil" (5) will undergo, Traill anticipates, a difficult acclimatization: "At first the strangeness of all things around them, the loss of familiar faces and familiar objects, and the want of all their little household conveniences, are sensibly felt; and these little things make them uncomfortable and peevish: but a little reasoning with themselves would show that such inconveniences belong to the nature of their new position, and that a little time will do away with the evil they complain of' (5). Traill readies women for the unrefined physical and social circumstances, or the "nature of their new position" in the backwoods. When it comes to failed transplants, no previous experience, education, or even husbands have prepared the women for the tasks at hand. Traill's "Female Trials in the Bush" demonstrates this re-contextualized understanding of cultivated femininity. Her initial reflections on women's domestic sphere echo Ruskin's delineation of "Queens' gardens" as the private terrains that women occupy and that men defend from the hostile outside world: "It is generally allowed that woman is by nature and habit more strongly attached to home and all those domestic ties and associations that form her sources of happiness, than man. She ... scarcely receives the same pleasures that man does from travelling and exchange of place; her little world is *home,* it is or should be her sphere of actions" (80). Whereas the man moves freely and confidently from place to place in the public realm, the woman encounters a more contained experience within the home; her very happiness seems predicated upon this singular domestic role. Traill's description foreshadows the unprepared state of the female emigrant whose sphere of influence and activity is about to expand drastically. "[T]otally unfitted by habits, education and inclination, without due warning of the actual trials she is destined to encounter" (81), the female emigrant is, in Traill's view, destined for a failed transplanting to Upper Canada because of a too severe hardening-off. In this context, the husband no longer possesses the Queen of the garden: "The wife finds she has been deceived, and becomes fretful, listless and discontented; and the husband, when too late, discovers that he has transplanted a tender exotic, to perish beneath the withering influence of an ungenial atmosphere, without benefiting by its sweetness or beauty" (81). Comparing the female settler to a "tender exotic," Traill implies that a failed transplanting will occur when a woman remains like an English flower: passive and delicate.

In Upper Canada there is a noticeable shift in circumstances and societal expectations, and if settlers do not respond, they fail to thrive. In *Roughing It in the Bush*, Moodie recounts numerous failed transplants, most notably that of Jeanie Burns, the "daughter of a respectable shoemaker, who gained a comfortable living by his trade in a small town of Ayrshire" (119).[8] When Jeanie emigrates from England to join her fiancé Willie Robertson, she discovers that in his impatience and ambition, Willie married another woman who had a "good lot of land in the rear of his farm" (124). Overwhelmed by the deception, delicate Jeanie lacks resiliency and is bedridden for weeks; the "the colour ... fade[s] from her cheeks" (126). Ultimately, she dies of heartache and cannot withstand the climate of neglect and romantic betrayal that follows her uprooting from England: "Puir Jeanie! she held out during the simmer, but when the fall came, she just withered awa' like a flower, nipped by the early frost, and this day we laid her in the earth" (127–8). Middle-class female emigrants such as Jeanie Burns seem particularly ill-suited to the hardships of the backwoods, which are exacerbated by the unforgiving environment. The resulting physical transformation is especially severe: "The Canadian women, while they retain the bloom and freshness of youth, are exceedingly pretty; but these charms soon fade, owing, perhaps, to the fierce extremes of their climate, or the withering effect of the dry metallic air of stoves" (217). Eventually, Moodie concedes, "the glowing tint of the Albion rose pales before the withering influence of late hours and stove-heat" (218).

Ultimately, the objective is to educate readers into agency, teaching them the skills of manual labour, the varied hardships of the backwoods, and a self-directing attitude so that they can thrive as true immigrants of their adopted home. In cases where women adapt to the new climate, successful transplants result, which means a more hardened, rather than refined, state of femininity. These women are no longer passive and exotic flowers, but active and enduring gardeners. In "Female Trials in the Bush," Traill recalls how one lady of "some fortune" was romanced by her fiancé to emigrate after being given the impression that she would become "the queen of the village of which he gave her so glowing a picture" (82). In reality, the new wife finds herself physically transformed by poverty and manual labour: "Though to some persons it might appear a trifling evil, there was nothing in all her sad reverse of condition that seemed so much to annoy my poor friend as the discolouring of her beautiful hands; she would often sigh as she looked down on them and say, 'I used to be so vain of them, and never thought to employ them in menial offices'" (83).

Extending this conventional gendered discourse, metaphors of transplanting and hardening-off render familiar perceived transgressions against nineteenth-century paradigms of femininity. Not lacking in self-reflection or humility, Moodie counts herself among the women who have been physically hardened when she recalls her own family's departure from the bush. Although she works to maintain her "cultivated" status and appearance within *Roughing It in the Bush*, her situation alters her self-characterization. When John Moodie finally procures the sheriff's position in Belleville, Moodie feels that she is no longer suited for the now unfamiliar town environment: "my person had been rendered coarse by hard work and exposure to the weather. I looked double the age I really was, and my hair was already thickly sprinkled with grey. I clung to my solitude. I did not like to be dragged from it to mingle in gay scenes, in a busy town, and with gaily-dressed people. I was no longer fit for the world" (501). This self-portrait appears near the conclusion of the sketch, yet earlier in this departure sequence, Moodie contextualizes the extent of her physical transformation and its social implications. Preparing to leave the bush, she worries about the possible change in situation for her daughter Addie (or Agnes), who has been living with a wealthy neighbour during Moodie's convalescence: "Mrs. H----, whose husband was wealthy, was a generous, warm-hearted girl of eighteen. Lovely in person, and fascinating in manners ... she dressed the little creature expensively; and, by constantly praising her personal appearance, gave her an idea of her own importance which it took many years to eradicate. It is a great error to suffer a child, who has been trained in the hard school of poverty and self-denial, to be *transplanted suddenly into the hot-bed of wealth and luxury*" (492, emphasis added). Moodie fears that in being transplanted into a position of wealth and finery, her daughter will no longer be suited to her own domain, which is a world of "useful occupation … scanty means and plain clothing" (492).

### *Pioneer Heroines, Mending Baskets, and Botany: Critical Models*

Although horticultural metaphors are central to Moodie's and Traill's revised gendered discourse, critics have, until recently, overlooked this recurring language, preferring alternative models to describe the sisters' accounts of settler life. There are generally two schools of thought reflecting on Moodie's and Traill's transformation into pioneer women: the first (which includes scholars such as Elizabeth Thompson, T.D. MacLulich, D.M.R. Bentley, and Virginia Watson Rouslin) argues that the Strickland sisters embrace the freedoms afforded by their new social milieu and consequently reject any constraining notions of femininity. In contrast, the second school (which includes, among others, Misao Dean and Marian Fowler) suggests that the sisters adhere to gender and class norms and, therefore, assimilate their unconventional pioneer lives into the British model of respectability.

According to the first school of thought, Moodie's and Traill's works depict the creation of new ideals that redefine domestic, maternal roles. In this regard, Elizabeth Thompson sees "a self-assured, confident woman, one who adapts cheerfully to adverse circumstances, one who is capable and active in an emergency, one who plays a vital role in pioneering" (4).[9] The environment facilitates the transformation into a successful, hardy pioneer, and MacLulich, Bentley, and Rouslin echo this argument for dramatic gender revisions in the context of a new society.[10] Upper Canada is a promised land of near-feminist potential where, according to Rouslin, women "could exercise their individuality," discover "the freedom of expression and self-development," and above all, cast away the restrictions of cultivated femininity with "more room to grow in a natural direction" (326).

A woman who grows "naturally" is unfettered by the engendering processes of British society; but for Misao Dean, the key spokesperson for the second line of thought, gender cannot be conceived "as an artificial limitation upon a pre-existent self which may be thrown off almost at will by daring individual women" (9). Using Judith Butler's theory of gender performance, Dean formulates an alternative interpretation: Moodie and Traill practice their gender consistently and struggle to naturalize pioneer femininity as they "mend the gap between inner self and outward practice" (28). According to Dean, *The Canadian Settler's Guide* serves as a discursive and "ideological mending basket" (12) for the maintenance of proper femininity: manual labour is declassed, de-masculinized, and realigned with the traditional, inherent feminine virtues of duty, modesty, frugality, self-regulation, and refinement (24).[11]

In response to these two opposing schools of thought – the one for radical gender freedoms and "natural" growth, the other for continued gender constraints – this study suggests that in their confirmation of and divergence from the discourse of "cultivated" femininity, Moodie's and Traill's garden writing assumes a complicated middle ground. As we saw in chapter one, Moodie's and Traill's actual gardens were composites: material palimpsests of their British horticultural practices and ideals, and the wilderness-settler environment. By extension, their figurative and literary constructions of the third nature of the garden are also inherently reflective of a combination of discursive, cultural contexts. Moodie and Traill can neither grow unencumbered by traditional British gender norms, nor absolutely maintain these norms within Upper Canadian society with its rough living and mixed society. The composition of their literary gardens reflects this paradoxical relationship through the transgressions and interlopers that eventually become commonplace within their backwoods plots.

One line of inquiry relevant to the paradoxical nature of the Strickland sisters' garden writing pertains to Traill's interest in botany as a source of informative metaphors for the pioneer experience. This resurgent interest in Traill's botanical writings has its foundation in Michael Peterman's (and others') early work on Traill as the "anachronistic" backwoods botanist and natural historian whose work "has fallen between the disciplinary schools of botany and literature both in her century and in our own" (183).[12] Peterman notes that Traill's love of plants, especially flowers, provides her with "an invaluable emotional continuity between past and present ... Suffolk and Upper Canada, and cultivation (civilization) and wilderness (the state of wilderness)" (179). In chapter one, we saw how actual plants in the form of seed exchanges between Upper Canada and England facilitated this ongoing social network. Following Peterman's invitation for further study of Traill's naturalist work as a kind of innovative autobiography, Lisa Stefaniak's "Botanical Gleanings: Susan Fenimore Cooper, Catharine Parr Traill, and Representations of Flora" (2001) and Margaret Steffler and Neil Steffler's "'If We Would Read It Aright': Traill's 'Ladder to Heaven'" (2004) contend that in Traill's botanical works, readers discern socio-cultural significance beyond the scientific application.[13] In writing about specific native and introduced species of plants, Traill attempts to root herself in her new home by "reinforcing rather than negotiating the limits of culturally sanctioned femininity" (as argued by Stefaniak, 239), or by acknowledging her colonizing power as a British settler and her colonized position as a woman (as argued by the

Stefflers, 138–40). While the Stefflers' highlighting of Traill's paradoxical position is relevant to my interest in the garden, theirs and Stefaniak's lines of inquiry are primarily interested in the naturalist works and Traill's role as "floral godmother," a phrase she uses to describe herself in *The Backwoods of Canada* (104), when identifying, naming, and interpreting nature. By complementing and diverging from such botanical scholarship, my study concentrates on the figurative expression of feminine adaptation not confined to descriptions of flora. Traill reads nature or plants according to her values as an amateur botanist, yet both she and her sister perform the inverse: interpreting and constructing settler characters as plants, gardens, and gardeners. It is essential to see these authors as "gardeners" (in addition to being amateur botanists) in order to examine the interconnections between gardening and creative writing, a relationship modeled and alluded to explicitly in "The Five Little Gardeners." Moodie and Traill obviously adapt the figurative language popular at the time to accommodate the female pioneer's revised gender roles, but they also structure their stories in innovative ways by spatially framing garden "plots" and characters specific to the backwoods experience.

## Garden "Plots" for the Female Immigrant

Moodie and Traill are successful gardener-writers because they foster purpose and relevancy in their manipulation of genres and literary conventions appropriate for a new country. They strategically situate female characters and even their own personae through garden "plots" at integral moments of gender and class negotiation. Because a literary topos (such as a garden) operates as a "fixed combination" of space and event, Mieke Bal argues that creative manipulations produce significant effects. Readers' understanding of literary conventions combined with a writer's need to use or diverge from them result in the expression of changeable circumstances and meanings. Bal notes, "The expectation that a clearly marked space will function as the frame of a suitable event may … be disappointed"; conversely, "information concerning space is often repeated, to stress the stability of the frame, as opposed to the transitory nature of the events which occur within it" (97). Here, Bal highlights the incongruence and temporality of events, in contrast to the stability of the frame, as one possible manipulation of a topos. In the case of Moodie and Traill, however, the garden frame works in a somewhat different manner. On the one hand, because of its continued association with the nineteenth-century rhetoric of cultivation, the garden is a reassuring, constant space that enables the reiteration of gender conventions, even as Moodie and Traill revise their notion of femininity in a pioneering context. On the other hand, the garden as narrative frame changes its form in response to its actual counterpart: the backwoods kitchen garden. When it comes to the garden "plots" of the backwoods, then, both the frame itself and the events that take place within it are significantly altered, thereby directing readers' attention toward profound shifts in gendered and domestic paradigms. Moodie's and Traill's "plots" serve, therefore, as bounded sites and narratives that paradoxically challenge the fixity of the garden topos: they defamiliarize English norms (or what is "second nature" within English society and its discourse of gendered and class propriety) and introduce unfamiliar conduct and characters through the critical third space of the backwoods garden. These innovative "plots" are, therefore, inherently tied to Upper Canada's cultural landscape and its alternative "second nature" of everyday pioneer life with its ongoing negotiations.

Moodie's and Traill's attentiveness to the spatial framing of their characters can be seen in garden plots set in both England and Upper

Canada. Both locations lend themselves to the staging of social transgressions, yet they do so in different and telling ways. The English stories highlight character foibles and class conflict because of unfortunate or unusual circumstances that temporarily disrupt normative behaviour and conduct. In "A Garden Party" (from *Cot and Cradle Stories*), Traill directs her story of relatively innocent transgressions towards children.[14] Moodie, on the other hand, in the stories of "The Miss Greens"[15] (from *Matrimonial Speculations*) and Noah Cotton[16] (from *Flora Lyndsay; or, Passages in an Eventful Life*) turns to garden settings in England to explore serious adult misdemeanors. Traill and Moodie wrote many of these stories after their emigration, but the kinds of gardens featured and the central concerns and outcomes of the narratives are unquestionably distinct from their backwoods counterparts. In all three stories, the less fortunate members of English society try to gain access to privileged garden space and all it represents. The gardens (which range from a childhood garden, to a middle-class suburban yard, to an illustrious landscape park) provide not only physical and ideological parameters for the communication of gendered and class-related propriety, but also (and paradoxically so) spaces where social codes can be tested and, eventually, re-instated. In these narratives, the social transgressions or falls from grace take place in gardens that are part of an unchanging socio-economic system, reflecting the relative fixity of English society. The socio-economic injustices featured in these stories form the impetus behind the Strickland sisters' own emigrations. In fact, both of Moodie's stories actually posit the Canadian colony as a potential solution to these English garden settings that accentuate a lack of personal freedom.[17]

While these English stories tell of fortunate escapes from, or travesties of, ignorance and greed, they are not suggestive of fundamental changes in class structure or gender paradigms. When Moodie and

Traill set garden plots in the backwoods, however, their employment of spatial frames differs. In their Canadian stories they focus on the day-to-day realities of a dramatically altered context with new sets of issues, all of which are concentrated in the third nature space of the garden. Class, property, and identity remain significant preoccupations in these narratives, but there is a shift in emphasis, as gender becomes the foremost concern through the near-solitary actions of female pioneers. While the transgressions may not appear as severe as those in the English narratives (no humans are murdered in the backwoods, for example, although a pet is), these garden plots nonetheless reveal profound social adaptations.

In *The Canadian Settler's Guide*, Traill claims that she is writing as a didactic homemaker, "contented to abandon the paths of literary fame" (xviii) in the production of her "homely" manual (xviii), yet she skillfully persuades her readers to revise their gender norms through a conspicuous narrative of discordant behaviour that disrupts the parameters of spatially defined femininity. In the middle of her manual, Traill relates a garden plot featuring the harsh realities of pioneer life and one woman's harvesting of the corn crop. This story of difficult adaptation and hardening-off takes place outside the domestic sphere, and Traill could not have included it in the opening sections of *The Canadian Settler's Guide*, where she inures her readers gradually to manual labour. Through references to garden enclosures both at the onset and within the telling of this story, Traill works to reframe the woman pioneer's work ideologically. First, she situates her subject within the domestic domain of cultivated femininity, describing her as an officer's wife, "a young woman who had never been accustomed to any other work than such light labour as the most delicate female may take pleasure in, such as the culture of flowers, and making pastry and preserves, and such matters" (114). When her female servant, husband, and man-servant all fall ill with fever, the woman takes to the corn fields to harvest the crop, noticing that the corn is "just ripe" but that "the fence [is] not very secure, and the hogs of a settler about half a mile off, came thrugh [sic] the woods and destroyed the corn" (114). With the crop in danger of being ruined completely because of the faulty fence, the immigrant wife must move beyond her usual sphere of domestic work. She sets out to harvest with baby in arms; "fortunately [the field is] close at hand, just beside the garden" (115).

The proximity of the garden is reassuring; nevertheless, the woman labours outside it, and this de-framing of her work and gender leads to a paradoxical reversal of the public/outside versus private/inside model of masculinity and femininity, respectively. The garden fence serves both spatial and rhetorical purposes as Traill directs and persuades her readers toward an acceptance of gender transgressions. With her baby seated nearby, the woman harvests the corn crop in the hot afternoon:

> She soon became interested in the work, and though her soft hands, unused to rough labour, were blistered and chafed, in a few hours she had stripped the cobs from a large portion of the corn, and thrown them into heaps, running back from time to time to speak to her baby, and amuse him by rolling towards him the big yellow golden pumpkins, with which in a short time she had effectually fenced him round, while the little fellow, shouting with joy, patted and slapped the cool rind of the orange-coloured fruit …
>
> Between gathering the corn, playing with the baby, and going to visit her sick husband, she had enough to do …
>
> In after years she has often with honest pride related to her children, how she gathered in the first Indian corn crop that

was raised on their bush farm. Possibly this very circumstance gave a tone of energy and manly independence of spirit to her children, which will mark them in their progress in after life. (115)

Traversing both physical and ideological boundaries, this woman occupies an ambiguous position: she is both maternal, in caring for her baby and sick husband, and paternal, in completing the harvest and "mark[ing]" her children with masculine independence. Traill's garden plot de-frames and re-frames, therefore, the feminine sphere, pushing outward into the masculine domain, which demands a forthright, even "interested" engagement with a difficult, labour-intensive world. The mother is the new protector of the home: she "fence[s] [her son] round" with pumpkins, while she, herself, remains outside the home and garden, setting a "manly" example by working in the field.

### A Contemporary Pioneer Garden Palimpsest

The ingenuity of Traill's garden plot and related gender discourse is made evident by the fact that it inspired Robert Kroetsch to create a palimpsest in his poem "Pumpkin: A Love Poem" (published in the collection *The Stone Hammer Poems*, 1975). Kroetsch never explicitly names Traill's text as the original source (a telling effacement that I will address momentarily), but the parallels are clear. The speaker situates himself in the position of the baby boy who is encircled by pumpkins as his mother works in the field. The major differences in this reworking of the story are that Kroetsch's overtly sexualized lyrical speaker is no longer an innocent infant or silent bystander, but rather a creative agent in his own right. Moreover, he now resides within a pumpkin, rather than being encircled by them:

Inside the pumpkin     I feel much better
I feel     loyalty to my pioneering
ancestors     I have entered

new territory     I feel a bit
sticky, yes, cramped     but I feel
much better     trying to smile (1–6)

In response to Traill, a literary foremother embodied by the female settler who toils outside the pumpkin, Kroetsch presents his speaker as expressing "loyalty" to his predecessors who broke new creative ground. At the same time, the speaker feels "cramped" or crowded by the previous generation and wants "new territory" by feeling out original, imaginative terrain for himself. As Robert Lecker suggests in his book-length study *Robert Kroetsch*, "Kroetsch places himself 'inside the pumpkin,' which has become both his brain and the universe, the overseeded realm of darkness waiting impatiently for light" (131). When the speaker enters into this introspective world, he engages with his ancestors, Lecker explains, in an almost physical, even sexual way: "the ancestors are actually being touched, made love with, gone inside of. Thus it is quite correct to say 'I feel / ancestors I have entered' or to insist that by doing so 'I have entered / new territory" (132).

This intimate encounter with the pumpkin, the female ancestor, and the imaginative territory speaks to Kroetsch's admiration for Traill's garden plot, which informs the ambiguous sexual imagery and spatial framing of his poem. Lecker notes that the speaker carves the pumpkin into a face, where the "mouth ... is subtly altered into images of male and female genitalia" (132). In the poem, the speaker describes his mouth as a veritable *vagina dentata*, "toothed and jagged / the slit" (27–8). This "mouth" also engages his erect and "pressing groin" (30) however, making, as Lecker argues, the mouth (or voice) "the resting place of seed" for this sensual poet-speaker who brings opposites together in sexually provocative ways (132). In addition to the pumpkin's ambiguous facial/genital features, the male speaker resides inside the pumpkin whereas the female pioneer toils outside it ("and she, outside   walking / in her garden" [37–8]), suggesting a reversal of traditional gendered space. The female pioneer addresses the speaker as an interloper, asking, "What are you doing     in my / pumpkin" (43–4), as he resides in what was previously her domain. Moreover, just as the speaker describes the pumpkin as his "head," implying that he occupies his brain, or the rational centre of the human subject that is typically masculine, the speaker alternatively emphasizes that he is immersed in what is normally the irrational, body-centred experience of the feminine. Continually repeating the phrase "I feel," the speaker focuses on emotions and senses (eyes, nose, mouth, touch). Further to this point, Lecker posits that the first half of the poem is "concerned with embryonic, 'cramped' introspection" (132), a reading that implies that while the speaker inhabits his pumpkin head, he simultaneously resides in a womb-like, bodily space of generative potential. In this regard, the speaker's pumpkin mouth also functions as a maternal "cradle" for his birth as a poet (32).

Kroetsch's young speaker inherits and revels in a literary tradition of transgression, or what the speaker refers to as his "recovered ancestry / of borders    bravely crossed" (40–1).[18] Just as Traill's original female pioneer works on the borderline between garden and field, feminine and masculine, convention and innovation, Kroetsch's speaker occupies the borderline of past and present, ambiguously gendered identities and spaces, and creative faculties housed in the body and the mind. The palimpsestic poem's erotic border-crossing is signaled by the bringing together of opposite worlds, as Lecker suggests:

"Outside, there is a Woman, a garden being wasted, a whole vista of 'pea vines snared in wire / and lettuce gone to towering seed.' The idea is to cross borders, bringing the inside outside and vice versa without losing sight of the potential fertility of each domain" (132). In keeping with this line of interpretation, then, it is not just the female pioneer who is a garden and gardener, but also the flourishing male speaker. He reveals his "unfallen / nature" (his erect penis and his "seeds" of poetic creativity; 39–40), and celebrates "husbandry    triumphant," with "husbandry" being both a successful planting and the cultivation of his garden poem (42). This decidedly male terminology for the literal and figurative work of cultivation denotes, however, a possible supplanting of the unnamed female pioneer's earlier work in both her garden and her writing, a territorial struggle between artists which is important to highlight.

Part of Kroetsch's borderline of creation and de-creation, as Lecker refers to it, is his wrestling with literary traditions that potentially inhibit Canadian writers. A writing and unwriting of the colonial past and its literary gardens are represented in the speaker's carving his identity in the pumpkin head when he attempts to "lift the old eye  to its new vision" (13) and "cut the new mouth" (25) while he "slice[s] out the old" (29). In carving out the old with the new, the speaker creates a second palimpsest, as there is both the palimpsest that is Kroestch's poem (a re-writing of Traill's garden "plot") and the palimpsest of the actual pumpkin in the poem. This multiplying of the palimpsest through different media is in keeping with strategies Kroestch uses elsewhere, such as in the long poem *Seed Catalogue*, or "Stone Hammer Poem."[19] Pamela Banting notes that for Kroetsch, "a palimpsest is more than a doubly or multiply inscribed text. A palimpsest can be located in other kinds of objects as well, even objects of utility. Moreover, a palimpsest can be deliberately created as such. In the process of the poet's excavation of it, for example, the stone hammer [in "Stone Hammer Poem"] becomes a palimpsest. But importantly, it does not become an inscribed text at the expense of losing its physical objecthood, its stoniness" (95). The manipulation of the pumpkin as palimpsest in "Pumpkin: A Love Poem" speaks to the fact that in an interview with Russell Brown, Kroetsch once described Canada as a relatively young country with few of its own literary models "Whereas what we've got to play off against is … the literal objects … [A] Canadian writer doesn't have that vast store of other books behind him to work out of, so he's still in the process of confronting very directly his environment, his time and place" (7). Kroetsch's reflection on a tradition of palimpsestic "objects" resonates with the fact that Traill also created a material palimpsest in her actual kitchen garden through her colonial tilling of the wilderness and her "overwriting" of this environment in a composite manner (see chapter one). However, while Kroetsch places the palimpsestic object (the pumpkin) front and centre in his poem, effectively effacing the textual source by never naming Traill, it is important to acknowledge that Traill formulated not only a material palimpsest but also an innovative literary model, a garden "plot" suited to her new cultural context and published in multiple editions of *The Canadian Settler's Guide*.

When Kroetsch's speaker begins to manipulate the pumpkin, carving out himself (and the past), the significance of Kroetsch's refusal to identify Traill's *The Canadian Settler's Guide* as the source for his poem cannot be underestimated. First, Kroetsch's effacement of Traill's identity as author is idiosyncratic when compared to other pioneer garden palimpsests: Margaret Atwood names Susanna Moodie in her title *The Journals of Susanna Moodie*, just as Lorna Crozier names Sinclair Ross' protagonist in her collection *A Saving Grace: The Collected Poems of Mrs. Bentley* (see chapter five).

By contrast, Kroetsch's poem denies even as it celebrates Traill's innovation as a writer. Kroetsch's pumpkin-carving speaker leaves behind his inherited colonial identity, yet in the process dis/figures himself, as he "slice[s] off / [his] nose" (21–2). In keeping with the idiomatic expression, the reader is tempted to complete the line with the words "in spite of his face" but Kroetsch's omission of the concluding phrase leaves the gesture ambiguous. Cutting off his nose may be successfully holding a previously established identity "in suspension" – a process that, according to Kroetsch in his essay "No Name Is My Name" is necessary in the Canadian literary tradition – but it could also be doing more harm than good (51). After all, the erasure, or cutting out, of one's past, while creating a productive "namelessness" from which to generate a supposedly more authentic literary identity and voice, can also lead to a solitary, frustrated stance, unproductive in its silencing of critical dialogue with the past. Indeed, this (inadvertent?) effacement of Traill and her garden "plot" potentially denies one woman writer's early, inventive contribution to the Canadian literary tradition through an unexpected genre that has, as we saw in chapter one, been frequently disparaged or dismissed by other writers and literary critics: the domestic manual.[20]

For both Traill and Kroetsch, ideological, spatial, and literary border-crossings are made especially visible within the bounded space of the garden that highlights so effectively the processes of creation, de-creation, and re-creation. Traill attempts to rewrite an inherited tradition of the cultivated woman when her female pioneer leaves a surprising legacy of "masculine independence" to her children in her garden "plot." In turn, Kroetsch's speaker tries (unsuccessfully?) to exert his own decidedly male, sexual, and literary independence from the  unnamed woman in the poem. From within the space of his pumpkin, he shouts at her to "go / away" as he concludes with his self-contained autoerotic play (46–7), a comedic "masturbatory movement" that Lecker sees at work throughout the poem when the immature speaker pursues "the impossible wish of finally impregnating himself" (132). Kroetsch's palimpsest is a far-from-straightforward tribute to Traill, yet it still demonstrates, even as it effaces her authorial identity, the significance of her pioneer work. That said, Traill is not alone in undertaking challenging conventions; Moodie also shapes her narratives through a strategic garden frame. The major distinction between the sisters' garden plots is that Moodie more daringly frames and re-frames herself, not just other characters, as a transgressive pioneer.

## Moodie's Garden Plots and Susanna's Transgressions

The consensus among critics is that *Roughing It in the Bush* exhibits a dual perspective, as "Moodie" the writer relates retrospectively "Susanna's" experiences as a naïve settler.[21] Dermot McCarthy notes that despite the autobiographical elements of *Roughing It in the Bush*, Moodie composes her text through "a number of devices of the kind found in imaginative literature" including changes in time, foreshadowing, and character sketch (8). This manipulation of genre is another kind of border-crossing, and McCarthy believes the subsequent "tension between fact and fiction" enables Moodie to develop an ironic stance in her self-depiction, "as [she] mocks her own naivete and romanticism" (8). On a similar note, Gillian Whitlock argues that "the Moodie sketches discredit and question their own narrator and, in some cases, offer a number of different narrators," resulting in a "complex textual interchange between the retrospective narrator and her inexperienced younger self" (39). Another part of her strategy is to manipulate the spatial frames of her garden plots to mediate and signal to her readers (an audience well-versed in the topos of the garden) the changes in her character and context.

In their discussions of Moodie's self-construction, critics argue for the persistence of landscape and a distant prospect. Susan Johnston pays particular attention to Moodie's nineteenth-century aesthetics and landscape paradigms: how the "phenomenal world ... eludes [Moodie's] control" and how "this subversion is consciously related" in *Roughing It in the Bush* (30). While Moodie's presentation of herself as Susanna enables her to explore her character's personal growth and revised preferences for nineteenth-century landscape aesthetics, Johnston concludes that "the perceptual paradigms ... are only superficially altered" (34–5). In Johnston's view, aesthetics remain deeply intertwined with economic concerns and the process of settling the land. Moodie never extends her questioning to the point that the wilderness becomes an independent entity over which human society loses control and which consequently invades Susanna's subjectivity as Atwood presents it in her poetic interpretation (42–3).

Although I concur with Johnston that Moodie is a more consistent figure than Atwood's radically transformed persona, I would argue that Moodie's use of the garden as an innovative narrative device mediates the gendered and class-related propriety of her characters. She constructs garden plots that allow for more than superficial disruptions of social paradigms. In his biography, *Susanna Moodie: A Life*, Peterman notes that when *Roughing It in the Bush* appeared in London in February 1852, Moodie's sister Agnes, who was circling among aristocratic society as a successful royal biographer, was shocked and outraged by the book's depiction of "vulgar people" (144), particularly because Moodie had dedicated the volume to her and Agnes detested being associated with it. Agnes was so mortified that she even wrote a scathing letter (dated 23 May 1852) to Moodie in Belleville, telling her sister exactly what she thought of the book: "I had the prudence to commit the whole four volumes to the flames ... that might have proved a scorpion to myself" (Strickland). Agnes proceeds to express embarrassment and unease with the content, particularly Moodie's unflattering characterization of socially respectable acquaintances: "I drank tea with your friends the Thompsons ... They enquired very kindly after you, so did Lydia and Susan Wales ... What they will say about Tom Wales, alias Wilson[22] I don't know" (Strickland). Peterman writes that Agnes demanded Moodie drop the dedication from all future editions. The conflict had a lasting impact as it not only influenced Moodie's decision to stop writing about life in the colony, but it also lingered regrettably in the memories of the Strickland family: "Years later [in a letter from 1874], another sister, the widowed Sarah, would recall the indignation at Reydon Hall that followed the appearance of the book. It was as if Susanna had descended to the depths and wanted to drag Agnes and the Strickland family down among the vulgar with her" (*Susanna Moodie* 145). Others objected to Moodie's exploration of middle-class immigrant failure and the socially mixed dynamic of the colony, but the most intriguing aspect of the text is precisely that she resists shielding herself as a character.

*Roughing It in the Bush* employs at key moments a garden topos to structure the narrative, to frame Susanna's actions, and to bring into focus the shifting boundaries of social propriety for middle-class women. In these narratives, the garden provides Moodie with the means to create a spatial discourse that communicates her feminine persona's unconventional experiences and actions in what would otherwise be a more flattering self-portrait. As a border territory and narrative that incorporates both the "cultivated" and "wild" features of the environment on a number of levels from the literal (actual plants), to the figurative (classes of people), to the conceptual (gender paradigms), the third nature aspect of the garden "plot" lends itself to Moodie's negotiation of Susanna's behavioural transgressions within the colonial settlement. In these instances, the literary garden renders what has been second nature – that is, England's class and gender norms – less stringent by exposing their constructed, rather than inherent, quality. Moodie inserts herself as a character into the ambiguous, third nature space of the backwoods kitchen garden to reveal her intimacy with less appealing members of her community. This frame enables Moodie to dramatize and mediate the subsequent impact on her character's feminine identity. Two episodes that demonstrate Moodie's use of the garden in this manner are Susanna's discovery of the murdered dog Chowder in her pea patch (in "The Fire" sketch), and Susanna's encounter with Malcolm Ramsay, who takes up a lengthy residence in her backwoods home and garden (in "The Little Stumpy Man").

In "The Fire" sketch, the border territory that is Susanna's backwoods garden operates as a space of "cultivated" gender performance that diverse intruders and custodians undermine. Moodie begins by indicating a level of decorum in keeping with a visit among educated, middle-class women. Susanna's friend Emilia shares in the polite ritual of tea and a leisurely stroll in the garden; Susanna is not aware, however, that her servant John has killed Emilia's pet. When the women discover the carcass among the peas, their spoken exchange facilitates a performance of respectability that conceals undeniable transgressions on Susanna's part. Rather than censuring the egregious act, Susanna becomes complicit with her lower-class servant's impulsive crime:

> After tea, Emilia requested to look at the garden; and I,
> perfectly unconscious that it contained the remains of the

murdered Chowder, led the way. Mrs. ----, whilst gathering a handful of fine green peas, suddenly stooped, and looking earnestly at the ground, called to me,

"Come here, Susanna, and tell me what has been buried here. It looks like the tail of a dog."

She might have added, "of my dog." Murder, it seems, will out. By some strange chance, the grave that covered the mortal remains of Chowder had been disturbed, and the black tail of the dog was sticking out.

"What can it be?" said I, with an air of perfect innocence. "Shall I call Jenny, and dig it up?"

"Oh, no, my dear; it has a shocking smell, but it does look very much like Chowder's tail."

"Impossible! How could it come among my peas?"

"True. Besides, I saw Chowder, with my own eyes, yesterday ..."

"Indeed! I am glad to hear it. How these mosquitoes sting. Shall we go back to the house?" (423)

Susanna performs through her proper manners and "air of perfect innocence," but surmises fully that the dog buried in her garden is Chowder. In accordance with class loyalties and social expectations, Susanna should appear in control of her person, her hired help, and her garden territory. She offers to have the mysterious remains dug up by her servant and later seems unaffected by the strangeness of the situation when she turns her attention to the insects and the need to return indoors for self-preservation on at least two levels: to alleviate her supposed physical discomfort being out-of-doors and to maintain her appearance of propriety.

Readers appreciate, however, that the Susanna who speaks with her friend Emilia and feigns innocence differs from Moodie who narrates the tale, admitting in an aside to her audience the awkward reality of the situation: "Murder, it seems, will out" (423). The fact that Susanna seems completely unscathed by her servant John's burying a decomposing animal in her vegetable garden, a garden that feeds her family and over which she is supposed to hold dominion, suggests that Moodie's writing and self-construction do not always uphold a refined nature or class distinctions. After having criticized Old Satan's family's utter disrespect for her own property in the earlier sketch "Our First Settlement, and the Borrowing System,"[23] Susanna is now party to the mistreatment of her own neighbour (not to mention friend). The irony is not lost on Moodie the writer; indeed, it is orchestrated by her. Her amusement concurs with and extends an earlier humourous scene regarding John's violent intentions towards Emilia's thieving cat, Master Tom. On that occasion, John was angered by the cat's "depredations in the [Moodies'] potato-pot" during its nightly prowls and by the fact that "potatoes dressed with cat's hair is not a very nice dish" (421). Moodie recalls her own character's response: "I could not help laughing, but I begged John by no means to annoy Emilia by hurting her cat" (421). In light of the Chowder incident, John twice ignores his employer's authority and instructions, and Susanna, rather than punishing him for his disrespect, takes pleasure in the predicament. Unlike the garden narratives set in England, where temporary transgressions are met with repercussions and a return to the status quo, these backwoods garden plots reveal the ongoing impact of a proximate, socially mixed community on the middle-class: that is, their appearance of propriety versus their actual conduct.

Moodie's doubled presentation of herself as both narrator and character in the Chowder garden plot inspired Margaret Atwood to include this episode in her celebrated palimpsestic book of poems, *The*

*Journals of Susanna Moodie*. Resonating with Kroetsch's palimpsest of Traill, Atwood's rewriting of *Roughing It in the Bush* similarly downplays Moodie's contributions as a gardener-writer in its twentieth-century preoccupation with a distinct Canadian literary identity. Atwood's objective is ostensibly to promote a wilderness-centred reading of the Canadian imagination, and her re-working of the Chowder incident in "The Double Voice" accordingly effaces Moodie's innovative use of the garden as it appeared in the original sketch. Atwood states in the Afterword that the poems "were suggested by Mrs. Moodie's books, though it was not her conscious voice but the other voice running like a counterpoint through her work that made the most impression on me" (63). In keeping with this interpretation, "The Double Voice" implies that Moodie's conscious, artistic voice "had manners" and could only express through "hushed tones," "uplifting verse," and "sentiment" (42). Atwood constructs Moodie the writer as artistically restrained by English propriety and outmoded literary conventions, while the subconscious Moodie, the "other voice" with its experience of the wilderness, perceives and revels in a horrific world: "The other found a dead dog / jubilant with maggots / half-buried among the sweet peas" (42). This brief portrayal plays on sharply dualistic imagery: a rotting, maggot-infested carcass (representative of the wilderness) and a perfumed flower garden (representative of an orderly, feminized, and civilized space). These images are Atwood's own embellishments, however, as the original sketch neither graphically illustrates the decaying Chowder (only the exposed tail and odour are mentioned), nor acknowledges any presence of flowers. In the original sketch, Susanna and her friend Emilia admire *green peas*, not sweet peas, since vegetables are the primary content of the practical backwoods kitchen garden. At first glance, these alterations appear minor, but Atwood's twentieth-century palimpsest significantly reinterprets the subtle yet innovative achievements of Moodie's original nineteenth-century prose and her re-contextualized use of garden rhetoric and spatial framing. Effaced in Atwood's poem are the mixed composition of the backwoods kitchen garden, the servant's liberal traversal and use of the terrain, and Moodie's own artistic, purposeful orchestration of an ironic "cultivated" demeanor for her own character.

Through her poetry, then, Atwood superimposes her wilderness vision in a formidable palimpsestic gesture as the class-related, spatial transgressions of Moodie's original "plot" are subsequently curtailed. The wilderness, not the garden, serves as the transformative force and authentic source of knowledge and national identity. In other words, in Atwood's hands, first nature (the wilderness), as opposed to third nature (the garden) acquires the critical, insightful role. Moreover, this dark source of knowledge disrupts from below: initially, from below the soil and the subconscious as her Moodie persona dreams "fleshy" and "pulsing" vegetables "down through the earth" in the poem "Dream 1: The Bush Garden" (34); and later, from this transformed pioneer persona, herself, as she lies buried, united with the land, speaking from the grave to present-day society "through subsoil" in the poem "Alternate Thoughts from Underground" (57).[24] Ultimately, Atwood's Moodie becomes the voice of the wilderness speaking to twentieth-century Canada, as Sherrill Grace concurs, "Just beneath the bold surfaces of our heated buildings, our weatherproof houses and malls, is 'the centre of a forest' … What does Moodie come back to tell us? The careful order of walls and ceilings … cannot deny the insistent reality of wilderness" (41–2). While the dark forces are irrepressible in Atwood's palimpsest, Moodie's original "plot" suggests a more conscious, subtle use of form and content inspired by the kitchen garden and its accompanying, re-contextualized narratives of social transgression. *The Journals of Susanna Moodie* may be, as Grace contends, "a Canadian myth and a dramatic incarnation of our past," in other words, a "Canadian classic" (33), but it is also a version of the past extensively reinterpreted during the early 1970s and, therefore, informative of a time in our literary history when the wilderness was paramount in thematic conceptualizations of the national imagination.[25] Paradoxically then, Traill's and Moodie's garden plots, which have been the inspiration behind other writers' celebrated literary palimpsests, have also been partially effaced, their visions overwritten. Traill's household manual goes unnamed, and Moodie's strategic use of the garden plot as a third nature is replaced by a gothic story of the wilderness.

While the incident of Chowder's demise operates as a brief, amusing sketch in Moodie's text (in contrast to Atwood's dark re-working of it); the garden topos becomes even more instrumental when Moodie uses the garden plot in "The Little Stumpy Man" not only to frame and structure the sketch of Malcolm Ramsay, but also to reposition her own character within the shifting backwoods paradigms of "cultivated" femininity. Perhaps not surprisingly, this sketch, which relies so thoroughly on the garden plot for its setting, narrative structure, and content, makes no appearance in Atwood's poetic palimpsest. The murdered carcass of a dog falls more readily within Atwood's wilderness-focused adaptation, rather than "The Little Stumpy Man" with its emphasis on shifting social conventions of gender, or that which becomes "second nature" within the wilderness-settler cultural milieu. Nonetheless, despite Atwood's omission of this sketch, "The Little Stumpy Man" has continually attracted critical attention, a testimony to its literary achievement and nuance. Exploring these gender-related tensions with respect to Moodie's status as a writer and her narrated role as a wife and mother, Misao Dean notes that Moodie uses narrative framing techniques throughout her work as a strategy of modest self-construction, or ideal performance of femininity. According to Dean, the sketch "The Little Stumpy Man" is no exception; Moodie and her retrospective narrating voice disappear from a supposedly autobiographical text when a secondary character (Malcolm Ramsay) creates his own dialogue and narrates his own story (38). Dean asserts that the nineteenth-century "stereotype of feminine self-effacement" coupled with the "numerous tales within tales" (37) within *Roughing It in the Bush* allow Moodie to downplay her public role as author and reassert her maternal, domestic qualities as she shies away from telling (or even appearing in) her own story and instead recounts the stories of others.[26] But Moodie's use of embedded narratives is not her only framing device, as the frame of the garden plot works to structure her narratives as well. Moreover, this garden frame, rather than being used for self-effacement, subtly redirects readers' attention onto the character of Susanna even when the narrative's focus appears to be elsewhere.

In the Malcolm Ramsay sketch, in particular, the garden plot demonstrates Moodie's contrary desires not only to safeguard Susanna's property and gendered propriety but also to explore her ongoing exposure to, and occasional complicity with, the uncouth of society who occupy her new home. As with Traill's narration of the corn-harvester faced with a feverish husband and a broken garden fence in *The Canadian Settler's Guide*, Moodie's sketch includes similar circumstances during the spring of 1836: her husband John is ill in bed and her garden fence is in bad repair. During this time when the family's well-being and security are compromised, Malcolm Ramsay – an unwelcome, passing acquaintance of John Moodie – arrives at the Moodies' door to spend the night. Nicknamed the "little stumpy man" by the Moodies' daughter Katie (405), Ramsay is as unpleasant and uncultivated in his behaviour and appearance as the tree stumps that form unattractive blots upon the landscape, inhibiting agricultural progress. Depicting him as a sudden intrusion, Moodie introduces Ramsay as a man lacking all respect for others' privacy; he not only announces his presence with a "violent knocking at the door" (388), but also presumes to enter the family's parlour without a proper invitation or introduction: "I immediately went into the parlour, where [John] Moodie was lying upon a bed near the stove, to deliver the stranger's message; but before I could say a word, he dashed in after me, and going up to the bed, held out his broad coarse hand, with, 'How are you, Mr. Moodie? You see I have accepted your kind invitation sooner than either you or I expected ...'" (389). Unfortunately for the Moodie family, Ramsay establishes himself comfortably within their home and stays for nine months.

Susanna dislikes Ramsay immediately, and her ongoing observations of him reveal the impact this man has on her domestic sphere and person as his cultivation of her garden coincides with a disruption in her sense of middle-class propriety and privacy. Susanna's initial assessment of Ramsay reveals her social bias: "I had taken him for a mechanic, for his dirty, slovenly appearance; and his physiognomy was so unpleasant that I did not credit his assertion that he was a friend of my husband" (388). Indolent and unwilling to work at clearing the land, a task suited to masculine fortitude, Ramsay turns to Susanna's garden on the pretense of appearing useful. He repairs the fence and plants vegetable seeds, and Susanna feels Ramsay's intrusion acutely:

> "At any rate," said he, "we shall no longer be starved on bad flour and potatoes. We shall have peas, and beans, and beets, and carrots, and cabbage in abundance; besides the plot I have reserved for cucumbers and melons."

"Ah," thought I, "does he, indeed, mean to stay with us until the melons are ripe?" and my heart died within me, for he not only was a great additional expense, but he robbed us of all privacy, as our very parlour was converted into a bed-room for his accommodation. (396)

Ramsay's desire for an improved diet and his decision "to make garden" (396) suggest his intention of a prolonged stay, veritably rooting himself within the family and particularly within Susanna's domain. Furthermore, Susanna cannot reconcile Ramsay's rough, inactive personality with his aptitude for gardening, a task she equates with her own sense of refinement and pragmatic accomplishment: "I procured the necessary seeds, and watched with no small surprise the industry with which our strange visitor commenced operations. He repaired the broken fence, dug the ground with the greatest of care, and laid it out with a skill and neatness of which I had believed him perfectly incapable. In less than three weeks, the whole plot presented a very pleasing prospect, and he was really elated by his success" (396). Ramsay's "industry," "greatest care," "skill and neatness," and above all his ability to create "a very pleasing prospect" through his garden aesthetics are all activities that Susanna associates with herself – an educated British woman – and not with Ramsay – a slovenly, disrespectful man. For Susanna, becoming a gardener of the backwoods has been a difficult process of adaptation: braving black flies, heat, and deprivation. Now, Ramsay readily supplants Susanna in her own garden and role, acting as an unexpected foil: both characters are gardeners, avid readers, and storytellers situated in the domestic and sharing a daily routine, all the while supposedly embodying distinct social classes.[27]

Susanna cannot easily categorize Ramsay as "cultivated" or not, and the ease with which he accepts his ambiguous status counters her own difficult adjustment to the socio-physical environment of the backwoods. As Peterman argues in *This Great Epoch of Our Lives: Susanna Moodie's Roughing It in the Bush*, Ramsay's continual rebuking of Susanna for her shortcomings disrupts her vision of herself: "Ramsay cleverly [keeps] her off balance by teasing her about her 'methodical' and prudish values ... and she [can] see how, under the circumstances, she [may] appear somewhat narrow-minded to him. As a woman proud of her liberal and open-minded values, such criticism [is] surely galling" (95–6). Having learned to milk a cow, for instance, Susanna feels unduly chided when Ramsay watches and insults her abilities, all the while enjoying his more enviable, cultured task of reading: "'You are a shocking bad milker' ... 'More shame for you! A farmer's wife, and afraid of a cow! Why these little children would laugh at you'" (*Roughing It* 397). As an officer's wife struggling to become a successful backwoods "farmer's wife," Susanna witnesses all her adaptations undermined by Ramsay's criticisms. In *Susanna Moodie: Voice and Vision*, Carol Shields argues that Ramsay's presence is so disruptive that he affects not only the character of Susanna within the story, but also Moodie the writer at the level of the story, as the prose deviates from its normal pattern: "The chapter about him is even more fragmented than her usual writing; she jumps from episode to episode in her frustration with him" (29). Vexation may be evident in the composition, yet Moodie is a writer working strategically with her garden plot. From this standpoint, the atypical fragmentation, as Shields reads it, is actually generated on purpose. The multiple movements between episodes, particularly the episodes that relate to the garden, subtly craft Susanna's flawed yet admirable persona of adaptable pioneer. In other words, Moodie's kitchen garden plot operates as a discursive domain of context-specific femininity;

it ironically frames Ramsay by de-masculinizing this "little stumpy man," and tempers Susanna's own "hardened-off" transformation.

Moodie purposely foregrounds the tension between Susanna and Ramsay through the home and garden, describing the relationship as one of "deep-rooted antipathy" (390). Susanna feels Ramsay's intrusion more intensely than her husband, as this lazy, ungentlemanly figure situates himself most comfortably in her domestic domain: "our guest did nothing but lie upon the bed, and read, and smoke, and drink whiskey-and-water from morning until night" (392). In addition, Ramsay does not assist Susanna with her strenuous chores: "He has often passed me carrying water up from the lake without offering to relieve me of the burden" (393). Ultimately, he decides to garden only after the hired man, Jacob, resigns, leaving Ramsay to feel "ashamed of sitting in the house doing nothing," while John Moodie undertook all the farming work (396). Moodie positions Ramsay unequivocally indoors, thereby repelling his criticisms of Susanna's ineptitude and promoting her own character's efficiency: "The season for putting in the potatoes had now arrived. Malcolm volunteered to cut the sets, which was easy work that could be done in the house, and over which he could lounge and smoke; but [John] told him that he must take his share in the field, that I had already sets enough saved to plant half-an-acre, and would have more prepared by the time they were required" (402). Moodie contrasts Ramsay's behaviour with that of John Moodie in spatial terms (specifically the garden versus the field), by way of communicating that Ramsay refuses to function within the expected domain of masculine labour: "[John] Moodie was busy under-bushing for a fall fallow. Malcolm spent much of his time in the garden, or lounging about the house. I had baked an eel-pie for dinner ... Malcolm had cleaned some green-peas and washed the first young potatoes we had drawn that season, with his own hands"

(404). Moodie's concluding comment "with his own hands" carries an unmistakable sarcastic tone that resonates with her own character's struggles to become accustomed to manual labour, such as the time Susanna builds the garden snake fence (see chapter one). Prior to this scene of dinner preparation, there is an exchange between Susanna and her houseguest where Ramsay voices his dislike for working in the field and complains that the hoe blisters his hands, to which Susanna responds, "'You are terribly disfigured by the black-flies. But [John] Moodie suffers just as much, and says nothing'" (402). Although Ramsay and Susanna are similar in many respects, Moodie claims the space of her text by subtly yet continually highlighting her own persona's self-sufficiency, perseverance, and industry. In contrast, the effeminate Ramsay is overly concerned about his physical condition, content not to labour, and ready to abuse the family's goodwill and generosity.

Moodie creates an admirable, adaptable version of femininity within her text, but the less controllable dynamics of the backwoods (in the form of other servants and settlers) destabilize the character of Susanna. In this way, Moodie uses Ramsay and the garden frame first to expose and then to mediate some of Susanna's unrefined behaviour within a socially mixed setting. The indecorous circumstances of the backwoods are such that Moodie goes as far as to show her own character laughing impolitely at the comical antics of a jumpy, molasses-dribbling neighbour, Mr Crowe:

[Ramsay] saw the intense difficulty I had to keep my gravity, and was determined to make me laugh out. So, coming slyly behind my chair, he whispered in my ear, with the gravity of a judge, "Mrs. Moodie, that must have been the very chap who first jumped Jim Crowe."[28]

This appeal obliged me to run from the table. [John] Moodie was astonished at my rudeness; and Malcolm, as he resumed his seat, made the matter worse by saying, "I wonder what is the matter with Mrs. Moodie; she is certainly very hysterical this afternoon." (403)

Instead of pursuing feminine self-effacement and middle-class respectability, Moodie uses the scene to draw attention to her persona. The sketch invites comparisons between Ramsay and Susanna, highlighting the lapses in not only gendered behaviour, but also class conduct. Malcolm's feigned ignorance – "I wonder what is the matter with Mrs. Moodie; she is certainly very hysterical this afternoon" – resonates with Susanna's own performance of false naïveté when Chowder's remains are unearthed by Emilia. During this visit with Mr Crowe, Susanna's social impropriety shocks her husband, as her peculiar affinity with Ramsay reveals a loss of self-control and "cultivated" refinement in keeping with their original English cultural norms.

Susanna embarrasses herself, but Moodie the author remains decidedly in control of her sketch by juxtaposing this scene of a lapse in decorum with a sudden and significant return to the garden frame. Directly following the infamous incident with Mr Crowe, Moodie writes, "The potatoes were planted, and the season of strawberries, green-peas, and young potatoes come, but still Malcolm remained our constant guest. He had grown so indolent, and gave himself so many airs, that [John] Moodie was heartily sick of his company" (403). The ensuing description of the garden's seasonal growth coincides directly with Ramsay's increasingly inappropriate, ill-mannered imposition on the Moodies' goodwill. Whereas Susanna opens herself to censure momentarily through her rude outburst, Ramsay's objectionable behaviour is prolonged (as measured through the garden) and more distasteful, as his fraudulent "air" of refinement is undermined at every turn by his very nature and appearance. Ultimately, Ramsay's rudeness and false sense of superiority are his undoing. One evening, John Moodie chastises Ramsay for insulting Susanna's cooking, prompting this usually self-indulgent man to leave the dinner table in a huff, his "fine peas and potatoes" (404) remaining untouched on his plate even though he had "washed the first young potatoes … with his own hands" (404). Later, an enraged Malcolm departs from the Moodie home when the young daughter Katie refers to their "houseguest" with the unflattering nickname the "*little stumpy man*" (405, original italics). For the purposes of the sketch, then, the garden plot provides readers with a familiar ideological and spatial context through which different kinds of transgressions, or border-crossings (to use Kroetsch's concept), take place. The garden plot facilitates a paradoxical construction of Susanna and Malcolm Ramsay, as Moodie examines the contradictions of refined, middle-class, gendered propriety within an alternative social milieu. The surprising intimacy between these disparate characters renders class and gendered distinctions not only unstable but also highly constructed, as the garden in its third nature role reflects critically on that which is supposed to be "second nature," revealing social conventions to be at once mutable and context-specific.

Critics such as Fowler and Dean read Moodie's and Traill's writing under the category of "feminine texts" (Dean 36) because they identify an unwavering reiteration of nineteenth-century gendered ideology. The Strickland sisters are undeniably situated in a traditional discourse of cultivated femininity, yet they nonetheless draw attention to the paradox of the transplanted woman pioneer. By virtue of being both actual and literary gardeners, Moodie and Traill devise context-specific creations, or an art of milieu, through the relevancy and adaptability of their figurative language and their innovative garden "plots." In their texts, boundaries are continually breached at the level of setting and incident, and on the level of the ideological parameters set forth in their narratives. These trespasses serve as the catalyst for their examinations of ruptures in proper and "propertied" feminine behaviour as espoused by both themselves and their society.

In the end, Moodie and Traill may be viewed as exemplary pioneers from a variety of perspectives. First, they created a rich foundation for the literary gardens that sprouted in Kroetsch's, Atwood's, and others' fertile imaginations that gave lasting shape to the Canadian imagination. In this regard, Moodie's and Traill's most obvious legacies stem, paradoxically enough, from their effacement and re-inscription within twentieth-century literary palimpsests inspired by their work and informed by Canadian cultural nationalism. In these extensive re-workings, the gardens of the colonial and gendered past are disrupted in order to formulate an authentically Canadian imagination founded in and through the wilderness. Alternatively, Moodie's and Traill's less apparent contributions, which merit reassessment, involve their own writing not about the wilderness, but about domestic terrain. Their actual and literary garden plots work in tandem, revealing how stories of the everyday have the creative potential to reflect significant cultural moments of transplanting and transition.

## CHAPTER THREE

# "Then a living house": Gabrielle Roy's Domestication of the Bower

A Chinese proverb says, If you want a day of happiness,
buy a bottle of wine and get drunk; if you want a week of happiness,
get married; if you want a whole life of happiness, plant a garden.
There's some truth in that, don't you think?
Gabrielle Roy, "Letter to Bernadette Roy," 40

When readers discover Gabrielle Roy's *oeuvre*, they enter highly sensual, idyllic gardens that express enchantment with the world. This vision does not preclude, however, the inclusion of adult experience and its complexities. Just as Susanna Moodie and Catharine Parr Traill employ images of transplanting and revised garden plots to communicate the difficult transition to an unfamiliar land, Roy explores the uprooting of her characters during the turbulent first half of the twentieth century. The most compelling of these depictions involves her adaptation of the bower genre to convey the problematic position of the displaced woman artist who feels isolated within her larger community and at odds with its narrowly defined views on gender. In accordance with this literary tradition and readers' expectations, her bowers are highly stylized enclosures or flowery abodes, acquiring symbolic value during the life journeys of her characters (and her own persona) as they search for space that will accommodate their creative endeavours and enable them to flourish.

Roy's description of a garden as integral to "a whole life of happiness" (quoted above) resonates in two of her later works: the autobiography *Enchantment and Sorrow* (1984), in which Roy traces her artistic maturation during the late 1930s; and the short story "Garden in the Wind," from the same-titled collection (1975), in which the dying immigrant Marta Yaramko contemplates the meaning of her existence through the comforting terrain of her prairie garden. Within the safety and beauty of these idyllic green-spaces – the one, a cottage garden in England; the other, a replicated Ukrainian homestead in northern Alberta – the young Gabrielle[1] and the aging Marta experience moments of profound introspection and transformation. These gardens are not simply cultivated earth, but rather bowers that construct and validate their roles as artists. In the context of Canada's nascent literary milieu at the time in which these narratives take place, Roy's association of bowers with other origins is hardly surprising; she transplants them as Moodie and Traill transplanted the English cottage garden tradition to the backwoods. Roy's female subjects long to connect with other locales in order to counter both cultural and geographical isolation as experienced in Canada during the first half of the twentieth century. In Roy's texts, the predicaments are specifically those of the French Canadian growing up in the rather insular, predominantly Anglophone province of Manitoba, on the one hand, and the immigrant settler residing in a remote rural village in Alberta, on the other. With respect to Roy's own circumstance, the fact that her bower is situated abroad is most certainly reflective of her historical context as a fledgling Canadian artist.

Recounting Roy's travels to France and England at the age of twenty-eight, just prior to her realization of her vocation as a writer, François Ricard notes, "The voyage to Europe for any young Canadian or American of the period with the slightest artistic or intellectual inclinations was a rite of passage in his or her worldly and cultural apprenticeship. No one could pretend to be a real painter, writer, actor, or intellectual, no one could claim to be 'cultivated,' without having made an Atlantic crossing and discovery of 'the Old Countries'" (*Gabrielle Roy* 163). But as much as these gardens facilitate Gabrielle's and Marta's expression by providing vital spaces of artistic inspiration and cultural belonging, they also work to contain and to limit, revealing the complicated demands of femininity and its rootedness in the domestic. These literary bowers demonstrate a difficult negotiation of the shifting boundaries of women's personal space and creativity within Canada's unaccommodating social "climate," especially with respect to traditional gender norms. In her garden settings, therefore, Roy combines the familiarity of the domestic, as a space of routine and gender paradigms, with the temporariness of the bower, as a space of brief encounter and transformation. In this way, she facilitates a transition for women artists moving from silence to voice, and from private to public roles. Through her re-working of bower conventions, Roy reveals and tests the limits of female artistry.

## Roy's Gender Politics of Space, Enclosure, and Gardens

Enclosure and entrapment, in which gardens play a part, are significant themes in Roy's writing, particularly when she explores urban and domestic worlds. In her essay "Female Spirals and Male Cages,"

Paula Gilbert Lewis argues, "There exists ... a profound influence of environment – defined as one's physical and, at times, social milieu – upon all Royan characters ... Whatever the surrounding location may be, there is a close rapport and even a communion between the individual and exterior space" (71). This interconnection between space and character is not always beneficial. All Roy's characters are delimited by their environment, but the women appear especially confined. Lewis argues that Roy's men possess a linear mobility that enables them to escape, albeit momentarily, from the oppression of the city. Conversely, the women are forever contained, "caught in the round" of "female structures of motherhood, crowds, and hereditary misery" (75). Markedly restricted in their freedom and movement, women are impeded by familial responsibilities and even their biology, a dilemma that Lori Saint-Martin explores at length in *La voyageuse et la prisonnière*. In *The Cashier*, for example, the mobility of the terminally ill Alexandre Chenevert is largely unaffected for key portions of the novel, but his wife, Eugénie, is physically incapacitated by severe menopausal symptoms (82). Similarly, at the conclusion of *The Tin Flute*, Azarius Lacasse makes a bleak escape from the poverty of Montreal when he departs on the train for war, but his wife, Rose-Anna, only glimpses the tracks from her window, compelled to remain at home because of the recent birth of their twelfth child. Roy's male characters may be trapped literally and figuratively by their urban existence,[2] but the women appear doubly contained within both the city and their gendered sphere.[3]

When depicting the garden, Roy similarly creates places that demand much from their inhabitants, typically girls, women, or domestic-focused men. Noting the restrictive gardens that Roy associates with childhood in her fiction, Carol J. Harvey writes, "Mais pour peu que le jardin devienne trop sécurisant, il risque d'étouffer l'individualité de l'enfant et son esprit d'aventure" (But if the garden provides too much security, it risks suffocating the child's individuality and adventurous spirit; 179). A young Christine in Roy's *Street of Riches* yearns to explore beyond the garden, pumping her swing high up into the air above the wall in order to see the unknown: "When I was high enough in the sky, I was happy, but each time the swing sank back, I found myself in a minute garden, shut in on all sides" (22). Here, the garden offers only imprisoning innocence; outside exists a spacious, informative world of experience with new horizons and intriguing neighbours. Gardens are not limited to juvenile characters, however, as Roy makes a critical connection with women's adult lives. Christine observes her mother rise early every morning "to go out in summer at the sun's first rays to care for her flowers" (142), only to be exhausted in the evening after a work-filled day: "She put me in mind of those flowers, so living by day which at night so sadly hang their heads" (143). Gardens demand permanent residence and continual care, conditions that preclude adventures beyond the home. In *The Hidden Mountain*, for example, the atypically domesticated gold-miner Gédéon feels isolated in his northern cabin and unable to join the other men who are exploring because he must tend to his garden: "So great was the torment of his yearning to see other men that the poor old fellow was often on the verge of setting forth in his homemade craft. But ... were he to leave, and were it not to rain during his absence, would his tiny vegetable patch on its barely cleared soil survive without water?" (4). Tellingly, in the far reaches of the north that beckon to adventure-seekers, the only other cultivators are nuns who reside in the convent of the mission at Fort Renunciation.[4]

The spatial circumscription of women and their stories has inspired much debate over Roy's interest in the feminine condition and in her gender politics. A number of critics argue that her fiction retreats from an overtly feminist challenge of the status quo. Phyllis Grosskurth contends, "Roy possesses a mother's-eye view of the world. The area of action in which her characters move is limited and conditioned both spatially and psychologically by the imposition such a focus places upon them" (7). Similarly, Lewis suggests that Roy is not a feminist but rather a traditionalist or "feminine humanist"[5] because her adult women characters rarely "relinquish their maternal and familial roles" ("Feminism" 29). In her book-length study, *The Literary Vision of Gabrielle Roy*, Lewis further develops this point, arguing that family-centred plots culminate in predictability, with women "trapped in the predetermined destiny and apparently resigned to or voluntarily accepting their fate" (95).

In contrast to those who argue that gender norms dominate Roy's fiction, many critics detect an awakening feminist consciousness in the sensitive, multifaceted depictions of women's circumstances and desires. Drawing on Rachel Blau DuPlessis's discussion of male-centred narrative structures in *Writing beyond the Ending*, Saint-Martin argues that Roy actually exposes the gender limitations of romance and offers other possibilities in their stead. Conventional marriage plots (such as that of the pregnant and unwed Florentine in *The Tin Flute*) are presented as "une forme d'enfermement" (a form of entrapment; *La voyageuse* 108). In Roy's later works, however, Saint-Martin perceives a break with tradition and an attempt to write beyond prescribed story-lines. Daughters leave behind their mothers and pursue other experiences: "Tous les livres sur l'enseignante et la femme-créatrice ouvrent ce 'chemin de liberté'" (All the books on the teacher and the woman-artist open this "path to freedom"), which means the domestic prisoner becomes "l'aspirante voyageuse" (the aspiring voyager; 110). Even Lewis, who categorizes Roy as a traditional writer, admits that Roy "clearly did not whole-heartedly support a woman who sacrificed her own life for others" (*Literary Vision* 95). In her influential article "Gabrielle Roy as Feminist: Rereading the Critical Myths," Agnes Whitfield argues that labelling Roy a "traditionalist" is confining in and of itself. Whitfield notes that while many of the female characters appear conventional, Roy, herself, was not: "In 1937, despite family opposition, [Roy] forsook the security of a traditional [teaching] position near her home in Manitoba, for the uncertainties of pre-war Europe where she eventually abandoned her dramatic ambitions for the equally precarious career of female journalist" (20). In this light, Roy and her texts can be considered "feminist in the broad sense of the word" (20) for a number of reasons,[6] but it is Whitfield's reading of "spatial tensions" (26) with respect to gender that holds particular significance in terms of Roy's recurring use of gardens.

Whitfield aptly observes that many of Roy's characters – men, women, and even children – express a paradoxical interest in both travel and a settled home life. Most often "these tensions have been related [by critics] to universal themes, such as man's conflicting desire for security and liberty ... [but] they may also reflect Gabrielle Roy's conception of the particular constraints of the female experience" (26). Some of the thematic critics who focus on universals, rather than on the specifics of gender, to whom Whitfield refers, are of particular relevance here, as they provide early and influential readings of the garden in Roy's writing. Hugo McPherson's 1959 article "The Garden and the Cage" and E.D. Blodgett's 1980 article "Gardens at the World's End or Gone West in French" associate idealism and even nostalgia with Roy's fictional garden motif. For both McPherson and Blodgett, the gardens speak to the polarized experience of both the Everyman and the French Canadian on the western prairie in their longing for an idyllic past, and their recognition of the uncertainty or decline of their present situations. Neither critic takes notice of the politics of gender with respect to the garden. In McPherson's case, "[t]he values of the garden, childhood, innocence, and the past, array themselves against the forces of the city, adulthood, 'experience,' and the present" (49).[7] Alternatively, but in a similar vein, Blodgett argues that Roy's gardens reflect central themes of western Francophone literature: mainly the idealization of the frontier, nature, and the *voyageur*, or *coureur de bois* (115–16). For these critics, Roy's profound veneration of the garden is intimately connected to the pastoral tradition (particularly through Roy's use of idyll) and the related sense of loss, as "[t]here can be no return to the garden" in a modern society, according to McPherson (55). These gardens occupy, in Blodgett's view, a space between the past and the future: "between the subjunctive mood of the way things might have been and the optative of how one would like them to be" (114).

The specifics of Roy's narratives reveal, however, that women and especially female artists are the most prominent inhabitants of her gardens. Moreover, whereas McPherson and Blodgett suggest that in keeping with the pastoral tradition, the archetypal return to the garden is impossible because maturity, change, and the future are all discovered through journeys beyond the garden's confines, some of Roy's female protagonists make pivotal returns to their gardens. These visits and, in some cases, continued occupancy are not static or regressive, but rather transformational. Complicating Whitfield's gendering of the anxiety over the need for both home and escape is an additional yearning, therefore, felt by many of Roy's female characters for a private retreat within, ironically enough, the home environs. These retreats are designated for the pursuit of creative expression and manifest themselves through the motif of enclosure. Consequently, Roy's gardens can be read not just as the ideal place for the modern Everyman, the western French Canadian, or the child, but as uniquely feminine terrain, in that these spaces capture not only the "constraints of the female experience" (as Whitfield describes it), but also the complicated, outward growth of women's artistic agency within an uncertain, changing world.

Roy's sensitivity to the development of her female characters – particularly artist figures – prompts the creation of gardens that enable both conformity to, and restrained dissension from, women's familial roles. Her use of the garden as an enclosing space aligns Roy with what Kerstin W. Shands perceives to be a central feature of the history of feminist discourse: spatial metaphors. According to Shands, while First Wave feminists of the nineteenth century reveal a preoccupation with metaphors of division (public versus private spheres), Second Wave feminists of the early twentieth century through to the 1960s and 1970s focus particularly on confinement and escape imagery. Central to the writing of such key feminists as Virginia Woolf, Simone de Beauvoir, and Betty Friedan is the "scrutiny of rooms and enclosures" (13) and, in the case of Woolf, the need for a woman to have a room of her own for independent, creative thinking. Roy's garden enclosures achieve a similar critical end as the oppositional themes of women's confinement and dormancy intersect with exploration and personal growth. Even as she turns to the pastoral mode and its idealization of the past, Roy refuses to forfeit the garden's potential to be a transformative space for women in the present and future who seek rooms (or bowers) of their own. Avoiding overt transgression or conspicuous questioning, Roy does not lay bare gender constructs in her innocent gardens but instead carefully promotes social norms, or what is second nature, in order to "naturalize" and mediate women's emerging agency. In this way, Roy's gardens facilitate a subtle opening out through the domestic-centred maturation and increasing mobility of her female artist figures, creating a comforting image of change within constancy. Roy's bower plot is, therefore, a modern extension of the subtle gender negotiation we see at work in the backwoods garden plots of Moodie and Traill (see chapter two). But while Moodie and Traill concentrate on the recontextualized domestic settings and roles of transplanted female pioneers, Roy contends with women's increasing desire for mobility in order to pursue other kinds of lives. While these three writers obviously differ with respect to their historical contexts and mandates, they all take full advantage of the garden plot's third nature by generating concentrated, artistic critiques of the larger socio-cultural landscape: its expected gender norms and circumstances of daily life, that "second nature" with which women must contend when imagining alternatives.

Nowhere is the garden's paradoxical role as both daily enclosure and creative refuge more apparent than in Roy's autobiography *Enchantment and Sorrow* and her short story "Garden in the Wind." Roy composes two idealized gardens that house female artist figures: Gabrielle, a young woman coming into her own as a writer travelling abroad; and Marta Yaramko, a Ukrainian immigrant who lives and gardens in northern Alberta. As highly literary terrains shaped by bower conventions, Gabrielle's and Marta's gardens provide spaces for introspection, creative freedom, and confidence-in-artistry to grow. In every conceivable way these bowers are distinct from other kinds of gardens (flower beds, window planters, vegetable plots) that Roy depicts elsewhere.[8] Consider Gabrielle's mother's flower pots in *Enchantment and Sorrow*: "Whatever worries or sorrows Maman had, as soon as summer came she'd drop everything to gather up the geraniums and fuchsias that had spent winter on the windowsills and plant them in the earth around the house" (31). Flower gardening is a typical part of female characters' seasonal work and pleasure, but by way of contrast, Roy infuses Gabrielle's and Marta's gardens with the extraordinary status of bower as she uses them to capture pivotal moments of transition and transformation for her women artists and their expression. She departs from traditional bower scenes, however, in that she chooses to domesticate these enclosures through their stylized presentations. As a result, Gabrielle's and Marta's safe containment is two-fold: these artists are surrounded not just by cultivated greenery but also by their "home" settings and associated roles.

The apparent novelty of the woman artist, then, and the need to naturalize her find complicated expression in bowers where gender norms are not radically questioned but surprisingly reinforced. Arguing that "the garden is ... a vehicle for reassurance" (34), landscape architect Ian L. McHarg believes that together the intimacy and familiarity of a garden maintain a pre-existing order: "In the home, furniture, memorabilia, and books provide a familiar and reassuring environment ... Affirmation of values is linked to reassurance. I believe that the garden combines both explicit and implicit statements of affirmation. Perhaps the most dominant statement is that nature is benign" (34). In Roy's case, bowers offer reassurance by shaping family-oriented scenes and recognizable feminine subjects. But while Roy's careful integration of the daily life of second nature is central to her bowers, the garden's third-nature role protects the tentative female artist by subtly revealing the limitations of women's placement within the settings of home and family. Roy's strategic containment of the bower within familiar constructs, then, paradoxically accommodates and promotes female artists' non-conformity: that is, their capacity for private introspection, desire for creative agency, and departure from domestic preoccupations.

## The Literary Genre of the Bower

According to its generic tradition, the bower serves an essential role in inspiring an artist-figure, usually a male poet, to realize his artistic potential. Writers characterize the bower typically as a site of repose, a brief respite where an artist has time to reflect and bring his creative vision and confidence to fruition. According to the *Oxford English Dictionary*, a "bower" is "an idealized abode, not realized in any actual dwelling," or "a fancy rustic cottage or country residence." It is typically "closed in or overarched with branches of trees, shrubs, or other plants; a shady recess, leafy covert, arbour."[9] The bower in Roy's *Enchantment and Sorrow* fulfills conventional expectations. When a young Gabrielle stumbles across Century Cottage, the dwelling is surrounded by a magnificent garden: "it seemed ... buried in a tangled profusion of flowers. I walked up a path winding this way and that, perhaps as dictated by the flowers themselves in their determination to grow and spread where it suited them" (306). Similarly, in "Garden in the Wind," the narrator describes her first glimpse of a garden-embowered home surrounded by the prairies: "The road, straight for so long, at last bends slightly ... Then a living house. And in the same moment, flowers. A mass of flaming colours that strike your eye, seize your heart ... I saw before me, under the enormous sky ... this little garden fairly bursting with flowers" (124–5).

In addition to these notions of an ideal, nature-adorned enclosure, a bower may refer more specifically to an inner room, or a "lady's private apartment" or "boudoir" (*OED*). Fulfilling this interior aspect of the bower's definition, the natural vibrancy of the exterior of Century Cottage as depicted in *Enchantment and Sorrow* extends into Gabrielle's "inviting country bedroom," as the mantel is decorated with Scottish heather and other dried flowers, and the large windows open to the downs (307). Marie-Linda Lord notes that throughout *Enchantment and Sorrow*, Roy uses as many as seventeen bedrooms to mark "des temps forts de son évolution psychologique" (some of the most powerful moments of her psychological evolution; 99) and to arrange memories aesthetically and spatially (101). Of all these rooms, the bedroom at Century Cottage is paramount because of its situation within the extraordinary garden and its facilitation of Gabrielle's ultimate transformation into a writer whose sudden flourish of creativity reflects the very nature of her fertile surroundings. Roy similarly extends Marta's prairie garden into her kitchen. The walls are painted "delphinium blue"; dried poppy heads hang from the low ceiling beams; and the tablecloth showcases "big red flowers on a blue and yellow background" (165). Ultimately, what both Gabrielle and Marta have in common is an enclosed domestic space that accommodates their artistic pursuits: Gabrielle works on her writing in her Century Cottage bedroom every morning, and Marta performs her daily domestic art in her garden and kitchen.

Because of its designation as an inner room, the bower, or "boudoir," carries erotic connotations. In her study of the tradition in "Troping the Subject," Rachel Crawford notes that the conventional depiction as an idyllic enclosure derives from the combination of two idealized concepts of place: the *locus amoenus* (pleasant or pleasure ground) and the *hortus conclusus* (enclosed garden; 258–9). While the classical *locus amoenus* implies "murmuring breezes, birdsong, shady trees, sweet-smelling flowers, and clear-running brooks or fountains," the Christian tradition of the *hortus conclusus* "provide[s] an allegory for the inviolate body of the Virgin Mary" (258). This "identification of the female body with the enclosed space" of pleasing, reposeful landscape results in a highly erotic, natural dwelling (259). Outlining the gendered features of bower scenes, Crawford observes that the enclosure is often "occupied by a female character or object, or is instilled with some feminine principle (for example the nurturing power of nature)" (261). This character occupies a secondary role, while a solitary male takes center stage. His entrance into the bower constitutes part of his journey toward self-realization; the bower is merely a stop along his way. In *Poetry, Enclosure, and the Vernacular Landscape, 1700–1830,* Crawford suggests that the romance epic furnishes the bower tradition with "the figure of the lone knight/hero whose dynastic quest is punctuated by digressive interludes of embowered, sexualized encounters with maids, sorceresses, or divine female figures" (226). When these idealized concepts of place and erotic enclosure combine with the romance tradition, the bower operates as a highly literary garden "plot." Edmund Spenser's *The Faerie Queene* serves as an early example wherein the knight Guyon encounters both the Bower of Bliss and the Island of Phaedria. Patricia Parker reads these bowers as ambiguous middle-ground for the male hero's transition: Phaedria's "sequestered spot, deep in the shady quiet of the dale, offers ease to both ear and eye, respite from 'noyse of armes'" (372), yet also threatens the progress of Guyon's quest as "an image of the appeal and of the dangers of repose" (374). The bower is a delightful, feminized place, but it can also take the questing male figure off course.

As the tradition evolves through the centuries, the knight/hero figure appeals to many male poets' reflections on their own journeys toward artistic self-realization, making the writing of the bower, according to Crawford, "highly conventional in that its primary reference is not to gardens but to the world of poetry" (*Poetry* 226). In these imaginative quests, the private and oftentimes erotic setting of the bower's "boudoir" facilitates a heterosexual encounter between the male artist and his female muse, a union where the "traditional analogy for conceptual productivity is provided by sexual reproduction" (Crawford, "Troping" 261). In keeping with the *hortus conclusus* that identifies the female body as the enclosed garden, the female muse takes the form of either a woman, or the "lap of nature," both are suitable ground for the demonstration of masculine potency (Crawford, "Troping" 261). Such an eroticization of the female muse and garden is evident (as we saw in chapter two) in Robert Kroetsch's "Pumpkin: A Love Poem." If we read this poem as a bower poem, then we see the speaker describe the female gardener as a "new territory" (4), or garden, that he has "entered" (3) in a manner reminiscent of Andrew Marvell's most famous work of this genre: "The Garden." Marvell's poem illustrates what Crawford outlines as the male artist's privileged, solitary possession of his garden enclosure. With Eve banished from this alternative paradise (just as Kroetsch's speaker yells at the female pioneer to "go / away" [46–7]), Marvell's speaker revels in his "happy garden-state," as Nature is an erotic substitute (57). The "luscious clusters" of vine (35), the "curious peach" (37) and ensnaring flowers constitute this lush, seductive atmosphere (35–40).

The particular inspirational appeal of the bower does not, however, always elicit the same response from male writers. While Marvell's speaker indulges in his bower, other male poets, notably those from the Romantic period, relate troublesome visions. According to Crawford, the bower can be "a space of dilemma, ambiguity, and frustration in the quest for subjectivity" ("Troping" 261). William Wordsworth's bower scene in "Nutting" demonstrates, for example, a difficult rite of passage through a boyhood discovery of a "virgin scene" (21) and the bower's final "[d]eformed and sullied" (47) state subsequent to an enraged destruction of it. Likewise, Samuel Taylor Coleridge's "This Lime-Tree Bower My Prison" captures a mature male subject's ambivalent response to a bower that does not offer repose, but rather despair and isolation: "Well, they are gone, and here must I remain, / This lime-tree bower my prison!"(1–2). The embowered poet yearns to wander the countryside with his companions, but creative renewal arrives only when he imagines himself beyond his idle state. As Michael Raiger argues, the source of poetic fertility springs more from the poet's mind and spirit than from the bower itself, as the poet "sought communion with both absent friends and absent nature" (73), and this active "vision has transformed the lime-tree bower from a prison of the senses into a playground for the spirit" (74).

Whether the bower provides a secure, sensual, or problematic environment for the knight/hero or male poet, it remains largely his privileged domain and story. Unfortunately, generic conventions pose a real dilemma for questing female subjects who desire their own bower experiences. According to Dorothy Mermin, an impossible situation results when the female subject has "to play two opposing roles at one time – both knight and damsel, both subject and object – and that because she can't do this she is excluded from the worlds her imagination has discovered" (65–6). The female subject is prohibited from entering the bower[10] or faces a prescribed role within it as eroticized object and muse. In response to these limitations, women writers negotiate this gendered terrain in ways appropriate to their socio-historical milieus. In her book, Crawford points to Felicia Hemans, a nineteenth-century writer who legitimizes the embowered female as artist, rather than as muse, by devising heroines who embody the "sexual regulative ideal of the passionless female ... thus forming an unexpected association between authorial power and the regulated female character" (244). Whereas Hemans treads carefully within the bower tradition by adhering to her historical ideals of womanly virtue, contemporary Canadian writer Phyllis Webb infuses her poem "Marvell's Garden" (1956) with a critical feminist vision, by openly and angrily protesting in her "hot glade" (6) the bower's exclusivity to male artists. The speaker laments women's erasure from the bower and their being denied this rite of initiation into poetic achievement. Undermining Marvell's original poem and dream of a solitary male paradise, she inserts feminine difference, a vision of "contradiction" (7), revealing "the shade green within the green shade" (8).[11] By the conclusion, however, the speaker denies men access to her own "garden" and mourns the gender division that precludes the possibility of exchange. Robert Kroetsch may similarly be read as lamenting a loss of fertile exchange in "Pumpkin: A Love Poem" by mocking his juvenile male speaker's banishment of the female pioneer and subsequent focus on masturbation. Such solitary behaviour is, of course, in direct contrast to that of Kroestch, himself, whose very use of the garden palimpsest engages in a creative dialogue with a woman writer from the past.

The extraordinary abodes in *Enchantment and Sorrow* and "Garden in the Wind" concur with typical bower settings and their sequence of events, but Roy strays from convention by choosing to domesticate the bower through the incorporation of gender paradigms: specifically, familial relationships, feminine virtue, and the self-less nurturing of others. Unlike Webb, Roy's purpose is not to defiantly address the gendered hierarchy of bower scenes; what she pursues instead is a careful elevating of the status of Gabrielle and Marta. They are not merely decorative fixtures within their bowers, but rather their own questing artist-subjects. Because of this change in role, their enclosures are necessarily sites of reassurance, affirming gender norms and rendering these female artists benign creatures. Artistic agency and solitariness are "brought home" – that is, aligned with nurturing femininity and those aspects of identity and experience that spring from one's maternal origins and families.

In this way, Gabrielle's and Marta's bowers are gender-appropriate for the fictional contexts of Roy's literary works, which both take place in the mid-twentieth century. Added to these stylized depictions, though, are significant differences relevant to a generational shift in each female artist's position, which is dependent on her particular circumstance and time frame as she either begins or ends her journey. While Gabrielle is a young artist (of words) with independence and mobility, Marta is an aging gardener (of flowers) tied to the home. Consequently, Roy formulates a clear distinction between expression that is informed by the domestic (art that responds to, but can move beyond the home) and domestically situated art (art that responds to, and takes place within the home). This difference speaks directly to the woman artist's tentative agency, reflected not only in her spatial characterization (beyond, or within the domestic bower), but also in the public extension or private curtailing of her particular mode of expression.

## *The Domestication of the Bower in* Enchantment and Sorrow

In *Enchantment and Sorrow,* Roy uses the bower as a subtle means of validating Gabrielle's artistry by mediating the tensions between her longing to circulate freely within the public domain and her need to account for socio-cultural norms that dictate domestic responsibility. First, within the bower of Century Cottage, Roy defines Gabrielle through a familial role, as opposed to making her a completely independent figure. Second, Roy objectifies her momentarily without jeopardizing this quest for self-development, thereby maintaining feminine submission within the bower in relation to Gabrielle's more novel creative agency. And third, Roy presents Gabrielle's resolution to nurture others through her art, thereby moderating the seemingly self-centred, unfeminine nature of Gabrielle's artistic pursuits that take her beyond the home and even beyond her own country.

Century Cottage appears at a pivotal point in Roy's autobiography, providing a much-needed refuge and place of maturation during Gabrielle's journey toward self-discovery. Leaving behind her mother and her Manitoba home, travelling to Paris to pursue an acting career, and finally residing in London, Gabrielle experiences mobility and independence previously beyond her grasp. In his biography, Ricard writes that "[a]s [Roy] had done in Paris, once she was settled in London she began systematically visiting the city and its environs, armed with her small camera" (168) and in this way, was able to "shake off all that still stamped her as a dutiful, submissive, little small-town girl" (*Gabrielle Roy* 170). Indeed, a number of the photographs housed in the *fonds Gabrielle Roy* give the impression of a young woman on a joyous adventure, exploring the English countryside (Figure 3.1) and public gardens such as the Kew Gardens in London (Figure 3.2). The feeling of female autonomy is evoked most compelling by an image of Roy's silhouette taken at Land's End, England (Figure 3.3). Eventually, though, this personal freedom is overshadowed by dismay when Gabrielle is overcome by her lack of dramatic inspiration and creative direction, and also by the abrupt end of her first love affair. In *Enchantment and Sorrow*, Gabrielle leaves the city on a whim and boards the "Green Line" bus that takes urban dwellers to the countryside. She arrives by chance at Century Cottage, which is owned by Esther Perfect and her father, a retired manor gardener. Instilling in Gabrielle a sense of renewal, wholeness, and security, this place proves to be the highly idealized bower of salvation that Crawford defines in "Troping the Subject" by offering both "the ground for an initiation into subjectivity" (261) and "the passageway to a vocation as poet" (262), or in Gabrielle's case, a writer of fiction.

When Gabrielle first encounters Century Cottage, Roy represents herself as a questing heroine in need of shelter and rest after an arduous journey. Gabrielle may happen upon the cottage by chance, but it is a destined turning point in her experience: "I came to a door of dark wood. I reached for the knocker but as if I'd had enough strength only to bring me as far as this doorstep, I suddenly drooped against the doorframe. I think I was so tired that tears came to my eyes, so exhausted I felt I was arriving ... from the agonizing uncertainties I'd been living with so long ... This was my last thought before letting my head fall against the door, no longer able to keep my eyes open" (306). Her emotionally vulnerable state draws attention to her typically feminine character, yet her independent status, as suggested through Roy's repeated use of the pronoun "I," highlights the unconventional

FIGURE 3.1 Gabrielle Roy on a bridge in Bibury, England, 1938

FIGURE 3.2
Gabrielle Roy
in Kew Gardens,
London,
England,
1938

FIGURE 3.3   Gabrielle Roy at Land's End, England, 1938

nature of her solitary journey as a woman artist. During her time in Europe, Gabrielle is decidedly removed from her familial duties and financial responsibilities. Paradoxically, then, the cottage bower realigns Gabrielle with some of these traditional gender expectations at the same time as it brings her to artistic fruition.

Grappling with the uncertainties of her life and vocation, Gabrielle discovers in Century Cottage a place of quiet self-reflection and an opportunity to withdraw from the world. Through the convention of the bower, Roy stages Gabrielle's initiation as an artist. John Lennox notes that the larger framework of Roy's autobiography works as a fairytale filled with archetypal scenes in which Gabrielle "plays" the role of heroine. The Century Cottage bower scene is no exception. In Lennox's reading, the first section "The Governor's Ball" (a ball to which Gabrielle's parents are invited but which they do not attend when they see the other guests' expensive attire) brings to mind the Prince's ball that Cinderella is barred from attending: "The metaphor of the ball suggests a fairy-tale pattern of usurpation, hardship, initiative, and restoration" (70). In fairytales, the heroine "is marked for greater things; her destiny is strong" (71). This sense of predestination finds its fullest expression at Century Cottage. At this point in the autobiography, the garden envelops Gabrielle instantly upon her arrival: "I must have disappeared ... among the tall delphiniums, giant hollyhocks, and Canterbury bells" (306). Imbued with a magical nature typical of most bowers, the little back garden filled with herbs and flowers feels otherworldly, out of time and space, with the "Canterbury bells bearing more big sumptuous bells than [Gabrielle has] ever seen anywhere else" (306). The garden is alive, burgeoning with plants, delicious aromas, and sensations. The scent of mint and rosemary float from the back corner of the garden; and "the air positively vibrate[s] with the buzzing of insects, the clamour of voices around a banquet table" (306). The immense fertility of the place promises a productive imagination. Roy even refers to her time at Century Cottage as a "fairy story"; it "was all [she] could possibly desire" (309).

As much as Century Cottage is an extraordinary bower, it is also a domestic setting of quotidian routine and familial ease that facilitates and naturalizes Gabrielle's artistry. Her initiation as a writer comes not from an erotic encounter that typically suggests "conceptual productivity," as Crawford outlines it, but rather from a comforting bedroom, doting parental figures, and childhood memories ("Troping" 261). The flowery abode is in keeping with the genre's conventions, but these innocent, familial circumstances are decidedly not. Gabrielle's discovery of her vocation follows, therefore, the pattern that Whitfield contends is so central to Roy's "feminist" writing: the oppositional pull of journey and home. With Gabrielle's craft at odds with the traditional domestic responsibilities modeled by her mother Mélina, Roy uses the third nature of the bower to reconcile these disparate roles. For example, just prior to Gabrielle's arrival at Century Cottage, she has tea at another cottage in the woods, a place that initiates a remembrance of and return to youthful innocence: "It couldn't be made for living in, I thought, just for playing at living in; the humble little Tudor cottage of Old England on the tins of fine biscuits my mother used to buy when I was a child ... The minute I saw it I felt I'd returned to the safety and peace of my early childhood" (301). According to Lennox, this petite cottage "mirrors an intimate part of Gabrielle's personality in its diminutive role-playing" (76), and this observation is equally relevant to Gabrielle's bower experience, which melds artistry together with a surrogate or make-believe family. In keeping with a return to child-like innocence, Roy compares the first morning at Century Cottage, the morning Gabrielle fervently begins to write, with a morning of an earlier time in Manitoba: "When I woke I was perhaps more at peace than I had been since ... the days of summer holidays at the farm when I'd wake on my first morning in my uncle's house not knowing where I was; then I'd ... know for certain I was happy again in the house I loved so much, where I'd known only peace and happiness ... With the return of this peaceful feeling so long absent from my life, I discovered just as suddenly a burning urge to write" (316). Through this parallel to her uncle's farm, Gabrielle is significantly "brought home" and subsequently able to pursue her writing. The virtuous protection of Esther and Father Perfect reinforces her reclaimed sense of childhood. In this shelter, the female artist may safely develop along appropriate gender lines that demand a woman's familial involvement.

By fashioning Gabrielle's initiation in such a manner, Roy mediates her vulnerable position as a woman writer whose vocation and travel run contrary to a sedentary home life and its obligations. In the autobiography as a whole, the combination of the domestic setting with the bower lends an organic quality and a sense of validation to Gabrielle's journey of self-affirmation. The Upshire bower is actually the culmination of a plant and garden motif that shapes the opening chapters. Throughout Gabrielle's life, her central preoccupation is with her heritage as an exile: her experience of being uprooted, or of uprooting herself. As Vincenza Costantino argues, "Une mobilité spatiale correspondant à une instabilité plus profonde lui rend difficile tout enracinement" (A spatial mobility corresponding to a more profound instability makes all rootedness difficult for her; 392). At the foreground are both Gabrielle's alienation as a young Francophone living in the mainly English-speaking province of Manitoba, and her choice to leave her family in order to travel to Europe and follow independent pursuits. The end result is a tenuous bond between identity and home. As a young woman attending the English-run Normal School in Winnipeg, she finds there is no opportunity for Francophone students to experience "'an opening out'" or a "'blossoming of the self'" (63). Seeking cultural and intellectual stimulation, Gabrielle admits that there is little that reflects or speaks to her French way of life, which leads "to a kind of withering" and makes her feel that she is "living in some walled enclosure" (109–10). The most difficult experience of uprooting is, however, her departure from both her mother and the familiar confines of home. Being transplanted to France leaves her "timidly" trying to "find [her] feet ... like some bruised plant in a protective layer of compost" (208). In the end, this garden imagery works to naturalize Gabrielle's desire to escape the confines of her original home and to pursue elsewhere her life as an artist.

Gabrielle's ambivalence over her concurrent need to uproot and to remain associated with the domestic is perhaps best expressed through the photograph featured on the original cover of the autobiography published by Les Éditions du Boréal. Identified on the inside leaf as "Gabrielle Roy, à vingt-deux ans, dans le jardin de Rue Dèschambault" (Gabrielle Roy, at twenty-two years, in the garden of Dèschambault Street), the image captures Roy seated on a parlour chair in the garden of her childhood Manitoban home (Figure 3.4). A whimsical image, the photograph blends both "indoor" propriety (through Roy's dress and lady-like composure) and the outdoor surroundings of a cultivated garden. François Ricard states that the publishers "chose that photograph on my suggestion, for two main reasons, if I recall: it was one of the very few photographs of a *young* Gabrielle Roy that were known at that time; and it was a photograph that had never been used before on a book by or about Gabrielle Roy" (Letter to author). In addition to providing a youthful image, the cover encapsulates the

FIGURE 3.4   Gabrielle Roy seated in her parents' garden
in Manitoba from the cover of Roy's *La détresse et
l'enchantement*, 1984

central preoccupations of Gabrielle the tentative artist as conveyed in the autobiography: her choice not to remain enclosed but to pursue her craft wherever it might take her, and at the same time, her continuing need to present herself as firmly tied to the domestic.

Gabrielle's quest beyond the home creates an interesting parallel with some of Roy's male characters who undertake similar independent journeys. A close examination of the details of these journeys reveals the gendered limitations that Roy appreciates as being real and unique challenges for the female artist. In *The Cashier* and *The Hidden Mountain*, Alexandre Chenevert and Pierre Cadorai respectively sever themselves from their homes and embark on solitary adventures. What distinguishes Alexandre and Pierre from Gabrielle, however, is the degree and ease of separation between the questing subject and home. Alexandre and Pierre find inspiration in moments of near-complete isolation. These men are not situated amid obvious familial surroundings, such as Gabrielle's Century Cottage, but rather a sparsely populated forest setting (for Alexandre) and the untouched reaches of the wilderness (for Pierre). Leaving behind his wife Eugénie, Alexandre locates his ideal retreat in the pristine forest of Lac Vert. In many ways, Alexandre's journey from Montreal to the country parallels that of Gabrielle. Just as Gabrielle boards the Green Line bus that takes Londoners to the country, a weary Alexandre and his fellow Montrealers travel by bus in a comparable excursion: "Alexandre had the impression … that all of them together were awaiting a return to their native soil. The home they all yearned for – was it, for the others as for him, merely some small, unknown patch of greenery?" (137). The "home," or seemingly contained "patch" of nature, that Alexandre ultimately finds is, however, quite different from Gabrielle's Century Cottage.

In *The Cashier*, Alexandre takes his respite not in domesticated nature and a familial setting, but in the isolated woods of Lac Vert and a rented cottage, which replicates the exotic, deserted Pacific island paradise for which he continually longs throughout the novel. In his forest cottage a "feeling of childhood swath[s] Alexandre" (153), and although he senses this place to be "his true dwelling" (160), this is not a familial setting of companionship and domestic routine. Instead, Alexandre imagines living alone in nature as his "heart seized upon that ancient human dream, the dream of Robinson Crusoe!" (163). At Lac Vert, Alexandre has little contact with the owners of the cottage, Le Gardeurs (which literally means the "herdsmen" but connotes guardians or protectors), the trapping and farming family. Alexandre is so completely immersed in his solitude that Monsieur Le Gardeur even pays a visit to the cottage to "root [Alexandre] out and see if [he is] still alive" after Madame Le Gardeur expresses concern for his anti-social behaviour as he "had refused to stop off a moment at their house" (165). In keeping with their name, the Le Gardeurs provide a protective, familial component to Alexandre's respite, but he spends little time with them, preferring to remain alone.

When Alexandre returns to the city, the wildness and complete isolation of Lac Vert remain his inspiration, sharply contrasting with the artificial urban landscape of "fake brick and fake stone" and garden plots "full of chickens, dwarfs, and Grecian vases made of pottery or concrete" (189). Furthermore, unlike Gabrielle who undergoes a veritable transformation at Century Cottage, Alexandre seems, despite his belief in self-renewal, not to have changed as a result of his journey: "[Alexandre] seemed to suffer just as he had before he left. Nor did it seem that he had really put on any weight. Looking at him with compassion – and with a certain irritation, too – [Eugénie] remarked: 'It doesn't appear that your holiday has done you much good.

Poor old chap! And the crazy notion of going all by yourself into the woods!'" (197). In addition to his lack of physical improvement, Alexandre also fails to express himself when he attempts to write a letter to a newspaper informing his fellow urban dwellers of his inspired experience in the country. At Lac Vert, Alexandre produces only "a series of erasures" (180) and "tag ends of phrases which seemed to trace back directly to his nickel newspaper, to the catch-lines in the streetcar ads" (181). Together, the lack of physical renewal and the stilted expression suggest a failed wilderness-bower experience against the overwhelming realities of modern life.

Like Alexandre, Pierre in *The Hidden Mountain* is a man disconnected from family and home. A solitary artist searching for his vision through the Canadian North, Pierre appreciates that "a hearth and home [are] not for him" (114). A man seemingly without family, Pierre comments toward the conclusion of the novel, "'I have always had good partners'" (183), yet he distances himself repeatedly from his help-mate friends: "That strange artist's dream of being alone with his domain, in his interpretation, alone in his creation – had not Pierre achieved it from the very outset?" (174). While Gabrielle surrounds herself with doting parental figures and the comforts of a homey cottage, Pierre looks for a shelter that reflects his isolation and facilitates total immersion in his painting. When finding an attic room to rent in Paris, for instance, Pierre's friend Stanislas describes it as "a real hole," but Pierre seems content with his choice: "Everything was eliminated that could uselessly burden a man. He would have his stove, something to eat. What more did he need?" (162).

Pierre's source of inspiration is wild nature, and when he finds himself living in the heart of Paris he continues to paint the North, finding little artistic appeal in the contained space of Parisian public squares and gardens. Marie-Pierre Andron writes, "La recherche d'intimité avec la matière inspirante est impossible, les squares et les jardins, comme parenthèses dans la frénésie urbaine, sont impossible. Il ne peut y avoir ni recueillement, ni retrouvailles, ni intimité" (The quest for intimacy with inspirational material is impossible, these public squares and gardens, like parentheses in the urban frenzy, are impossible. There is no possibility of room for contemplation, reunion, or intimacy; 86). For the solitary male artist, his independence is reflected in the uncontained nature that inspires his self-focused quest. In direct contrast to Pierre's impossible experience of introspection and insufficient connection with the urban surroundings during his time in Paris, a fleeting glimpse of the Tuileries Gardens from a bus window sparks Gabrielle's revelation regarding her talents: "What I can't forget is that seeing the beautiful garden of Paris … made me

FIGURE 3.5 Luxembourg Gardens, Paris, France

realize I had a faculty for observation I hadn't really been aware of before, together with an infinite longing to know what to do with it" (228). Following this epiphany, Gabrielle experiences a necessary reprieve in the Luxembourg Gardens following her uninspiring acting rehearsals: "With great relief I sat listening to [the old women] talking about everyday things among themselves over their knitting. The more I saw of the theatre, the more I was drawn by people's simple, everyday lives and their everyday language ... Though I didn't realize it, I was approaching what would prove to be the right, the only school for me" (231). Even in this early stage of Gabrielle's journey toward artistic self-realization, the depiction is gender-appropriate: associated with enclosed, cultivated nature and family-oriented scenes. While she appreciates the Tuileries pond "with children playing around it" and "the impeccable rows of round-headed chestnut trees" (228), Alexandre and Pierre are drawn to that which is wild, solitary, and relatively uncontained, preferences in keeping, coincidently, with Northrop Frye's wilderness model of the Canadian imagination. In *The Hidden Mountain*, Pierre's art instructor tells him to "see what [he] can do with commonplace subjects" such as houses and public squares (145), but in "study after study there emerg[es] a Paris shivering under an Arctic glow" (149).[12] Unlike her depictions of Alexandre's and Pierre's predisposition for expansive nature, Roy seems compelled to relate her own character and her writing to the intimate space of house and home.

The pressures of gendered propriety push Roy to construct her artistry through traditional associations, but the creation of this bower is not without its challenges. Gabrielle enjoys the familial comforts of her bower, but it is not her privileged domain, which sets her apart from the experience of many male artists. Gabrielle's former lover, Stephen, arrives unexpectedly at Century Cottage, and during this scene, she seems in danger of slipping into the conventional position of female muse within a masculine-centred narrative of a questing hero. Roy admits, "Nothing happened to break the spell [of Century Cottage] for several weeks" (332), until Stephen appeared, travelling "the long way through the forest" and "suffering from the oppressive late-morning heat" (333). In his study of women's bowers in eighteenth-century fiction, J. David Macey notes that, typically, male intrusions preempt the privacy of these green spaces, as female heroines realize that the garden is "far from an absolute retreat" (76). These "scenes of discovery" consequently transform the women into objects of amorous male interest (76) and draw attention to the "theatrical quality of the bower scene" (90), suggesting that privacy is "conventional rather than actual" as women continue to perform according to gender and genre norms (92). This performative aspect of the tradition suits *Enchantment and Sorrow* well, as Lennox identifies a larger motif of theatricality informing both the structure and content in a "constant association between acting and writing" (72). During Gabrielle's encounter with Stephen, he assumes the heroic role, re-enacting her past experience: "As I had done when I first arrived in Upshire, [Stephen] was looking above the doors of the cottages for their names ... He came to our gate and paused to rest his laden arms on it" (333). Presented as another arrival scene, Stephen's intrusion jeopardizes Gabrielle's artistic quest, as he practically supplants her from her own story.

With Roy's inclination to naturalize the female artist, her bower must afford reassurance as much as it invites independence. Accordingly, Gabrielle performs a dual role as both developing artist and muse, or love object, to Stephen through Roy's staging of traditional femininity. Roy carefully navigates the bower's role as natural "boudoir" to initiate an acceptable, virtuous female artist and bring her quest physically and figuratively "home." A chaste familial model minimizes the erotic, a difficult task since Gabrielle's character must accommodate a seductive male presence. When Stephen arrives, Gabrielle sits above in her bedroom window like a conventional embowered muse, yet Roy revises this discovery scene by supplying a unique point of view. Maintaining possession of her bower plot, rather than allowing her character to become the object of the male gaze, Roy takes advantage of her heroine's position (looking down from the bedroom window upon an unsuspecting Stephen): "Spying on him from the windows so to speak, I felt none of the pathetic magnetism that had passed between us" (333–4). From her privileged position, Gabrielle avoids becoming the love object, minimizes Stephen's seductive power, and maintains her status as the female artist (334). In a later scene in the parlour, Gabrielle actually focuses Stephen's attentions away from romance and onto her own progress as a writer, showing him the royalty cheque from her first publication and allowing him to read her latest manuscript (336).

The erotics of the bower eventually find a place in Roy's narrative, yet she maintains a sense of innocence through the security of her domestic scene. Although Roy distances her character from the role of muse, Stephen's "burning, intense way" (336) of looking at Gabrielle prompts the former lovers to leave the Cottage garden and walk through the forest where they become "entwined, clinging to each other as though [they] were the last of our species left together on earth" (338). Roy stages the love scene *outside* the idyllic shelter and uses the familial setting of Century Cottage to frame Stephen's presence, curtailing the sexualization of Gabrielle. Esther reminds Stephen "of a beloved Ukrainian great aunt" (334), and during lunch both Father Perfect and Esther assess the young couple in the manner of concerned surrogate parents: "[Father Perfect] and Esther were delighted to find me less alone in the world than I might have seemed, and their eyes kept straying from me to Stephen and from Stephen to me as if to show me they approved of my choice" (335). Here, the erotics of the bower are safely contained within a courtship scenario. By the conclusion of the chapter, Stephen leaves to participate in the impending war, and his departure solidifies Gabrielle's romantic independence, a status that seems necessary for her artistic pursuits.

Roy's careful containment of the illicit bower, or "boudoir," enables her to foreground familial obligations and to downplay the unconventional, even immodest, independence of the modern female artist. The young Gabrielle's creative outpouring is not the result of a sexual exchange; instead her writing springs from a domestic model that depends upon the selfless nurturing of others. Ricard suggests that Century Cottage provides Roy with an "exemplary image of what writing is: a shelter from the world; and what it needs: quieted passions, total availability, and obliviousness to all material preoccupations" (*Gabrielle Roy* 174). According to Ricard, for the remainder of Roy's career, "[w]riting remained tied to the 'Upshire complex'" (*Gabrielle Roy* 361), by which he means a quiet, rural retreat tended by a caring individual to support the daily work of the writer. In fact, Ricard notes that during the last twenty-five years of Roy's life, she spent every spring and summer writing in her cottage in Petite-Rivière-Saint-François, Quebec (365) (Figure 3.6). While Roy's husband Marcel Carbotte visited on weekends and tended to the garden (366), her devoted friend Berthe Simard provided daily companionship and managed the household tasks (366–7) – all of which facilitated Roy's pursuit of her craft. Quoting a letter Roy addressed to her sister-in-law, Ricard stresses that for the writer, this little cottage, which was the first property she had ever owned, represented "'the only real refuge I've had in my wandering life since Dèschambault Street'" (365) (Figures 3.7 and 3.8). Roy's realization of the necessity of a domestic

FIGURE 3.6  Gabrielle Roy's cottage at Petite-Rivière-Saint-François, Quebec

retreat for the pursuit of her craft remains forever connected, however, to her original bower experience as depicted in *Enchantment and Sorrow*. In the context of the narrative, Century Cottage garden is undoubtedly an ideal shelter for Gabrielle as a young writer, but the "total availability" and freedom from "material preoccupations," as Ricard describes the scenario (174), seem partially at odds with Roy's domestication of her bower, an approach that ties the female artist to familial life and its obligations. With the re-enactment of her childhood at Century Cottage, Gabrielle is, of course, able to disengage from domestic duties as she benefits from, as Ricard

FIGURE 3.7 Gabrielle Roy standing in her flower garden at Petite-Rivière-Saint-François, Quebec

FIGURE 3.8. Gabrielle Roy reading in her garden
at Petite-Rivière-Saint-François, Quebec

observes, "the presence of some kindly and protective, discreet and yet
utterly devoted figure": Esther Perfect (174). With Esther's practical
help and affection, Gabrielle has the freedom to pursue her writing,
just as Roy's male artist, Pierre Cadorai, immerses himself entirely
in his painting through the assistance of his friends. But while Pierre
retreats from relationships, finding his inspiration in the uninhabited
reaches of the Canadian North and the barest apartment in Paris, Roy
situates Gabrielle in a domestic setting, which begs the question: Is
Roy's construction of her *role* as a woman writer as subtly enclosed

within gender paradigms as the terrain of her bower? Gabrielle may be free of material concerns, but her continued preoccupation with the home is expressed in other ways, as she assumes an alternative familial responsibility.

## Marta's "Garden in the Wind"

Pivotal to an appreciation of Roy's construction of the female artist and her domestic role is Marta Yaramko and her prairie bower in "Garden in the Wind." Catherine Rubinger believes that Roy's "*Un jardin* n'est certes pas le chef-d'oeuvre qu'est *Bonheur d'occasion*, mais il contient la quintessence de son art" (*Garden* [*in the Wind*] is certainly not the masterpiece that is *The Tin Flute*, but it contains the essence of her art; 124). Published toward the end of her career, "Garden in the Wind" preoccupied Roy for over three decades, during which she drafted a number of different versions.[13] In the short story, the travelling, nameless narrator, who is a writer and closely aligned with Roy herself, happens upon the practically abandoned Ukrainian settlement of Volhyn in northern Alberta. Roy's inspiration for "Garden in the Wind" came from an actual encounter she had in Saskatchewan as a journalist touring western Canada during the summer of 1942. In the article "Turbulent Seekers After Peace," which was originally published in December of 1942 in *Bulletin des agriculteurs* (a farmers journal) and was subsequently reprinted in Roy's *The Fragile Lights of Earth* (1978), Roy describes a Doukhobor woman named Masha and her "plethora" of flowers: "To reach her house I had to go miles and miles along rough paths, across a desolate plain. She lives in a region so remote that it seems like the world's end. Yet she has also spent her life planting flowers" (41). In the fictional version of this story, the isolated location of Volhyn is the place of fairytale itself, and indeed the nameless narrator describes it as "what once upon a time tried to be a village" (123). In this drought-ridden space, the domain of exiles, the narrator discovers an extraordinary yet modest "little garden" on the outskirts of the town (125). With its mass of scarlet poppies, lupines, geraniums, and snapdragons, the garden seems out of place, juxtaposed against, and in spite of, its surroundings, as if "a dream" (125). Its otherworldly quality and fecundity elevate it to the status of magical bower, particularly as this garden contains a female figure at its centre. Surrounded by flowers and colours, Marta either works or "sit[s] on a stool right in their midst" with a searching soul, surprising herself with the profound nature of her contemplation (137). This prairie garden is not only a retreat for Marta's introspection, but also her artistic product. Marta "compose[s] her intricate designs with groups of plants" and in this final year lets the flowers grow "according to chance" (137). She may be merely a farmer's wife but Marta is also an artist whose "dull life [has] had this richer side, a little mad and fanatical" (128).

In many ways, Marta's garden "bursting with flowers" seems both incongruent and frivolous in relation to the farming settlement struggling for survival. Nevertheless, Roy instills this bower with immense purpose through its capacity for nurturing. As with the bower of Century Cottage, Marta's garden "dream" provides daily comfort and facilitates life (125). Marta creates beauty and order amidst desolation, as she brings "a harmony of colours that immediately seemed a home, as much so as the horizon of the clouds. A house in its own place, a flower where it belongs, a tree where one is needed" (150). Spotting a newly emerged leaf, she "help[s] this birth along" almost like a midwife, "brushing away a twig that could hinder it" (127). Marta's bower does not simply serve as a site of transition or temporary repose on a journey that takes place predominantly elsewhere; rather, it is a site of self-realization and a process of continual work that has occurred for thirty years. Now, as she contends with failing health and physical pain, Marta discovers that her garden is crucial to her expression and growing self-awareness: "She no longer had the strength for heavy tasks. Now she gave herself solely to her little garden, and as she did so her thoughts, like plants well cared for, also sprang free from silence and routine … Sometimes she was astonished to find they were her own … But from whom else could she have had them? Perhaps she had always had them, but locked deep inside her, as indistinct as the flower-to-come in the heart of a dull seed" (128–9). Marta's garden serves her as an artist in a profoundly personal way and is her privileged domain, not simply because of its isolation, but because of her creative work. Like Marvell's speaker in "The Garden," who revels in his solitary green musings, Marta surprises herself with the organic germination of her thoughts, reflected in the growth of each seed. In contrast to Marvell's speaker, however, this creator exhibits a nurturing integrity that benefits not just herself but rather the whole community of Volhyn.

Although the younger generations have abandoned the isolated Alberta village for the city, and those left behind, such as Marta's husband Stepan, are full of anger and unproductive despair, Marta's garden plays a vital third-nature role in sustaining and highlighting what remains. In contrast to his wife's diligent care, Stepan gives the wondrous garden merely an "irritated glance" and wanders the untidy farm "scattering to the ends of their land the raging sound of hostile words" (130). Even the Ukrainian church with its "onion-shaped steeple" (123–4) is in a state of neglect, full of spider webs and "the dust of old bouquets of wildflowers" that lie at the feet of the depicted saints (124). Other settlers have long since deserted both the village and their faith, leaving Marta as "the only one in recent times to have cleaned [the church] up at all" (142). She remains steadfast and nurturing, perpetuating her dream for a home and community. As a young woman, Marta urged her family to immigrate to the western prairies, only to recreate their former home. Roy writes, "Not until today, after thirty years of living in Volhyn, did Marta realize that she and old Stepan, perhaps unwittingly, had reproduced almost exactly the atmosphere of the poor farm in their native Volhynia from which they had come" (131). In this ghost-town, Marta's extraordinary garden supplies a "buoyancy of spirit" (150) and creates a living legacy: "From that dear old friend in Codessa, whom she had not been able to visit, alas, for so long, [Marta] had received a rose of India taken from [Lubka's] garden ... From this one flower, hung from her ceiling to dry – head down, as it should be – Marta had been able to recover some three hundred seeds, which had given Volhyn almost as many roses, and each of these in turn had produced hundreds. Marta lost herself in her calculation of the infinite descendants of a single flower" (151). Through this seemingly perpetual regeneration, the temporal boundaries of Marta's garden expand and counter the demise of the village of Volhyn.

Nicole Bourbonnais notes that Roy positions Marta's garden as preeminent space: "le petit village pitoyable qui n'a pu accéder à l'existence est graduellement supplanté par un site également de dimensions réduites, mais triomphant et euphorique: le jardin multicolore de Martha Yaramko" (the pitiable little village that could not assure its existence is gradually supplanted by a site of equally reduced size, yet triumphant and euphoric: the multicoloured garden of Marta Yaramko; 369).[14] Marta is attentive to the needs and fragile continuity of her garden, immigrant community, and home. Just as she encourages the "delicately pleated faces" of the poppies to grow in the wind (125), she cleans the neglected church icons, "[their] eyes, dusted clean" (147), and later "dig[s] out of her trunk their old wedding photograph so as to see Stepan's face" (133), which has now grown dark and inaccessible under a "briar patch" of hair and "tangled eyebrows" (133). Marta's domain includes, then, both literal and figurative gardens, and through her artistic work she nurtures sources of identity and joy that might otherwise be neglected, forgotten, or lost. After all, while Marta may officially be "a part of Canada" (14), she and the other Ukrainian farmers of this isolated community have spent their lives "in some vague zone of wind and loneliness that Canada might yet embrace" (140).

In the emptiness and "savage silence" of northern Alberta, Marta affords the third nature of her garden great purpose (131), as she functions as an embowered female muse, inspiring others during their own journeys toward self-realization. In this regard, Marta and her art solidify Roy's dilemma regarding the role of the female artist who must be "brought home" but not necessarily remain enclosed within domestic space. Significantly, the narrator of "Garden in the Wind" is not Marta, but rather a woman writer who begins this story by relating retrospectively her own experience when she was young. In the opening paragraphs of the story, the writer-narrator describes her encounter with Marta's garden as a critical moment in her life: "In those days I often said to myself: what's the point of this, what's the good of that? Writing was a chore for me. Why bother inventing yet another story ... Who still believes in stories? And in any case, haven't they all been told? That's what I was thinking that day when, toward evening on that road which seemed to lead me nowhere, I saw in the very emptiness of drought and desolation that surge of splendid flowers" (125). Barren of creative ideas and artistic purpose, the narrator mirrors the drought and despair of the landscape surrounding Volhyn. She ultimately finds her direction, however, through Marta's example. In this domestic model of artistry, the narrator realizes that in tending to those otherwise neglected aspects of one's identity and familial heritage, the artist, and in this particular case the woman artist, creates invaluable expression. According to Saint-Martin's article "Portrait de l'artiste en (vieille) femme," Roy's pairing of the young writer-narrator with Marta positions women's domestic work as a source of creative agency, thereby extending the seemingly inconsequential private domain to a larger realm of influence: "Il est vrai que les pulsions créatrices des femmes ont été longtemps limitées à l'espace domestique; exclues de la sphère publique, les femmes ont oeuvré à l'embellissement du foyer et du jardin où elles se sont vues enfermées. Mais … Gabrielle Roy ne privilégie pas le public par rapport au privé … nulle hiérarchie ne s'élève. La quête éperdue de la beauté, l'amoureuse attention accordée à la matière, la solitude qui accompagne forcément toute création véritable, sont les mêmes" (It is true that women's creative impulses have for a long time been limited to domestic space; excluded from the public domain, women have worked on the embellishment of the home and garden where they were enclosed. But … Gabrielle Roy does not privilege the public over the private … no hierarchy emerges. The boundless quest for beauty, the passionate attention devoted to the material, the solitude that forcibly accompanies all true creative acts, are the same; 517).[15] Through the example of Marta, Saint-Martin perceives not a closing in, but rather an opening out for the female artist, as "Gabrielle Roy accorde à des activités féminines séculaires une visibilité et un prestige nouveaux" (Gabrielle Roy gives these secular, feminine activities a new visibility and prestige; "Portrait de l'artiste" 519).

While Roy grants Marta's garden work visibility and prestige, as Saint-Martin suggests, she also problematizes the position of this entirely home-based artist and muse. First of all, with a life so remote from modern society, Marta "[has] to make an effort to believe that beyond Volhyn there [are] cities and vast populations" (136). Roy implies that the embedded nature of Marta within her domestic circumstances ultimately means profound creative limitations, as there is no larger audience to witness or be transformed by her garden. Marta is the isolated wife of an immigrant farmer whose habitual rages deny the value of his wife's work, just as his ungenerous spirit prevents her from seeking the medical treatment in Edmonton she so desperately needs. The end result is her inability to continue her gardening. Marta is not an artist destroyed by self-absorption in a creative project, as is the case of Pierre Cadorai in *The Hidden Mountain*, who gives himself entirely to art and leaves nothing of himself for another person. Instead, at the centre of "Garden in the Wind" is the dilemma of a domestically situated woman artist restricted in her agency.

Because of this depiction, the majority of critics commend "Garden in the Wind" for its challenging of the gender norms seen elsewhere in Roy's texts. According to Rubinger, this character "est une nouvelle création dans la galerie impressionante des personnages féminins de cet auteur" (is an innovative creation in this author's impressive gallery of female characters), as Marta is neither contained within doors, nor burdened, at this point in her life, with child rearing (124). Christine Robinson similarly notes that between the multiple drafts of "Le printemps revint à Volhyn" (or "Spring Returned to Volhyn" [an unpublished manuscript]) and the publication of "Un jardin au bout du monde," ("Garden in the Wind"), Roy eliminates the character of Irina (Marta and Stepan's adult daughter) and instead "décide de centrer l'histoire sur le portrait de Martha" (decides to center the story on the portrait of Marta; 65). In their studies of the genesis and numerous pre-texts of "Un jardin au bout du monde," both Robinson and Sophie Montreuil see a narrowing of focus onto the main female protagonist, her garden, and the associated themes of beauty and creation. Analyzing the pre-texts that begin in 1942 and end with the final published story in 1975, Montreuil argues that the versions move from being "portraits sociaux" to "portraits individuels" (communal portraits to individual portraits; 366), as a number of social exchanges are eventually omitted and Roy concentrates instead on the gardener-artist.[16] The erasure of this communal life adds, in Montreuil's estimation, to the powerful impression Marta makes. Roy's narrowing of focus onto the main character and increasing emphasis on social isolation do not, however, entirely support Marta's status as an exceptional, resilient artist, as Montreuil claims. Rather, her solitary state and vulnerability expose her problematic position even as her achievement is celebrated.

Roy venerates Marta and her prairie bower, yet she also demonstrates the distinctive limitations of her expressive agency because of its relationship to space and time. The final title of the original French publication "Un jardin au bout du monde" (which literally translates as "A Garden at the End of the World" or "A Garden at the World's End") implies a garden not only isolated in the extreme, but also existing out of time or at the end of time.[17] Tended for thirty years, the prairie bower encapsulates the history and authentic experience of Marta's immigration to the prairies. As a living art, subject to the elements and dependent upon a creator who is nearing death herself, the garden's survival is more than precarious. A temporary reprieve arrives only when Stepan realizes the value of his wife's work during the last days of her life. He tidies the farmyard and protects the flowers from the frost with Marta watching these acts of tenderness from her upstairs bedroom window: "Then, as she pulled the curtain farther back she saw close by the house a big, calloused hand lifting the little paper cones with which the plants had been capped the night before ...

The whole pile of Codessa newspapers must have gone that way. Now the poor old fellow would have nothing to read in the chill, lonely November days" (173). Marta's nurturing capacity as an artist inspires even her despairing husband to become a gardener. As Kathleen M. Madigan observes, "Stépan has stepped out of character in walking onto Martha's sacred ground; rather than dominating his wife by trying to silence her, he takes on a role of reciprocity in the end, a key ideal of the feminist project" (74). Despite this change in Stepan, however, the story does not conclude in a triumphant or joyous manner. Marta retreats to her upstairs bedroom, an ominous kind of bower that denies fecundity, as she prepares for death: "She climbed the remaining steps. She changed the linen, lay down on the bed and, her eyes on the ceiling, experienced again the feel of the vast, living sky she had just seen. 'Why, oh why, did I have my life?' asked Marta" (166). This terminally ill woman moves further and further away from the active role of embowered artist and toward the passive position of isolated muse, framed by the curtains in the window of her sickroom, watching her garden until she resigns herself to her deathbed.

Although Stepan is last seen caring for the garden, Marta places her trust neither in her husband nor in her bower, but in the wind to tell her story: "if as [the wind] crossed the land he said something of her life – that would be enough for her: the wind in his loneliness consoling himself in her, and she in his errant spirit" (175). Recounting the initial 1919–20 settlement of Volhyn peasants, "most of them illiterates" (124), the writer-narrator implies in the opening chapter that Marta's legacy and story, if based solely in the garden, will not be sufficiently preserved. A written account, although still uncertain and materially vulnerable, is required as a more lasting record: "Her full name: Maria Marta Yaramko. At least on her grave, hidden among the tall wild barley and meadow grass, on the wooden cross that barely rises clear, that's what is written, letter after shaky letter, as if by a hand that scarcely knew how to write" (126). Whereas the epitaph safeguards Martha's name, the garden is the fleeting source of her expression: "for in a sense it *told* the real history of her life" (149, emphasis added). The typescript of Alan Brown's English translation of *Garden in the Wind*, which he first translated under the title "Exiles," reveals that originally he interpreted this line as "for it was, in a sense, the real history of her life" (Roy, "Exiles" 147) in keeping with Roy's original French passage: "[ce jardin] était en quelque sorte la veritable histoire de sa vie" (*Un jardin* 185). The hand-written revisions on Brown's typescript reveal a subtle alteration in the wording from "was" to "told" the history, shifting the artistic agency away from Marta and onto the garden itself.[18] As a result, the garden is not purely an artistic product (the true story of her life), but a story-teller, and an extremely vulnerable one at that, subject to the wind. The connotative difference between the original French and the English translation is in keeping with a key aspect of Roy's story: the isolated prairie garden assumes a tenuous preeminence relative to Marta's failing status. Marta represents maternal, selfless nurturing, yet she is also, more than anything, a figure of the past, ultimately denied the freedom and agency that Roy implies are necessary for the modern female artist.

Whereas Marta dies alone, enclosed within her sickroom, the story of her garden survives through the travelling writer-narrator's brief encounter with and inspired re-telling of it. In light of the retrospective past tense that opens the first chapter, the writer-narrator has clearly journeyed beyond Volhyn and found a renewed artistic purpose, as she has become a teller of stories. Robinson observes that this narrative technique is unusual in Roy's fiction: "Dans les trois avant-textes et le texte publié, une narratrice extra-homodiégétique apparaît dans le premier chapitre, puis cède la place à une narration à la troisième personne, procédé rarement utilisé dans l'oeuvre royenne" (In the three pre-texts and the published text, an extra-homodiegetic narrator [a first-person narrator in the story] appears in the first chapter, then gives way to third-person narration, a process rarely used in Roy's work; 65–6). In addition to employing this nameless writer-narrator, Roy frames "Garden in the Wind" by including an introduction to her collection that briefly recounts her actual encounter with a woman planting flowers on the western prairies: "*Garden in the Wind was born of a passing vision I had one day of a garden filled with flowers at the very outer limit of cultivated territory, and of a woman working there, in the wind ... who looked up and followed me with a long, perplexed and supplicating gaze which never left my memory and never ceased to demand – for years and years – the thing we are all asking for, from the very depths of our silence: Tell about my life*" (10). What this double framing technique suggests is that on two levels (in the text and of the text), the narrator's and Roy's written accounts, and not the garden, become the ultimate sources of expression for Marta, the artist-gardener. The writer-narrator and Marta differ decidedly in their expressive agency and mobility, but together these women both share in and promote a common artistic purpose by creating art that serves others in its attentiveness to family, heritage, and home.

### Leaving the Garden: Gabrielle's Return "Home" through Writing

The relationship between Marta and the narrator in "Garden in the Wind" demonstrates Roy's understanding of the problematic position of the female artist divided between familial work and the pursuit of self-expression. This dilemma relates directly to *Enchantment and Sorrow* and Roy's self-portrayal as a young woman struggling with conflicting loyalties. In contrast to Marta's enclosed experience, Gabrielle departs from Century Cottage to continue her journey of artistic self-realization. She travels, as does the writer-narrator in "Garden in the Wind," to pursue her craft, telling the stories she takes with her to a larger audience. In this way, Roy advocates feminine artistry that is not forever confined by the domestic setting, yet profoundly attentive to the needs of others.[19] The bower genre perpetuates the convention of a solitary male quester; in response, Roy's artist characters uncover discrepancies between gendered experiences of creative independence. Whereas Alexandre and Pierre work in relative solitude and with minimal regard for the domestic and all that it entails, Gabrielle is not afforded this level of freedom; hers is a relational art delimited by familial responsibility.

Near the conclusion of the bower episode in *Enchantment and Sorrow*, Gabrielle feels reproached for having neglected her personal affairs back in Canada while taking refuge at Century Cottage. Guilt weighs heavily for having left her mother, Mélina, behind in Manitoba and resurfaces upon receiving a letter. The following reflections reveal her entrapment: "I always trembled when [Mélina's] letters came, not because I was afraid of reading reproaches or complaints – there never were any – but because seeing her writing was enough to open the door to memories of all the suffering culminating in me. Surely I shouldn't be the only one to escape, I would think, and I'd feel condemned to suffer, as if it were a duty" (329–30). Gabrielle's mother figures largely in this journey of self-realization through a prevailing sense of care and duty that works on a number of levels. The retrospective narration of the autobiography aids Roy in devising a path of maturation for her protagonist in which the successful author (Roy) nurtures and protects in an almost maternal fashion the character and role of the developing young writer (Gabrielle). This same approach has been noted by Saint-Martin in "Gabrielle Roy: The Mother's Voice, The Daughter's Text" to operate extensively in Roy's fiction through her mother characters, "transforming tenderness into a 'literary quality'" (316).[20] In *Enchantment and Sorrow*, Roy turns this strategy of "tenderness" onto herself: that is, her self-portrayal as a female artist in exile coming to writing through a domestic-styled bower. Gabrielle may be separated from her original home, yet she assumes responsibility through the form of a written continuance, creating a literary homage to family and heritage within her art.

In addition to Century Cottage, the familial garden in *Enchantment and Sorrow* that looms largest in Roy's memory is that of her grandmother in Manitoba. Reminiscent of Marta and her attentiveness to community, Roy's grandmother "used to grow the same flowers in her garden that she'd had in Quebec" (17). From the "mansard roof" and chimney to the "plants around it, the home and garden proclaimed Quebec very loudly in Somerset, which in those days was at least half English" (35). This garden demarcates a territory synonymous with Roy's Francophone identity. Unfortunately, its final image is one that Roy recalls encountering later in life when a more mature version of her Gabrielle character returns to visit Manitoba in a romantic quest for ruins. Roy relates her younger self finding a "tumble-down ruin," "deserted and mournful," "abandoned ... crumbling" (35). Sensing her unfulfilled responsibility, Gabrielle feels "reproached" by the deserted maternal home (35). In this scene, Gabrielle, having long ago uprooted herself in a search for her vocation, and Roy, the established writer reflecting on her career, stand together in the narrative's conflation of time. The dual perspective magnifies the problematic position faced by Gabrielle and Roy, as the female writer's domestic and artistic roles seemingly counter one another. While the relatively younger Gabrielle contemplates the purchase of the property until her cousin questions,

"'And what would you do with a house here when you live in Quebec?'" (35), Roy (as narrator) declares, "I knew that little house. This was the one I had more or less in mind when I wrote 'My Almighty Grandmother' in *The Road Past Altamont*" (34). This scene occurs early in the autobiography and foreshadows Gabrielle's departure from her own home, the overwhelming sense of abandonment, and the ultimate purpose of her vocation: the literary preservation of the family legacy. Despite having contemplated the purchase of the property in the past, the mature Roy implies that in her role as writer, she has assumed domestic responsibilities of an alternative form, much like that of the narrator in "Garden in the Wind" who writes on Marta's behalf. When an elderly Englishman who lived in the Somerset home eventually dies, Roy writes that the last time she was in Manitoba she "came close to buying it" (35) because of her nostalgia and guilt. The final image of loss so clearly resonates with the image of Marta's garden in the wind: "But more than the crumbling house I'd so wanted to buy because it touched the very heart of my most precious memories, perhaps it was the sound of the wind that voiced all those generations of longing for a home so often sought and so often lost" (35–6).

Gabrielle's difficult visit to her grandmother's ruined home foreshadows the ultimate scene of leave-taking and transition towards female independence: her departure from Century Cottage. In contrast to Marta, Gabrielle's containment within her bower is negotiable, and the continuation of her journey of self-discovery presents a more liberated feminine mode of artistry. Century Cottage provided a vital shelter for Gabrielle's transformation, but she must move beyond her idyllic bower in order to observe and write critically about the world. In a comment to Gabrielle, Esther Perfect indirectly reveals that Century Cottage is not conducive to the writer's further development: "[Father Perfect has] lived in a kind of Garden of Eden and the woes of mankind haven't touched him as they have most people. And there really isn't much left to say about Eden once the story's been told, is there?" (313). Deciding that "[t]here was no closing one's eyes any longer" (343), Gabrielle leaves to confront the impending war. She exits a world of innocence – the Eden of Father Perfect – and enters into a fallen world of experience. The change suggests that a key function of a writer is to expose herself to the mutability and disparity of the modern world. Roy tempers this transition, however, by carrying the garden motif forward, creating both continuity and disruption between her persona's gendered and artistic roles. Upon returning to London just prior to the outbreak of the Second World War, Gabrielle describes walking through Hyde Park where men "were digging trenches": "They … were mining beneath the world's most lovingly nurtured lawns. Sometimes a shovelful would splatter into a bed of flowers. Children brought there by their nannies were hugely entertained by the transformation of the gardens into a battlefield. Playing at throwing grenades, they were hurling lumps of mud in one another's faces. Adults went this way and that, saying and seeing nothing" (345–6) (Figure 3.9). The "globs of clay" and "splatter" stand in sharp contrast to the cottage garden left behind by Gabrielle. Once a garden "lovingly nurtured," a place where children were brought to play, Hyde Park becomes the domain of war. Re-invoking the garden motif, Roy grounds the maturing Gabrielle in her vocation, but the extreme juxtaposition of images further clarifies the direction of the woman's craft. That is, Gabrielle needs to be immersed in, rather than isolated from, her milieu, observing first-hand as only the perceptive eyes of a writer can. The adults of Hyde Park may drift aimlessly, "saying and seeing nothing," but Gabrielle is there to witness and relate.

Venturing forth, Gabrielle appears to launch on a more masculine quest into a turbulent world; Roy reveals her enduring concern for

FIGURE 3.9 Workers digging trenches in Hyde Park, London, England, with a crowd of onlookers, 1938

gendered propriety, however, by concluding her narrative with the domestic garden motif, naturalizing this newfound independence. Following her European travels, Gabrielle decides not to return to Manitoba, her mother, and her teaching career, but to live and write in Montreal. This additional step towards autonomy is necessary for the pursuit of her craft, yet Gabrielle is also keenly aware of the need to be "at home" as a woman artist. Costantino reflects on Gabrielle's new Montreal setting and asks, "Va-t-elle s'enraciner ici?" (Will she root herself here? 392). At first, seemingly rootless, Gabrielle shirks family obligations, writing to her mother that she will not be returning.

The solitariness of her journalism and writing career counters more traditional models of femininity. The content of Mélina's letter upon Gabrielle's arrival in Canada reveals exactly what is expected of this young, unattached woman: "Mon enfant ... so you're back in Montreal, not so far from home now. Home isn't a house any more, of course, but with the bit of money I have left and what you'll be earning [from teaching] we'll be able to live pretty well, you'll see. And with you so independent and me probably too possessive, I'll try to get used to letting you lead your own life. I imagine I can expect you home soon" (406). Ever attentive to social pressures, Roy works, even at this late point in the journey, to cast her character's unconventional choices in an organic light.

Montreal may not offer the profusion of flowers and security of Century Cottage, but it becomes a kind of alternative bower for Gabrielle, an urban haven where she cultivates her expression. In the autobiography, the city grants Gabrielle the "feeling of having come home" (410). The French "words and expressions of [her] people, of [her] mother and grandmother" comfort the solitary young woman who rents an apartment across from Windsor train station (407). Working as a journalist for the farming publication *Bulletin des agriculteurs*, Gabrielle hones her talent for observation and pursues her own impulse for fiction, as she "began to build on the reveries germinated beside the old [Lachine] Canal [one] April evening" (410). In the original French edition of *La détresse et l'enchantement*, Roy writes "des rêveries nées ce soir d'avril au bord du vieux canal" (of dreams born this April night along the old canal; 505), which is not as clearly linked to the garden motif as the translated verb "germinate." The French text conveys, nevertheless, the springtime birth and growth of Gabrielle's writing. In her newly adopted home, Gabrielle tends not only the garden of her writing, but also the garden of her familial heritage by immersing herself in Quebec society and her mother tongue. As the questing woman writer, Gabrielle has been, once again, "brought home." Instilling in Gabrielle's writing this nurturing quality, Roy somehow compensates for the unconventional but necessary quest that took her away from family and even her own country, leaving her haunted by the deserted home of her grandmother, the "wind ... plucking at the vestiges of [the] garden" (36).

## CHAPTER FOUR

# "A Saucer of Green": Carol Shields and Domestic Paradise

*I have tended to … take my passions and give them to my characters …*
*I'm interested in living things, I'm interested in plants.*
Carol Shields (Ying 14)

Carol Shields once wrote that the "language that carries weight in our culture is very often fuelled by a search for home" ("About Writing" 262). Although she believes this search to be the most relevant story in literature, she also recognizes that not all narratives, even when shaped by this particular desire, are equally weighted. In her speech "Narrative Hunger and the Overflowing Cupboard," Shields contends that although "stories … sustain our culture" they sometimes "fail to correspond with our lives" (19). Only certain individuals are privileged to tell stories, limiting the range of content and perspective; meanwhile, formal conventions restrict the kinds of stories that come to fruition (28). In Shields' view, alternative voices need to be heard, particularly those of women; otherwise the loss is incomprehensible and "narrative hunger" remains: "I recently read a book called *Ruby: An Ordinary Woman*, made up of diary extracts of one Ruby Aliside, so ordinary a woman that you probably would not recognize her name ... [The diaries] were rescued by a granddaughter and put into print. How many other such accounts go to the dump? Accounts that like Ruby's will change forever the way we think of women's lives" (31). Shields' own fiction serves as a recuperative gesture. She refuses to allow women's life stories to "go to the dump," literally and figuratively, and in this regard writes with a similar purpose as that of Gabrielle Roy (as we saw in chapter three), when the writer-narrator in "Garden in the Wind" serves as a witness to Marta's gardening artistry. Despite this shared desire to record the unwritten domestic life, the two writers ultimately differ in that while Roy approaches the garden as a temporary destination that facilitates the creative life of the modern woman artist, Shields works to reclaim the domestic with its vernacular garden as the site of story itself.

Because she wants to illuminate the everyday, Shields admits in an interview that she is not interested in a typical linear story focused on a single climactic moment, but rather narratives that communicate quotidian lives: "Yes, I am always interested in biographies – the idea of trying to catch a life in some way. The arc of a whole life when it curves. I don't think in terms of plot very much ... but I think that the arc of the human life is a plot and it is enough plot, for me" (Maharaj 11). This particular description of "plot" combines readily in Shields' fiction with that ever-prevalent story that is the search for home – that "metaphorical place" of true companionship and belonging – that she sees as central to the narrative tradition as a whole ("About Writing" 262). These interrelated concerns find their most compelling expression within a habitual setting of Shields' fiction: the home and garden. One consequence is that the "human life plot," as Shields understands it, integrates with a "garden plot," that is, a garden setting and garden-inspired story that work in tandem. This not only situates and shapes characters according to their particular circumstances, but also reveals, in the process, Shields' mandate for recuperating and celebrating the domestic.

## Notions of Domestic Paradise

When Shields counters "narrative hunger" by relating stories of domestic life, she achieves her objective by reaching, ironically enough, for one of the most enduring and central myths in literature and Judeo-Christian culture: the myth of paradise. In drawing on this symbol, Shields makes a daring but also highly appropriate choice. After all, what is the search for paradise if not the search for the ideal home? As Clare Cooper Marcus contends, "The garden was where God first created order out of chaos; it was the home of the first man and woman. But the Garden of Eden, the place where we had our beginnings, was also Paradise, the place to which we would return. The myth of origin became fused with a myth of blissful homecoming" (26). As the ultimate search for home, the paradise myth highlights a complex inter-relationship between space and narrative, garden and story. As revealed in the introduction to this study, the paradise myth has a foundational presence in nineteenth-century Canadian literature by shaping stories of the "new world" and its pristine wilderness; where Shields innovates is in her re-contextualization of this national myth within the supposedly banal domain of middle-class homes and suburban lawns during the latter half of the twentieth century. Moreover, in using these everyday garden settings as idyllic but critical third natures, Shields interrogates the varied and changing ideals that constitute the paradisal homes of her characters.

The enclosed perfection that is paradise constitutes a self-sustaining, fecund environment, a domain where all needs are fulfilled. Tied to the traditions of the *hortus conclusus* and *locus aoemenus*, "paradise" derives, according to the *Oxford English Dictionary*, from the Old Persian word *pairidaēza*, which originally referred to "an enclosed park, orchard, or pleasure ground." [1]

Although "paradise" carries religious connotations in its signification of the Garden of Eden, the heavenly paradise of the afterlife, and even the enclosed grounds of a convent, the secular applications of the word are prevalent. "Paradise" refers literally to a place "of surpassing beauty or delight," and figuratively to "a state of supreme bliss or felicity." [2] The definition of paradise is, therefore, multilayered in that it involves both an ideal place and an ideal mode of being. In *The Architecture of Paradise: Survivals of Eden and Jerusalem*, William Alexander McClung concurs that the "search for Paradise is … an effort to discover the correct relationship between man, nature, and craft" (2). To McClung's definition, I would also add the correct relationship between individuals, as companionship is an essential part of the original design of paradise and its promise of fulfillment.

At its most fundamental, then, paradise offers an ideal vision of domestic partnership in which all needs are satisfied through the supportive presence and work of an other. John Armstrong equates the garden's idyllic nature with Adam and Eve's relationship; they are "creatures of unsullied goodness, who are completely fulfilled and have no vacuity in their lives or cause for restlessness" (3). This "paradise" of daily companionship is captured in Genesis, where Eve is Adam's "help meet" (2.18) and together "they shall be one flesh" (2.24). In *Paradise Lost*, John Milton creates a scene of marital bliss and partnership, housed most symbolically within Adam and Eve's "nuptial bow'r" (8.510). The couple's complementary roles facilitate an ideal domestic world of leisurely work and reciprocity. Just as Eve's role is "to study household good, / And good works in her husband to promote" (9.233–4), Adam is Eve's "best prop" (9.433) and he "guards her, or with her the worst endures" (9.269). This partnered vision of paradise resonates with Shields' own understanding of "home" as being that "metaphorical place where we can reach out and touch and heal each other's lonely heart" ("About Writing" 262). In much of her fiction, finding companionship and profound intimacy is central to discovering personal fulfillment. A case in point is Stu Weller, Larry's father in *Larry's Party* (1997), who cannot fathom life without his wife, Dot, after she accidentally kills her mother-in-law with botulism-ridden beans, "that treasonous vegetable" (53). Just as Adam laments the unbearable prospect of living alone in Eden ("to lose thee were to lose myself") following Eve's biting of the apple (Milton 9.955–9), Stu "uproot[s] himself" (52) from his original home in England and moves to Winnipeg out of love for his wife, as their "flight from the home country has the flavor of Old Testament exodus" following Stu's father's grief-stricken accusations against Dot (52). Thus, for Shields, paradise denotes, above all, a domain (whether an original home or another abode) where an individual's desires are shared and needs are fulfilled in the presence of a true companion.

By turning to paradise, the preeminent garden trope, and adapting it to her own fiction, Shields makes a bold statement in terms of reclaiming and sanctifying the domestic. But hers is not a straightforward celebration or simplistic idealization; on the contrary, Shields indicates both the freedoms and restrictions in her characters' fleeting realizations of literal or figurative "paradises" through their various modes of being, their domestic spaces, their relationships, and the temporal spans of their lives. She is particularly attentive to exploring and critiquing a full spectrum from paradises naïvely constructed and

superficial to those founded upon genuine self-knowledge and profound happiness.

Shields' understanding of what constitutes the paradisal in her
fiction relates to her own political "awakening" as a young wife and
mother when she first read Betty Friedan's *The Feminine Mystique*
(1963).[3] Bringing feminist consciousness to bear on her writing, Shields
appreciates that the home is a problematic physical and conceptual
space, impacted by societal pressures, inter-personal conflicts, and
restrictions on the self. Her fiction particularly reverberates with
Friedan's ground-breaking argument that media images of American
women from the 1950s and 1960s demanded that women fulfill their
feminine nature or "mystique" to the point that their lives were closed
to other possibilities. In this way, the home was utterly infiltrated by
commercial ideals and social conformity (Friedan 37–8).[4] Shields
ultimately distinguishes herself, however, from Friedan's assertion that
a woman only achieves self-realization through a life beyond the role
of suburban housewife. Certainly, just as Milton's indomitable Satan
promotes free will in his statement, "The mind is its own place, and in
itself / Can make a heav'n of hell, a hell of heav'n" (1.254–5), Friedan
advocates that a woman "can affect society, as well as be affected by it"
and that she "has the power to choose, and to make her own heaven or
hell" (10).

In an interview, Shields admits that when she first started writing,
her focus on the home was quite out of fashion: "This was the 70s, during the women's movement, women were leaving home and not having
children ... I wrote the book I always wanted to read ... but could not
find" (D'Souza 16). In a political gesture, Shields willfully chooses to
associate her idea of "heaven," or "paradise," with the domestic, but her
portrayals are far from innocent because they encompass all the di-
lemmas, deficiencies, and beguiling "serpents" readers come to expect

with such stories. The two novels in which she engages the most extensively and explicitly with this archetype are *The Box Garden* (1977) and *The Stone Diaries* (1993). Together they provide an informative trajectory of Shields' experimentation with the "garden plot" as she reasserts the importance of home in the (Canadian) literary tradition, questions middle-class assumptions about the domestic, and exposes the fact that notions of paradise are fragile, tenuous, and most certainly in need of close scrutiny.

## Relocating Quests for Paradise in The Box Garden

Shields once referred to *The Box Garden* as "the one book I would rewrite," and most critics agree that it is her weakest novel, which explains the minimal attention it has received (Ying 15). During this early stage of her career, Shields lacked the confidence to resist editorial input that steered her away from crafting what would later become her hallmark, the "plot" of an ordinary human life.[5] Reviewers at the time noted the disjunction between the book's dramatic narrative and domestic focus: "Shields was writing a delightful little back garden of a novel," Sandra Martin comments, until she "felt compelled ... to dress up the plot with the most absurd series of coincidences and contortions" (15–16). In the novel, the divorced protagonist Charleen Forrest (née McNinn) travels by train from Vancouver to Toronto with her orthodontist boyfriend, Eugene, to attend her widowed mother's wedding. Struggling to come to terms with her mother's remarriage, her childhood, and her ex-husband Watson (who has been contacting her under the alias of a monk named "Brother Adam"), Charleen faces the kidnapping of her teenage son, Seth, by a friend who is supposed to be looking after him during her trip east. *The Box Garden* is obviously not in keeping with Shields' usual emphasis on the "small ceremonies" of life, but if readers shift their attention away from the dramatic kidnapping plot and instead consider the "little back garden of a novel," they discover Shields interrogating domestic ideals and their place, or lack thereof, within a national mythos focused too much on the natural environment (the wilderness) and not enough on day-to-day twentieth-century Canadian society.

When Shields embarked on her career as a novelist in 1976, her decision to focus on suburban homes and women's lives as homemakers was a conscious and daring choice, not only because it seemed counter-intuitive to the feminist movement but also because it explicitly challenged the foundational myths of the Canadian literary imagination that were popular at the time. Reflecting on Shields' early works and her engagement with thematic criticism in both her first and second novels, Faye Hammill notes that Shields parodies the authenticity of a so-called "native genre" (87) that incorporates recognizable symbols (92) and "national traits" (93).[6] Shields questions the schematization of Canadian literature, yet at the same time recognizes that archetypes and myths have a role to play.[7] Even Charleen, the highly critical protagonist in *The Box Garden,* admits that "symbols have their uses" (60). *The Box Garden* relocates symbol and myth from the proverbial wilderness and into an alternative and unexpected place: home, replete with a banal patch of lawn. One cannot help but wonder if Shields had Margaret Atwood's "bush garden" and Northrop Frye's "garrison mentality" (terms that were circulating in the literary world at the time) in mind when she coined the title *The Box Garden* for her 1977 novel. In a parodic reinterpretation of these formative symbols, Shields' protagonist grows a box of grass in her Vancouver apartment, imposing geometric order upon unruly nature, as the grass *"struggles against the sides of the box"* (86, original emphasis). Wanting narrative to correspond with the ordinary, Shields presents the box garden not as an image of the wilderness (or first nature), but instead, as a symbol of society's relationship with its own socio-economic points of reference and self-constructed habitat, or second nature: twentieth-century urban and suburban Canada. Just as Charleen cultivates her box garden in sandy-coloured earth in her Vancouver apartment, her mother, Florence McNinn, tends a Scarborough bungalow, "a brick box on a narrow, sandy lot" (44).

In addition to possible allusions to the bush garden model of Canadian letters, the other national literary myth that Shields particularly redresses is that of paradise, as it informs *The Box Garden*'s narrative structure, imagery, and characterization. A successful poet, cognizant of Canadian literary traditions and circles, Charleen comments on the predominance of this myth when she alludes to the near mass-production of certain symbols: "symbolism is such impertinence, the sort of thing the 'pome people' might contrive. (God knows how easily it's manufactured by those who turn themselves into continuously operating sensitivity machines"; 60). With "pome" being a pun on "poem," Charleen attributes the symbol of the apple to poets, their works, and their desire to infuse meaning and substance into the world around them. The apple as the fruit of knowledge loses its veracity in this instance, however, as this paradisal association becomes endlessly "manufactured" by artists whose machine-like efficiency lacks originality and insight. While Charleen disparages overused tropes, Shields paradoxically adopts the paradise myth, purposely giving into this "manufacturing" impulse by rapidly producing multiple versions of the box garden image and its evocation of enclosed paradisal terrain. These "box gardens" range from Florence McNinn's suburban neighbourhood and home (in both their past and present states), to Charleen and Watson's brief marriage in Vancouver, to Brother Adam's one-room apartment "Eden" in Toronto, to Charleen's small indoor box of grass and box-set of published poems. By virtue of being either objects or images of enclosure, Shields' box garden motif is particularly well suited to placing in close relation both what is truly paradisal, and what is not, for the reader's reflection.

Although many of these successively smaller box gardens seem at once contrived and artificial, they do function as critically reflective third natures, delineating the characters' understandings of their socio-physical environments. According to Matthew Potteiger and Jamie Purinton in *Landscape Narratives: Design Practices for Telling Stories*, a garden's actual boundary serves both a physical and conceptual purpose by creating "the interpretive space for the story to be told" (169). Miniature gardens, in particular, offer concentrated, imaginative spaces that communicate "the desire to re-create what has been lost or to redefine the world within controlled bounds. In relation to the miniature, humans become giants who can move and mold the small pieces of a created world" (169). Shields' novel effectively works, then, to re-create what is either lost or desired at the individual level when it comes to the search for fulfillment undertaken by her characters, some of whom are focused far too much on either the superficial ideals of suburbia or the convenient national literary myths of identity (such as the wilderness or the solitary eden) which appear divorced from twentieth-century realities. By coming to terms with these various "box gardens," Charleen eventually appreciates that all "paradises" are in fact constructed; the real challenge is to move beyond appearances and to discover fulfillment in the everyday.

The novel's reworking of the paradise myth finds its initial and unexpected location in Scarborough, Ontario when Charleen belittles her childhood home in ways that resonate with many critics' examinations of Canadian suburbia.[8] In their historical analyses, J.M. Bumstead and Veronica Strong-Boag concur that the suburbs fostered a division of gender roles that proved unsatisfactory for many: men worked in the city and women remained at home to raise children. In addition, suburbanites faced both an environment and existence of social invariability through mass-produced housing and a culture of consumerism. With limited engagement with the outside world, the "suburbs of the post-war period," Bumstead notes, "acquired more than a bit of bad press, becoming exemplars of a vast identa-kit wasteland of intellectual vacuity, cultural sterility and social conformity" (n.p.). As a published poet, Charleen censures suburbia precisely because of these limitations, equating the monotony of box homes with the residents' narrow perspectives and lack of education. She remembers Scarborough as a place where women, in particular, faced predictable lives with few options, as "girls in the neighbourhood were going on to secretarial school or studying to be hairdressers" (142). Charleen admits that her "mother alone had been cursed by strange daughters," as she and her sister, Judith, strayed from convention through their strong-willed independence and "bookish" pursuits (142).

Further complicating Charleen's gender-related critique of the suburbs is the issue of class, which Shields carefully brings to light through the fact that an individual's economic status impacts whether he or she defines the suburbs in positive or negative terms. For the less affluent, the suburbs represent the achievement of a private paradise, not an unattractive habitat for the masses. Focusing on the decades following the Second World War, Strong-Boag argues that while many residents were middle class, the "suburbs always attracted ambitious working-class and immigrant citizens as well. One daughter remembered that 'as refugees from Hungary,' her parents 'could hardly wait to leave' downtown Toronto 'for ... [the] lavish splendor of the suburbs'" (486). Working-class and lower-middle-class families, in particular, viewed their new environment in largely idyllic terms.[9] Shields captures this alternative perspective in *The Box Garden* through the older generation. As a young woman, Florence McNinn aspired to life in Scarborough because of its improved living conditions and social caché. Charleen admits that prior to her mother's life as a suburban homemaker, Florence was a poor farm girl:

> My mother had not wanted to remember the muddy thirty acres where she grew up, the roofless barn, the doorless outhouse, the greasy kitchen table where the family took meals … Hadn't my mother, in spite of all this, finished grade nine and hadn't she gone to Toronto to work … Hadn't she married a city boy, someone who worked in an office, and hadn't they, after a few years, bought a house of their own, paid for it too, a real house in Scarborough with a back yard and plumbing, hadn't she kept it spotless and proved to everyone that she was just as good as the next person, hadn't she shown them? Yes. (124)

The coveted privileges of privacy and material comfort inspire Florence's yearning for property (a backyard), cleanliness, and respected (and respectable) boundaries, all of which stand in stark contrast to the mud and "doorless" surroundings that constituted life on the farm.[10] Despite outward appearances, the box-like bungalow's paradisal status as experienced in the beginning of Florence's married life is called into question by the younger generation when Charleen repeatedly refers to it as a "void" (48–9). In reality, the lack of personal fulfillment that both Florence and her daughters housed within themselves for so many years finds expression in the various empty "boxes" of this suburban setting: the endlessly re-decorated rooms that brought only superficial renewal, and the kitchen breadbox that contained scanty loaves of bread, offering only "[m]eagreness" (87).

By accounting for both idealism and socio-cultural limitations, Shields reveals that women have complicated, mixed responses to their suburban environments. Charleen expresses disdain for the suburbs, yet she also admits that her mother's experience of Scarborough is distinct from her daughters'. In this way, Shields' fiction reflects what Strong-Boag concludes, "Suburban dreams had captured the hopes of a generation shaken by war and depression, but a domestic landscape that presumed lives could be reduced to a single ideal inevitably failed to meet the needs of all Canadians after 1945. In the 1960s the daughters of the suburbs, examining their parents' lives, would begin to ask for more" (504). *The Box Garden*'s multi-generational presentation of the McNinn family's experience suggests that the seemingly predictable, banal suburbs are, in fact, dynamic, complicated, and reflective of an ever-changing society when it comes to issues of gender, class, and even ethnicity. An older widow, Florence McNinn may have "lived on the block longer than anyone else" (143), but the face of the suburbs continues to change, as Charleen observes: "All the houses in our neighbourhood are filled with Jamaicans now, with Pakistanis, with … unidentifiable southern Europeans who grow cabbages and kohlrabi in their backyards and rent out their basements" (143). The implication of these many perspectives and temporal contexts is that Shields uses her novel to position the suburbs as a significant narrative space for both women's lives and Canadians in general, especially when many contemporary writers (as depicted in Shields' first two novels) misguidedly search for identity in other quarters: primarily the wild, natural landscape.

Eighteen-year-old Charleen, for example, initially pursues a quest for fulfillment through her marriage to Watson. Her fascination with him parallels writers' and critics' promotion of a distinctly Canadian imagination and identity through both the wilderness and paradise myths. Watson's last name, *Forrest*, provides Charleen with a convenient symbol: "After being Charleen McNinn for eighteen years it seemed a near miracle to be attached to such a name. Forrest. Woodsy, dark, secret, green with pine needles, exotic, far removed from the grim square blocks of Scarborough" (3). Watson represents an alternative mode of being compared to Charleen's previous existence. He whisks her away from her parents' suburban home, creating a near-paradisal life in Vancouver: they produce a child appropriately named Seth, after a son of Adam and Eve, and purchase a house and garden. Charleen even dismisses her maiden name, McNinn, as "a bundle of negative echoes, minimum, minimal, nincompoop, ninny, nothing, non-entity, nobody" (3). Her subsequent adoption of the name "Forrest" resonates with the Miltonic Eve who surrenders her infatuation with her own insubstantial reflection and instead derives her identity from Adam:

A shape within the wat'ry gleam appeared
. . .
Of sympathy and love; there I had fixed
Mine eyes till now, and pined with vain desire,
Had not a voice thus warned me, "What thou seest,
What there thou seest fair creature is thyself,
With thee it came and goes: but follow me,
And I will bring thee where no shadow stays" (4.461–70)

In this scene, Milton recreates through a role reversal the Classical myth of the self-loving youth Narcissus and the pining nymph Echo, who is reduced to her voice when Narcissus fails to return her affection. Captivated with her shape "within the wat'ry gleam," Milton's Eve is both "vain" and insubstantial (but a "shadow") until she is told to locate her role and identity in Adam: "Whose image thou art" (4.472). Following Milton's lead, Shields rewrites the myth of Narcissus and Echo, as Watson provides substance and shape (and a new last name) to Charleen's life. He lives according to an "Adamic impulse to give name," as Kroetsch theorizes it in "No Name Is My Name" (41), since Charleen herself admits that her identity as a poet "was grafted artificially onto her lazy unconnectedness, and it was Watson – yes, Watson – who did the grafting. Watson made me a poet" (150).

Just as Charleen is cast into a creative role, Watson formulates his own appealing array of personae from graduate student, to political activist, to amateur boxer. Being "a bit like a snake ... in his ability to continually shed his skin" (153), Watson eventually rejects his identity as husband and father and instigates the downfall of the superficial domestic paradise he has created with Charleen. He abandons his family and journeys back east in his own narcissistic quest. In the first stage of this quest, Watson attempts to live as part of the "Whole World Retreat," an organic-farming commune in Ontario composed of young couples who "dropped out of the whole city thing" (163).[11] When Charleen later visits this back-to-nature retreat during her trip to Scarborough, she discovers that Watson deserted it some time ago, as he "got disenchanted ... with the whole scene, the whole group thing" (163). In many ways, Watson's eventual separation from society and solitary turn towards nature are reminiscent of Frye's model of creative individualism, a necessary state in the gradual breakdown of the "garrison mentality" and the development of an original national mythology. Shields parodies this break from others and especially familial responsibilities, however, as Watson constructs another kind of "boxed in" perspective, a rooming-house Eden, or garrison, built for one.

Estranged from her former husband and still living in Vancouver,

Charleen unwittingly becomes involved with Watson and his latest garden "plot" when he assumes the monk persona of Brother Adam, preaching the virtues of garden grass from his Toronto apartment. After reading his article on the plant's sociological benefits, a paper rejected by the *National Botanical Journal* for which she works, Charleen begins an intimate correspondence with this supposedly religious man. Obsessed with symbolism, Brother Adam manufactures seeming paradises, one of which captures the imagination of Charleen in the form of a gift: a small box planted with grass that grows at an unbelievable rate. Describing the eccentric miniature garden to her sister, Charleen outlines Brother Adam's vision: "He's trying to prove that where people don't have any grass, just concrete and asphalt and so on, then the whole human condition begins to deteriorate" (81). This "life-giving, life-preserving grass" (85) quickly becomes suspect, however, as the box garden appears an empty, superfluous symbol to others (but not yet to Charleen) by having no real use in everyday life. Puzzled, Judith enquires, "But what ... does one do with a box of grass?" (85). Naively seduced by such symbols, Charleen defends what she believes to be the originality of Brother Adam's back-to-nature philosophy:

> "That's partly why he loves it, I think. The fact that grass is so humble. And no one's ever celebrated grass before."
> "Walt Whitman?"
> "That's different. That was more of a symbolic passion." (82)

Paradoxically, as a Canadian "Adam" figure alone with nature, Watson's latest obsession with "democratic" and "ubiquitous forms of plant life" (150) evokes American poet Whitman's *Leaves of Grass*. This conflation of national literary figures speaks to the fact that, as Alex Ramon argues, the American-born "Shields dismissed attempts to distinguish between American and Canadian fiction in terms of thematics as *'quite irrelevant'*" (15), even though her own fiction frequently plays with "the notion of 'Canadianness'" (15). Coincidently, while both Watson and Whitman celebrate grass, the comparison ends there, as the two men use this symbol in dramatically different ways and not according to Charleen's erroneous conclusion. Whitman's poetic persona is the all-encompassing, democratic "I," who enables each and every American to find expression in and through him, just as his inspirational grass "Sprout[s] alike in broad zones and narrow zones, / Growing among black folks as among white" (107–8). Watson, on the other hand, as a solitary, unoriginal Canadian Adam, increasingly alienates himself from people despite his supposed interest in "popular" plant life. In his letters to Charleen, Brother Adam actually voices "his distrust of cramped, urban, industrial society" (116), an entirely ironic statement since his promotion of nature finds its realization in the heart of Toronto, suggesting the impossibility of separating oneself entirely from the reality of modern, urbanized Canada. In many ways, Watson serves as the target of Shields' humourous censure of predominant national literary myths and archetypes that remain divorced from the lives of typical Canadians.

While Shields posits Watson's solitary journey as superficial and self-absorbed, Charleen's trip east to Scarborough is a true homecoming, grounded in humble self-awareness and the everyday imperfections of family and home. But before Charleen makes this realization, Shields invites readers to enter into Watson's Toronto "rooming-house Eden," a transitory garden setting that ultimately serves to reinforce the value of the McNinn household (188). Fearing that Watson has kidnapped Seth, Charleen and the police locate this self-proclaimed "Brother Adam" living in a one-bedroom apartment in a dilapidated building. The room is Watson's solitary paradise, the garden he has constructed for himself after leaving the Whole World Retreat:

> A small square room under the eaves, and yet my first impression was one of blinding, dazzling space. It was the mirrors ... huge mirrors mounted on two facing walls and lining the sloping ceiling, so that the small space seemed endless and unbelievably complex, like the sudden special openings that sometimes occur in dreams ...
>
> The whole room, except for a neatly made-up army cot, was carpeted with grass. In the rebounding arrangements of mirrors and lights, the grass stretched endlessly ... like a pocket of perfect and perpetual springtime where there was no night, no thought of cold or death. (186–7)

The endlessly reflected growth creates "another dimension" (187) where time and death no longer matter. Despite the perfection of Watson's miniature "paradise," it remains – as do Charleen's square tray of grass, her failed marriage, and her mother's endlessly redecorated suburban home of the past – a mere box garden existing through highly artificial conditions, like the "interior of a greenhouse" (187). As "king of his rooming-house Eden," Watson lacks all grounding in everyday life and its responsibilities. Worried about her missing son, Charleen questions whether her former husband knows of Seth's whereabouts, but Watson shows no compassion and is more upset about the intrusion into his private garden. Having regressed into the role of Narcissus, Watson-as-Brother-Adam is captivated solely with himself and his infinitely mirrored reflections, as Charleen remembers his "terrible need for an audience" (192).

While the unraveling of the mystery behind both Brother Adam's identity and Seth's abduction is undeniably melodramatic, Shields nevertheless achieves a critical shift in her paradise motif. The myth of the solitary Adam is rendered ridiculous, and Charleen welcomes a modest life rooted in family, a sheltering openness that will not "box her in" with false ideals. She may have been seduced for a time by Watson's idyllic gardens, but she admits that "something – my cramped Scarborough girlhood no doubt – ties me to the heaviness of facts" (60). By the conclusion of *The Box Garden*, Shields chooses, therefore, not to reject myth and symbol outright, but instead to re-imagine paradise. Formerly susceptible to her own superficial ideals of suburban life, Florence McNinn now becomes a model for her daughter by creating a paradise of substance through the *bower-like* companionship of the aptly named Louis *Berceau* (the French word "berceau" translates as "bower"), a former priest who has left his solitary religious life in order to marry Florence. This newfound paradise does not appear wholly ideal or overly romanticized, as Louis plants a "mock" orange shrub in the garden (198), Florence declares that her wedding bouquet of lilacs is "just weeds" (205), and the couple is married "in front of the artificial fireplace" (209). The suburban home may be renewed by the preparations for the ceremony, including Seth's mowing of the lawn (which marks a return to order) and the impromptu bridal shower (which furnishes Florence's tired kitchen with brand new utensils and tea towels), but the constructed artificiality of suburbia remains, just as the living room still "looks barren" (199). Although Shields impresses upon her readers that no domestic paradise is truly perfect or "natural," Florence's home has become open to change and the promise of fulfillment, as demonstrated by Louis' comment, "Good healthy roots on this one" (198), when planting the orange shrub, a symbol of generosity (Waterman 153).

When Charleen observes this elderly couple, their figurative garden of companionship appears genuine and founded upon routine: "Later, when he had finished planting, he went inside the house. He and my mother sat at the kitchen table talking a little and drinking coffee ... Seeing them sitting there like that I had a sudden glimpse of what their life together would be like. It would be exactly like this; there would be nothing mystical about it; it would be made up of scenes like this" (198). After witnessing the ease with which her mother accepts Louis into her life and home through the third nature of the Scarborough garden, Charleen now approaches her own quest for paradise with a different vision. Surmising that her self-contained box garden back in Vancouver has died from neglect, Charleen turns away from this symbol and instead opens herself to a new "garden" of intimacy and practical considerations when she flies home to Vancouver with Eugene and Seth by her side: "Eugene, peering down through grey mists, says, 'What we should do is buy a farm. A few acres. For weekends, you know. Maybe grow some vegetables, have a horse for the kids. Might even be a tax advantage there'" (213). Ultimately in *The Box Garden,*· paradise is what characters create and share with others within realistic settings and circumstances, and not what they construct through far-flung ideals that neither function nor hold purpose in the real world.

## A Return to Paradise in *The Stone Diaries*

While *The Box Garden* is a prime example of Shields' incorporation of myth and symbol in her fiction, she also avoids the schematization of such devices. Consequently, when the paradise motif re-emerges sixteen years later in Shields' most acclaimed novel, *The Stone Diaries*, readers witness a writer no longer preoccupied with foundational myths of the Canadian literary imagination (and particularly the model of a solitary Adam at one with nature), but instead interrogating what a "domestic" model of paradise actually means and requires. Whereas *The Box Garden*'s Brother Adam independently constructs an array of paradises depending on his changeable whims, *The Stone Diaries*' married and maternal "Eves" (in the form of Mercy Goodwill and Daisy Goodwill Flett) exhibit agency that is relatively contained. For the most part these female characters find themselves placed within, or facilitating, the ideal "gardens" of others, while their own fulfillment remain troubled or less certain. Dave Williamson contends that when it comes to the chronological progression of her novels, Shields demonstrates a penchant for pairs as a means of exploring similar issues and events from different points of view.[12] However, an alternative and productive relationship emerges when comparing *The Box Garden* with *The Stone Diaries*, as both involve a search for paradise, albeit undertaken by protagonists from different generations. Despite an obvious discrepancy in their sophistication and literary accomplishment, the novels display an affinity through the way in which Shields conceptualizes the two works and through her borrowing of details from her second novel to aid in Daisy's characterization as a woman in search of fulfillment.

In *The Box Garden*, the motif of box gardens – empty, unfulfilling "enclosures" that are both real and symbolic – are at the forefront of the novel. With respect to *The Stone Diaries*, a novel that also foregrounds a lack of fulfillment and the various narratives that contain Daisy's life, Shields describes it as a series of boxes: "the novel 'is a box within a box within a box … I've made the big box; Daisy is the box inside, and the box inside Daisy is empty'" (Graeber 3). While this model pertains directly to Shields' narrative technique, empty or unfulfilling garden settings and imagery are central to *The Stone Diaries*, suggesting that form and content work together in this garden "plot" of Daisy's life.

Furthermore, Shields links her two novels explicitly by reproducing in *The Stone Diaries* the motto that appears in *The Box Garden*. Florence McNinn believes "people 'should keep to themselves'" and instructs her daughters to "tend to their own gardens" (123). In *The Stone Diaries*, Daisy's grand-niece, Victoria, reads a similar phrase on a Victorian wall-plate during her research trip to Scotland:

Happiness
grows at our own
fireside and is
not to be picked
in strangers'
gardens (302)

Interpreting Daisy's love for her own Ottawa garden, Leona Gom agrees with Victoria's assessment in the novel that her great aunt would "endorse this sentiment, but she will not" (Shields 302). Gom writes, "Perhaps [Victoria] has learned from Daisy that seeking happiness only at one's own stone fireside makes for too limiting a life; for women of Victoria's generation, life means exploring the gardens of strangers" (26). If readers consider the unhappy void of Florence McNinn's life and her eventual opening of her boxy suburban home to Louis Berceau at the ripe age of seventy, then Shields demonstrates that even the most enclosed "gardens" can open to change. Unfortunately, in *The Stone Diaries* readers never hear Daisy's thoughts on this directive for the achievement of happiness. After all, this plate hangs in the Grey Stones Hotel in Scotland, not in Daisy's Ottawa home. What readers do have to scrutinize, however, is Daisy's life experience. In its extensive critique of the complexities and disappointments of the domestic, *The Stone Diaries* suggests that in order to realize a "garden" of personal fulfillment, it is not simply the individual who needs to be open to others, but rather the very concept of the ideal home that must be redefined.

Whether they are celebrants of or skeptics about her work, critics of Shields often assume that the domestic for her typically and ideally entails a cohesive nuclear family (constituted by a marital, heterosexual relationship) living in a middle-class, single-family dwelling.[13] In actuality, Shields' interrogation of how we conceptualize "home" and where we locate it for happiness is frequently more extensive than critics give her credit. More recently, Ramon has rightly argued in *Liminal Spaces: The Double Art of Carol Shields* that much of Shields' work "constructs 'family' as an awkward and disabling contrivance" (5). In this regard, the literal and figurative gardens of *The Stone Diaries* play a crucial third nature role by subtly exposing how social norms and expectations largely predetermine the composition of Daisy's domestic life, but do not necessarily result in personal fulfillment.

As with *The Box Garden*, *The Stone Diaries* employs throughout a motif of paradise that is highlighted in the opening pages of the novel when the narrator Daisy Goodwill Flett declares, "Every last body on this earth has a particular notion of paradise" (2). A vague idea or fancy, a "notion" changes according to an individual's imagination, experience, and knowledge. What is held in common is the search for personal fulfillment, companionship, and a sense of home, with "home" being open to interpretation with respect to its appearance and circumstance. As we saw with Gabrielle Roy's autobiography, sometimes one's own family is not the most fulfilling or even supportive, and a surrogate is (temporarily) required. In a similar vein, Shields suggests that where one feels most at home may be in an unexpected place and beyond social conventions, those "second nature" formulations of house, husband, wife, and children. When recreating the story of her parents and their deepest desires as a young married couple, Daisy imagines what constitutes paradise for Mercy and Cuyler just prior to her birth. Noting the heaven motif that begins the novel in chapter one (and later contrasting this scene with the hell motif of chapter five), Wendy Roy argues that Mercy's assembly of the Malvern pudding provides "an imaginary rendering of the joys of domestic life" (136). Through Daisy's description, readers glimpse immense pleasure, or what Roy notes to be the "'heavenly'" aspect of Mercy's "preparing and eating food" within her kitchen (136). As the scene progresses, however, Daisy, as narrator, exposes Mercy's over-eating as unhealthy: "Eating was as close to heaven as my mother ever came. (In our day we have a name for a passion as disordered as hers)" (1–2). Although Mercy's cooking is creatively fulfilling and in harmony with the environment through her incorporation of natural ingredients, her solitary paradise is constructed around a feeling of emptiness.

Described in conjunction with the miraculous kitchen scene is husband Cuyler's own notion of paradise. For the two years of his married life, Cuyler revels in the abundance of Mercy's body and the domestic setting she creates. When Cuyler was living with his parents, his mother's pathetic garden was merely "a few weak rows of cabbages, some spindly wax beans" (274). By contrast, in his life with Mercy, he feels that he "has been transported to a newly created world" (35), his marriage more "an enclosure he'd stumbled upon than a legal arrangement he formally entered" (275). Prior to his marriage he imagined "nothing but misery within" (36) the homes of the Galician immigrants that line his walk home from his job at the limestone quarry, but now Cuyler perceives redefined domestic worlds within these walls: "Now he knows better. Now he has had a glimpse of paradise and sees it everywhere" (36). Although profoundly experienced and world-altering in their effects, Mercy's and Cuyler's "notions" of paradise are incongruent with each other; Shields uses disparate visions to suggest a decided lack of connection in the couple. Rather than being "Imparadised in one another's arms" like Milton's Adam and Eve (4.506), Cuyler and Mercy experience major incompatibilities. Whereas Mercy revels in food, Cuyler is a "pick-and-nibble fellow" who does not partake in the same joy as his wife (1). As for Cuyler, he exhibits great ardour in the bedroom, his paradise being sexual intimacy: Mercy's "own fingers have once or twice brushed across his privates, touching the damp hair encircling his member and informing him of the nature of heaven" (34). Unfortunately, Mercy experiences no sexual pleasure and pretends for Cuyler's sake, compensating for her own bodily and emotional needs by devouring bread: "Her inability to feel love has poisoned her, swallowed down along with the abasement of sugar, yeast, lard, and flour; she knows this for a fact" (7). Paradise symbolizes ultimate fulfillment, a place and mode of existence where all needs are readily assured, yet Shields characterizes Mercy and Cuyler's relationship – their figurative "garden" home – through deficiencies: their lack of self-knowledge, mutual recognition, and shared pleasure.

With the couple's respective visions being at once isolating and temporary, the paradisal scene that opens the novel quickly unravels into Mercy's sudden and difficult labour. Roy reads the opening scene as a creative moment, an act of genesis for both Mercy and Daisy: "By representing the life-giving properties of the mother's breath" during the birth scene, Daisy, the narrator, "reappropriates the female creative ability that has long been patriarchally appropriated in the biblical rendering of a male God breathing life into dust as a means of generating human life" (132). But if this scene is one of female-directed creation, then Daisy expands her familial story of "genesis" to include the narrative of The Fall, the advent of mortality, and the loss of Eden for all characters involved. Mercy's culinary and Cuyler's domestic heavens are both dismantled by Daisy's birth, Mercy's death, and Cuyler's utter bewilderment: "His small dark face and sinewy body burst through his back door, the tune he has been whistling dying on his lips as *he falls upon this scene of chaos*" (38, emphasis added). Mercy's lack of physical self-awareness and innocent deception regarding her pregnancy result in Cuyler's sudden descent into disorder. Through this opening chapter, therefore, Shields positions the domestic as something that both is, and is not, paradise. Together, the alluring vision and its ultimate decline launch Daisy on her life's journey, which entails her own search for fulfillment. Unfortunately, the discrepancies that Daisy imagines as existing between her parents' mutually exclusive "notions" of paradise foreshadow for the reader the difficulties that she encounters in her own life plot and search for belonging.

As in *The Box Garden* with its ongoing construction of enclosed but unfulfilling "gardens," *The Stone Diaries* compiles numerous narratives that position and contain Daisy, the empty box, as Shields describes her, at the centre of the novel. Connected to this narrative strategy is Shields' portrayal of various idyllic "plots" – both literal spaces and stories – that are individualized not merely to reflect the specific desires (or "notions" of paradise) carried by each character, but especially to underscore the consequences for Daisy. For instance, following the disintegration of Mercy and Cuyler's flawed domestic paradise, Shields places a young Daisy within the real and imagined gardens of Clarentine and Barker Flett. Clarentine endows Daisy with her floral name and uses her as the impetus behind a new life and garden business in Winnipeg; alternatively, Barker sexualizes the pre-pubescent child with her "budding breasts" (111) as an exotic "sub-species," a floral temptress, "laughing, calling to him" from a far branch of his taxonomic system (77). With this abundance of garden and flower imagery circulating in the novel, critical commentaries abound pertaining to Daisy's personal development, relationships, and family heritage.[14] Gom observes, for instance, that the garden motif is central to the novel's life-encompassing narrative of growth and degeneration, while Marie-Louise Wasmeier contends that the "relationship between life (flower) and text (stone)" are at the forefront of the novel, "converging in the image of the fossil ... the tangible but dead proof of a past life, and the material on which to develop imaginatively an idea of what that life could have been like" (440). Such readings are supported by the novel, itself, when Daisy's daughter Alice declares, in reference to the verdant Ottawa yard, "That garden of [Mom's], it functioned like a kind of trope in her daily life, and in ours too" (236). But while it is tempting to assess the novel's images primarily in terms of a model of life's natural processes, as opposed to the model of artistry and construction captured so compellingly through Cuyler's stone tower (a tower which critics see as central to the novel's form rather than Daisy's own artistic inclination for gardening),[15] readers need to take a more critical look at Shields' use of the garden. After all, Alice refers to the garden as a "trope" and it is precisely that: a figurative device. It serves to communicate a life narrative that relies heavily on the persuasive guise of nature: in other words, the imagery here works to naturalize conventions of domestic life that may at times be far from paradisal.

If we reflect for a moment on *The Box Garden*, we see Shields positioning the garden as a highly manufactured space and oftentimes superficial ideal. A young Florence obsessively redecorates her suburban paradise with the meticulous care of "any set designer" (47), and Watson's rooming house "Eden" exists through electric lights and mirrors, the tricks of illusion. These notions of paradise are veritably staged; indeed, Watson's "paradise" with its many mirrors caters to his "terrible need for an audience": his narcissistic self (192). In *The Stone Diaries*, Shields executes a sophisticated revision of this plot by extending her use of constructed gardens, and even garden theatrics, into the seemingly idyllic, "natural" spaces of Daisy's life. One of the strategic ways that Shields employs the garden as a third nature is in positioning it as a kind of social theatre: an ideally manipulated but critically informative space that highlights the many roles Daisy assumes either unconsciously or consciously throughout her life.

Many of the garden plots contained within *The Stone Diaries* serve as effective means of accentuating Daisy's adherence to social expectations and related gender performance. When it comes to Shields' less studied dramatic works, Chris Johnson notes that Shields is drawn to the notion of "social theatre" – that is, the public or private places that operate as "venue[s] for the theatrical sense that enlarges ordinary lives"(252).[16] In Shields' fiction, gardens similarly facilitate such interactions and are therefore in keeping with what John Dixon Hunt emphasizes as the garden's ability to function as both a formal and informal theatre. In *Greater Perfections*, Hunt observes, "We talk casually of garden 'settings' or 'scenes'; the etymological connection to the theatre is no accident" (166–7). Historically, gardens have often contained platforms or green spaces for dramatic and musical entertainment, yet they also provide informal space for social exchange and display. Hunt writes that during the eighteenth century, "Gardens offered themselves as spaces where stage and auditorium, theatre and world, were constantly interchanged, where socially imposed roles could be played out before an understanding if critical audience, and where social artifice was 'naturalized' amid the garden's greenery in ways that it could never exactly be within doors" (163). The very fact that gardens are often the setting of choice for portrait paintings, or in the case of Shields' fiction, for characterization, further reveals the garden's uncommon status as a space of heightened performance of the self. As Hunt contends, "The very decision to depict owners and/ or their guests in a garden ... is an invitation to show them behaving self-consciously or with that extra verve or spirit that comes from registering a special place and moment" (165). This theorizing of the social drama of garden "scenes" holds great relevance for a writer like Shields, who looks to highlight certain moments in her characters' everyday lives, revealing Daisy's acting out of, or against, social roles according to the expectations of others and her own personal needs. In this way, Shields' theatrical use of the space resonates with Susanna Moodie's own feigned propriety in her kitchen garden in *Roughing It in the Bush*. The primary difference, though, is that while Moodie must account for the altered context and composite form of her backwoods garden (and the subsequent influence on the transplanted woman pioneer), Shields, in *The Stone Diaries*, has consistent, highly "naturalized" garden settings that potentially limit opportunities for performances that move beyond the socially prescribed, well-established roles and ideals of twentieth-century domestic femininity.

As Daisy matures, Shields incorporates the social theatre of the garden in increasingly pronounced ways in order to stage her character's varied powers of performance. For example, when Daisy embarks on a romantic relationship in the chapter "Marriage, 1927," she assumes an unexpected maternal role by catering to the needs of her fiancé, Harold Hoad. During a luncheon on the veranda, Daisy's future mother-in-law, Mrs Hoad, provides detailed instructions on how to "mother" the groom. In a later scene, readers witness Daisy performing this role when the young couple strolls through a public garden:

> "Don't do that with your stick," she said to him.
>
> Idly, he had been swinging a willow wand about in the air and lopping off the heads of delphiniums, sweet william, bachelor buttons, irises.
>
> "Who cares," he said, looking sideways at her, his big elastic face working.

"I care," she said.

He swung widely and took three blooms at once. Oriental poppies. The petals scattered on the asphalt path.

"Stop that," she said, and he stopped. (116)

Pointing to this exchange, Gom applauds Daisy for being "a caretaker of the garden, its advocate": "The scene works to give us an easy characterization of Harold, but we also see Daisy, usually so placid and agreeable, assert herself, not on her own behalf but on behalf of the flowers. And she wins. He stops" (25). Daisy may be the garden's protector when faced with a destructive Harold, but this garden scene is not entirely about her successful self-assertion. Although Shields presents the scene as a private moment between the affianced couple, it takes place in "Bloomington's public gardens" (116). This blurring of public and private space is key to understanding how gardens accommodate role-playing through the creation of a heightened awareness of space and time. Shields creates a "scene" not simply through the couple's tense emotions as they quarrel in the garden, but more importantly through an abrupt shift in the presentation of the text itself. Following a recounting of Cuyler's wedding gift to Daisy (a carved garden gnome) and his long-winded convocation speech to the graduates of Long College (115–16), Shields switches immediately to a new setting and employs dramatic, rather than linear and explicit, narration. The effect is that the brief incident of the flower decapitation becomes distinctly separate, set apart from the previous narrative line in the text, as Shields stages a "scene" in the full sense of the theatrical meaning of that term.

Shields posits Daisy (with Harold) as a social actor who understandably performs because, in the context of Hunt's theory, "the garden invites, even requires ... its owners or its visitors to 'perform', to entertain a new self or to exploit the full potentialities of an old one" (165). Hunt's use of the verbs "entertain" and "exploit" suggests a degree of personal freedom and experimentation when it comes to garden theatrics; Shields' depiction of Daisy highlights, however, performative agency underscored by gendered limitations. Following the dramatic exchange of dialogue, Shields summarizes the new role that Daisy has just performed in relation to Harold by providing *his* desired counterpart: "He knows how much he needs her. He longs for correction, for love like a scalpel, a whip, something to curb his wild impulses and morbidity. She honestly believes she can change him, take hold of him and make something noble of his wild nature. He is hungry, she knows, for repression" (117). Daisy may be nature's guardian in this scene, but she also acts according to Mrs Hoad's instructions, becoming Harold's maternal chastiser. Scripted into a garden performance pre-determined by familial obligation, Daisy acts within appropriate parameters. The social "theatre" that is Daisy's life in the garden facilitates modes of being in which personal desires (her love and protection of the flowers) and the pressures of social conformity (her new role as Harold's fiancée) find complicated, inter-related expressions.

If theatrics are part of the "plot" of Daisy's life, then how are we to interpret firstly, Daisy's Ottawa garden, and secondly, her performance as Mrs Green Thumb? For many critics, the Ottawa garden is a feminine oasis within a society that has always entrapped and defined Daisy. Lisa Johnson views gardening as Daisy's mode of empowerment, her "space of self-actualization" (207). Naomi Ellen Guttman equally contends that the garden represents "an escape from the rigid confines of the home and … culture's expectation of ideal womanhood" (25); here, Daisy creates a sacred space of spiritual renewal, childhood innocence, and personal fulfillment, countering the many voids in her life.[17] Mercy (almost) found and lost paradise in the kitchen, and now Daisy (seemingly) regains paradise in her backyard. Gom similarly agrees with these conclusions: "If Daisy's garden is Edenic … then what really is Daisy? Is she God? A kind of bewildered, troubled God, nurturing what she has been given and ignoring the rest? Well, why not?" (25). These critics' celebratory appraisals are in keeping with the care Shields takes in establishing the garden's heavenly quality, even using the term "Eden" explicitly: "Visitors standing in this garden sometimes feel their hearts lock into place for an instant, and experience blurred primal visions of creation – Eden itself, paradise, indeed" (196). Shields wanted Daisy's unique skill to be appreciated, as she playfully admitted once to using her own Ottawa home and its "pokey little garden" as a model with a slight change in address and embellished appearance (Sibbald n.p.)[18] (Figure 4.1). But does Daisy truly succeed in realizing fulfillment through her garden? As we saw in *The Box Garden*, overt declarations of a place or mode of being as "Edenic" often prove to be illusory. In turn, *The Stone Diaries* reveals through its complicated, highly naturalized presentations of domestic "paradises" just how difficult it is to find fulfillment.

One way of reassessing the Ottawa garden is by considering how Shields frames readers' entrance into this setting (and related chapters) by recounting Daisy's idyllic journey to Canada from Bloomington, Indiana at the age of thirty-one. Reminiscent of Charleen's naïve elopement into the west with Watson in *The Box Garden*, Daisy's journey north is presented as the ultimate home-coming, as the hopeful, young widow sees Canada in purely ideal terms: a "healing kingdom," a "cool clean place" of "polite" people (133) teeming with "heavenly" scenery (146). Here we see Shields drawing again upon what Ramon highlights (through Peter Dickinson's term) as a "border consciousness" as her "texts increasingly work to contest American attitudes towards Canada" (15).[19] Shields quickly undermines Daisy's girlish expectations when

FIGURE 4.1 Carol Shields' Ottawa home, 582 The Driveway

registering her disappointment with the Niagara Falls and the Dionne
Quintuplets (the girls are a spectacle for paying tourists who visit their
Callander, Ontario garden; 134). Daisy's over-zealous, Americanized
outlook and eventual disappointment intimate that caution is required
in assessing the Ottawa chapters of Daisy's life. Whenever "notions"
of paradise appear in *The Stone Diaries* they prove to be problematic
because of major inconsistencies; ultimately, Canada will not prove
to be the promised land. This premise extends in a number of ways

to Shields' varied depictions of the Ottawa garden, a garden which readers never actually see, as the photograph included in the novel and labeled "583 The Driveway" (the address of Daisy's Ottawa home) is a literal interpretation: a picture of a car parked on a winter street. On the one hand, this ensures the garden's status as an ideal by protecting it from visual scrutiny. The garden exists only in readers' imaginations through the awe-struck description that spans over two pages. On the other hand, the inclusion of the banal photograph is puzzling in its clear effacement of this "miracle" (195), Daisy's urban gardening achievement.

## The Deficiencies of Daisy's "Eden"

Reflecting on both the Ottawa garden and the much-loved position of garden columnist, Shields states in an epistolary interview with Joan Thomas that Daisy "stumble[s], for a time, into meaningful work. Her garden offer[s] her a form of creative expression" (81–2). This sense of purpose and pleasure stems, of course, from the continued gender performance associated with the garden. When Daisy assumes the persona of Mrs Green Thumb for the *Recorder*, she acquires a new role that allows for a degree of self-realization. After spending her life fulfilling the needs and desires of others, Daisy seems to have "veered, accidentally, into her own life" and demonstrates a real talent for writing (237). Alice observes her mother's amazing concentration in this new venture: "She gets lost in what she's doing and doesn't even hear the phone ringing; none of us ever guessed she had this power of absorption" (239). As evidence of Daisy's success, fan letters compose a portion of the chapter "Work, 1955–1964" with Mrs Green Thumb receiving everything from gardening questions, to compliments on her prose style, to poetic declarations of affection from an anonymous admirer. Daisy (as columnist) connects with people through her writing, and her audience responds to her performance. As one fan "Fed-Up-With-Weeds-And-Bugs-in-South-Ottawa" writes, "You've got a real gift for making a story out of things" (222).

This surprising aspect of Daisy's character extends well beyond her new profession, though, as she enters a significant time of creative independence and unconventional behaviour in her personal life. Now widowed for the second time, Daisy welcomes into her home her pregnant, unwed niece, Beverley, much to Alice's chagrin: "Let me say right off that you've completely lost your marbles about this baby business" (212). The household slips into disarray to the extent that Daisy even neglects her beloved plants: "She got way behind on the vacuuming. Everything. Even her beloved African violets dried up, even her ferns" (237). And finally, she involves herself romantically, readers suspect, with her editor Jay Dudley. Ironically enough, during this overtly performative yet self-concealing phase of her life as "Mrs. Green Thumb," Daisy pursues her own interests, expressing herself in a less scripted manner.[20] Alice recalls this "Work" period as an immense but welcome disruption in her mother's commonplace existence: "In 1954 we were a nice ordinary family, Mr. and Mrs. Barker Flett and their three tractable children. Then – it seemed like a lightening flash had hit our house – there was just one parent (distracted, preoccupied) and an unwed mother and a baby with colic and three teenagers ... You'd have thought my mother would be wildly unsettled by all this, but you would be wrong. She let the chaos that hit our household in 1955 roll right over her like a big friendly engulfing wave" (238). The sudden "chaos" of the Flett household is reminiscent of Cuyler's fall into chaos in the opening chapter, but here disorder becomes, paradoxically, a kind of "paradise." In this wave of change, Daisy "bob[s] to the surface, her round face turned upward ... happy" (238). Fulfillment is found not in the orderly domestic "paradise" of traditional married life with Barker, but rather in a kind of domestic disorder combined with the unexpected opportunity of an impromptu performance as a garden writer.[21]

But if Daisy's stint as an advice columnist is a liberating experience that breaks the predictable pattern of her development, something is decidedly lacking in this phase of life: Daisy, herself. Shields composes this chapter entirely through the words of others. Readers see letters addressed to Daisy or to Mrs Green Thumb, but are never privy to Daisy's (or for that matter Mrs Green Thumb's) own thoughts, feelings, or predilections. If this chaotic time and mode of being represent "paradise" in Daisy's life, then she is unsettlingly silent, her performance neither dramatized (as we saw in the public garden scene with Harold) nor depicted (none of her columns is included).[22] When Daisy eventually loses her position to the underhanded and appropriately named journalist "Pinky Fullham" – an egotist impressed with his talent for botanical illustration, but less qualified as a garden journalist by being endowed with only a "pinky," rather than a true "green thumb" – readers are forced to re-evaluate Daisy's brief contentment, particularly because of her absence from this critical sixth chapter of her life plot. Furthermore, the fact that Daisy's newfound paradise is so readily usurped by another implies she was not truly in possession of it.

In the ensuing chapter, "Sorrow, 1965," Daisy enters a period of depression and (continued) silence, and Shields subtly implicates both the role of Mrs Green Thumb and the Ottawa garden in her unhappiness. The chapter "Work, 1955–1964" (the seemingly most rewarding period of Daisy's life) and the chapter "Sorrow, 1965" (the most unfulfilling time), are connected through a shared narrative style that unsettles this particular garden "plot." Sifting through the opinions of other characters, readers cannot confer with Daisy as to whether or not family members, friends, colleagues, lovers, or fans communicate her experience appropriately or justly. When a depressed, now unemployed Daisy enters her garden in search of comfort, readers hope for rejuvenation but are met instead with a sad predicament. Alice recounts her mother's despairing state: "I find my mother seated in the garden, gripping the arms of a wicker chair, her chin oddly dented and old, her mouth round, helpless, saying, 'I can't get used to this. I can't get over this.'" (240). In this brief passage, Shields creates another critical garden scene featuring a moment of heightened self-consciousness: Daisy is a woman in crisis who seeks comfort in her garden but finds little solace there. Readers may choose to agree, or not, with Alice's theory that the source of Daisy's grief is the loss of her job and alternative role: "She was Mrs. Green Thumb, that well-known local personage, and now she's back to being Mrs. Flett again" (240). Ultimately, Daisy's despairing declaration demands further consideration within a much broader framework.

As much as the Ottawa garden and related role of Mrs Green Thumb provide sanctuary and outlets for creative expression, they also accentuate Daisy's persistent isolation and deficient self-development. In keeping with most interpretations of Daisy's idyllic retreat, Guttman celebrates the "freedom from self" the Ottawa garden provides (103), and indeed, Shields states that the garden "perceives nothing of [Daisy], not her history, her name, her longings, nothing – which is why she is able to love it as purely as she does" (196). In her private garden, Daisy is apparently not at risk of being cast as surrogate daughter, girlish temptress, maternal chastiser, matronly mother, or garden columnist in order to suit the needs of others and facilitate their own garden "plots," both real and figurative. If Daisy's garden is her own "Eden," however, this paradise is rather unfeeling and cold. The people in Daisy's life undoubtedly misperceive her at times, yet Daisy's garden presents a similar dilemma. Daisy may revel in anonymity in the garden because there she escapes unsolicited scrutiny and imposed social scripts but she still remains unknown and, at times, profoundly unfulfilled. Conferring much of her own self into the creation that is her garden, Daisy only "understands, perhaps, a quarter of its green secrets, no more" (196). Daisy yearns to read and understand the "signs" of her garden just as readers, critics, and even other characters in the novel attempt to "read" Daisy and interpret the meaning of her life: "She may yearn to know the true state of the garden, but she wants even more to be part of its mysteries ... she has opened her arms to it, taking it as it comes, every leaf, every stem, every root and sign" (196). Daisy attempts to embrace both her garden and her own otherness, those unexamined mysteries of her innermost self. Unfortunately, the scene of bewilderment featured in "Sorrow, 1965," where she sits uncomforted, problematizes what once seemed pure perfection. Daisy cannot realize true happiness and fulfillment in her Ottawa life and garden because she remains within it a stranger to both herself and to others.

Nowhere is this sad realization regarding Daisy's life more evident than in the final chapter, "Death," as Daisy's adult children lack appreciation for their mother's real pleasures and interests. In a series of dramatized exchanges of dialogue, the casual disregard for Daisy's life is palpable. Having earlier recognized her mother's transformation into a creative, independent woman as Mrs Green Thumb, Alice now dismisses what readers can only imagine is a prized, bequeathed possession – Daisy's garden trug:

> "She left you what?" Joan shouted over the telephone. (A bad transatlantic connection.)

"Her trug," said Alice, grimacing.

"What in God's name is a trug?"

"That old gardening basket of hers. That old mildewed thing with the huge hooped handle?"

"I think I remember. Vaguely. But why?"

"I don't know. Same reason you got the silver asparagus server, I suppose."

"Lordy."

"She really kind of lost it at the end, didn't she?" (347–8)

The concluding scene of the novel similarly emphasizes the lack of thought and attention others bestow upon Daisy throughout her life and even in her (imagined) death. Two unidentified speakers comment on the funeral spray:

"The pansies, have you ever seen such ravishing pansies?"

"She would have loved them."

"Somehow, I expected to see a huge bank of daisies."

"Daisies, yes."

"Someone should have thought of daisies."

"Yes."

"Ah, well." (361)

Taking into account that Daisy "once … said she liked pansies at a funeral" (a statement made a few pages earlier in the chapter), readers appreciate that one of Daisy's final wishes has been respected, if not fully understood, by those in attendance (356). Because the flower symbolizes memory being a "messenger of affectionate thoughts" (Dumas 112), Daisy appreciates their appropriateness for memorial services, particularly since she paid her own respects to her adoptive mother, Clarentine, by "float[ing] her to heaven on a bed of pansies" (77). The pleasing sentiment of the flower is undermined, however, as the speakers betray their callousness through the comment, "Ah, well," a short, dismissive response that sadly concludes Daisy's entire life story. The fact that Daisy's floral namesake is absent from the service is at once fitting and ironic, as the flower is the symbol of her unperceived life: "A daisy really is a bit like an eye when you think about it, round and fringed with lashes, staring upward. Opening, closing … And we require, it seems, in our moments of courage or shame, at least one witness, but Mrs. Flett has not had this privilege. This is what breaks her heart. What she can't bear. Even now, eighty years old" (339). From the moment of her birth to her (imagined) death, Daisy is assessed and interpreted by her family according to their needs and desires but rarely perceived in her own right. Like her parents (and especially her mother Mercy) before her, Daisy is understood superficially by those who should have known her best, including herself.

The fecundity of the Ottawa garden makes it seem a veritable paradise, but its unperceiving, unknown nature perpetuates the self-effacement and anonymity Daisy experiences throughout her life. Shields provides a potential counterpart to this Ottawa garden, however, when Daisy takes up residence in the Bayside Towers retirement community in Florida. Here, Daisy discovers (yet again) that a domestic "paradise" sometimes requires unconventional formulations in order to facilitate true companionship. The initial description of Bayside Towers is that of a contained, superficial residence.[23] Daisy feels that "[e]verything she encounters … lack[s] … weight. The hollow interior doors of her condo. The molded insubstantiality of the light switches. The dismaying lightness of her balcony furniture" (280). Reminiscent of the empty McNinn home in *The Box Garden*, the hollow quality of Bayside Towers is unappealing, and Daisy surveys her surroundings with ambivalence: "In the foyer of Bayside Towers stands an artificial jade plant, and she is unable to walk by this abomination without reaching out and fingering its leaves, sometimes rather roughly, leaving the marks of her fingernails on the vinyl surfaces, finding sly pleasure in her contempt" (280). Surely, readers surmise, this place, a retirement condominium for seniors, cannot be paradise when set alongside the visually stunning, natural Ottawa home and garden.

Within this artificial décor, however, Daisy realizes an alternative "garden" of profound fulfillment that does not leave her solitary, or held at a troubling distance in her role as Mrs Green Thumb. Together, the four elderly "Flowers" of Bayside – Daisy, Lily, Myrtle, and Glad – form their own kind of garden (on a first name basis) of shared pleasures and acknowledgement. In this integrated community of women who possess similar life experiences, readers sense that Daisy has finally found a paradisal "home" to belong to: "The four Flowers are fortunate in their mutual attachment and they recognize their luck. Lily's from Georgia, Glad from New Hampshire, the breezy-talking Myrtle from Michigan – different worlds, you might say, and yet their lives chime a similar tune. Just look at them: four old white women. Like Mrs Daisy Flett, they are widows; they are, all of them, comfortably well off; they have aspired to no profession other than motherhood, wife-hood; they love a good laugh; there is something filigreed and droll about the way they're always on the cusp of laughter" (318). The narrator commands, "Just look at them," and readers must perceive and recognize, as the Flowers do, that in this "garden" exists profound, fulfilling bonds of companionship. Possessing sought-after popularity, Daisy and her fellow "Flowers" provide entertainment to the other residents in the form of daily, garden-inspired witticisms, deriving, in turn, their own enjoyment from these small ceremonies. Finally, Daisy cultivates a meaningful, deeply personal social life. And although the Flowers may seem like an exclusive domain as other Bayside residents "envy their relaxed good nature," and the four women occupy the best bridge table, which "is the Flowers' table and no one else's" (318), Shields implies that this modest paradise is ultimately open and accepting. In the event that one of the Flowers dies, the group has already decided to invite "the unspeakable Iris Jackman ... to fill in at the round table even though Iris has the worst case of B.O. in captivity" and is useless at cards (319–20). After having entered the real and figurative gardens of others and of her own making, Daisy has lived according to internalized societal expectations, remaining for the most part unrecognized, a veritable stranger to both herself and her family. At this round bridge table, a table of equals, Daisy now communes with others, and while her retirement persona as one of the "Flowers" is another assumed role, it is interactive, spontaneous, and familiar, occupying a truly shared "garden." Daisy has realized a domestic paradise and its location is neither a typical family home nor an idealized locale situated in the country of her origins, but instead a retirement institution in the United States.

In the garden plots of Shields' fiction, paradise can be elusive in its temporality and deceptive in its artificial or "natural" expressions, destabilizing readers' expectations as to how it should appear and what it should offer. In this way, Shields refuses to foreclose on the relevance of "home" to our literary tradition as one of the most complex sites and dynamic factors in a character's search for fulfillment. Reflecting on Shields' extraordinary ability to situate her characters to the extent that their experiences and surroundings function interdependently, Giardini writes, "My mother takes one foot off the ground, rarely both" (11). Having one foot on the ground when that ground is a suburban lawn or kitchen linoleum is a position not always viewed as progressive, especially by some feminists who locate equality beyond the role of homemaker. Such negative scrutiny of Shields is usually founded upon conventional perceptions of the domestic as a static, uninformative site. In "Still in the Kitchen: The Art of Carol Shields," an article whose very title suggests waiting and stagnation, Laura Groening writes that "to call Shields a feminist ... is to place her distinctive fiction in an alien land" (14), as she "has no use for instruments of social change" (17). What needs to be acknowledged and explored by both her detractors (who tend to dismiss her work) and supporters (who tend to over-idealize it) is that Shields' domestic worlds have a remarkable capacity for gendered resistance, social critique, and above all, transformation. Her use of the paradise myth reveals the esteem with which she holds these kinds of narratives: their challenging subject matter and ever-changing composition. For Shields, "paradise" means profound companionship between like-minded individuals, wherever that kind of metaphorical homecoming is realized. The most meaningful quests and stories take place within the spaces and routines of daily life, and the fulfillment that is paradise is realized only through the most intimate sharing of each other's gardens, in whatever form they may take.

## CHAPTER FIVE

# Turning the Earth:
# Lorna Crozier the Gardener-Poet

Over the course of her career, Lorna Crozier has acquired a reputation
as Canada's "garden poet." Her notorious sequence "The Sex Lives of
Vegetables" has been a great source of controversy as well as laughter.
In an interview in 1988, Crozier commented on the astounding success
of her sixth book of poems, *The Garden Going On Without Us*, which
contains the sexually explicit sequence, and at the time had gone into
a third printing with sales of 2,500 copies (in contrast to the average
sales of 200 or 300 copies for a Canadian poet): "'Nobody expected it
… I was absolutely thrilled. It's a bestseller in poetry terms. It seems
to have hit a market that wasn't merely composed of regular poetry
readers.' She laughs. 'People, I think, bought the book for friends who
happened to be gardeners'" (Adachi M3).

In more recent years, Crozier has continued to tap into an audience with a "gardener" demographic by appearing with her husband,
writer Patrick Lane, in the 2002 episode "Reflections of the Soul" from
the *Recreating Eden* television series on Canada's Home and Garden
network (HGTV). In the episode, which takes place in the couple's

garden near Victoria, British Columbia, writing and gardening go hand-in-hand, as the documentary traces Lane's recovery from alcoholism. Lane steals the spotlight: a troubled Adam taking stock of his life and his neglected terrain as he works toward both his and the garden's renewal. Meanwhile, Crozier appears the intelligent helpmate: a strong Eve who welcomes this new opportunity of sobriety. In an article Lane wrote for the popular magazine *Canadian Gardening* (2006), he reflects that their coastal garden "had its beginnings in my boyhood when I watched my mother creep on her hands and knees into her flower beds as she weeded under the Okanagan sun"; he adds, "With the help of my wife, poet Lorna Crozier, I have tried to do the same here with its clouds and rain" (52). The companionship of Lane and Crozier's garden captures what is most central to Crozier's poetry: the garden as a site of ongoing construction, an expression of individuals' critical and inspired perceptions, and a dynamic social space that communicates the complexities of human relationships.

Just as Susanna Moodie, Catharine Parr Traill, Gabrielle Roy, and Carol Shields look to the garden as a means of negotiating women's changing domestic roles and agency both within and outside the home, Crozier is similarly preoccupied in her garden poetry with re-examining the quotidian: its pleasures, dangers, and above all, powerful influence on women's identities and ways of being in the world. With Shields, in particular, Crozier shares a recuperative feminist mandate, as she finds her inspiration in what she describes as the many unexplored silences in literature: "I write because I want to tell myself the stories I never heard as a child, as a grown woman, the stories I still can't find in books" ("Who's Listening?" 25). Following Shields' passing in 2002, Crozier spoke on the CBC radio program *As It Happens* about Shields' influence on her own writing practice, summarizing their shared vision: "Everything happens over the kitchen sink" (Finlay).

By exploring the domestic's unspoken stories, Crozier generates her own poetic form of garden "plots," and while initially this term may seem out of place, pertaining more readily to narrative fiction than to poetry, it is important to note, here, that Crozier envisions many of her poems as stories. In her essay "Comic Books, Dead Dogs, Cheer-leading: One Poet's Beginnings," Crozier recounts her working-class roots and notes that while her parents did not own any books, her older brother had an extensive comic book collection: "Maybe it was in those colourful pages of cheap paper that my poetry education began: I learned the value of the succinct, densely-packed narrative and the compact, meaningful line replete with words that exploded from boxes – POW! SHEBANG! BAM!" (n.p.). Within poems that, according to Crozier, typically "unfold in a series of images" as she writes them (n.p.), readers discover concise narratives that frequently draw inspiration from the garden, bringing this vernacular landscape into view in unexpected ways.[1]

Crozier's explicit desire to recoup untold stories is intricately connected to what critics have identified as two fundamental, inter-related aspects of her writing: her pluralist feminism and her understanding of writing as a process of re-vision. In a review of *The Garden Going On Without Us,* Janice Kulyk Keefer argues that Crozier's "'pluralist' feminism ... acknowledge[s] and revalidate[s] traditional female qualities and skills – nurturing, caring; emotional responses to experience and intuitive ways of knowing" (64). Crozier works to honour the many selves previously negated or dismissed, and at the same time resists constructing the domestic in a purely idealistic way. Intimately tied to Crozier's pluralist feminism is her emulation of American writer Adrienne Rich and her strategy of feminist "re-vision." According to Rich's essay "When We Dead Awaken: Writing as Re-vision," a woman writer benefits both intellectually and creatively when she "enter[s] an old text from a critical direction" in a "drive to self-knowledge" through alternative constructions of the feminine (35). In an interview with Barbara Carey, Crozier acknowledges Rich's concept as a guiding principle in her poetic practice: "One of the things I absolutely delight in is what Adrienne Rich calls 're-visioning': looking at the old stories but looking at them in a new way; adding women to the story when women have been left out; or adding a set of episodes to give a story a different slant; saying, 'There's another story, and then again, there's another, and there's also one more'" (17).

Crozier approaches her re-visioning, then, from a strategy of plurality: she re-creates and re-tells through many possible versions. In her foundational essay, "Let Us Revise Mythologies: The Poetry of Lorna Crozier," Susan Gingell highlights the multiplicity inherent in Crozier's craft: she "contend[s] with some of the dominant myths that govern our sense of who and where we are" and offers "in their stead not a single sacred feminized vision, but rather a plurality of possible ways of understanding human beginnings" (67). What is of particular interest here is how these two aspects – Crozier's pluralist feminism and re-visioning – intersect with her literary gardens. Both Gingell and Nathalie Cooke (in her monograph) acknowledge that Crozier's recurring focus on "the many selves" (94) is often connected with the theme of the garden.[2] Scholars have not, however, considered this at length, even though garden-related imagery appears in practically all of Crozier's collections to date.

## Crozier's Garden Poetry: The Interplay of Product and Process

Through Crozier's continual, creative engagement with the garden (a process in and of itself), she has arrived at an extensive realization of its third nature role. Over the course of her career, she has explored and reworked this relationship and in doing so, come to recognize its ability not only to represent but also to reflect critically upon what we take to be "second nature" which, in her case, most often refers to "the old tales that we grew up with, that have influenced so much of our lives. There's a great wealth of things to be said again from a different viewpoint, in a different way" (Barbara Carey 17). In the interview with Carey, Crozier reflects that much of her poetry "tries to prick holes in the false comforts we've surrounded our society with" (16), yet she also uses the garden to enable us to see what we take for granted in our everyday lives, what we fail to register until we finally see it in an alternative light. When speaking with Clarise Foster, Crozier reflects, "Language and attention can uncover the extraordinary in what we often overlook. It can honour what exists outside us ... What I am trying to establish when I write is a movement back and forth between the profound and the ordinary ... The beautiful is often in what we usually don't notice" (9). In previous chapters, we saw how Moodie, Traill, Roy, and Shields turn to the formal aspects of the garden (i.e. its spatial frame, its capacity for staging scenes) and its particular processes (i.e. transplanting, naturalizing) as means of expressing women's everyday lives, changing gender roles, and agency. Crozier, perhaps more than any of these other writers, turns to the garden as a model for writing by drawing upon its capacity to be both product and process. Indeed, Crozier's mandate to look "in a new way" or "from a different viewpoint" (Carey 17) intersects with the garden's third nature role, which is to provide a critical, and even defamiliarizing perspective, or as John Dixon Hunt describes it, to offer "fresh visions and versions of ... abiding concepts" ("*Paragone*" 67).

One line of inquiry that has shed some light on why the garden holds persistent, changing appeal for Crozier and how it informs her re-visionist poetics is ecocriticism. According to Marilyn Rose,

Crozier demonstrates an innovative approach to nature and its processes. She introduces Crozier as a "nature poet" and a "lyric poet of the new order" (62) who often curtails the subjective ends of her writing and promotes an ecological vision (55). Citing poems such as "Inventing the Hawk," in which the speaker must wait for the hawk's cry to enter her body, and "The Garden at Night," in which the speaker glimpses a mole tunneling through the dark earth to the light, Rose reads an eco-philosophy quietly at work: Crozier recognizes an "interdependent world" of nature to which the human subject must be receptive in order to experience illumination (62). This ecocritical interpretation holds great relevance for the garden poems, as a garden is constituted by natural processes of growth and decline, as well as many species of animals, plants, and insects. Crozier herself acknowledges experiencing this kind of interaction: "How do we erase the species line between us and other creatures, whether it's between us and trees or us and domestic pets? I have two cats ... and they teach me things. If I sit with them in the garden and I look where their eyes are looking, I suddenly see what they are seeing – a raccoon in the fir tree, for instance. I wouldn't have seen it if I'd been on my own" (Foster 10). A further distinction needs to be made, however, between Crozier's "nature" versus "garden" poetry to account for the fact that a garden is also a subjective, socio-cultural product – a human creation.

One poem that captures this sense of discovery in and of nature, yet also gestures toward the potential influence of the gardener, is "In Moonlight," a piece that supplies the title of Crozier's first collection of previously published and new works, *The Garden Going On Without Us*. "In Moonlight" posits the garden as both a site and a process of continual change and activity. On a first reading, nature's life forces seem to exist almost independently of the human subject, who is figured as a mind not quite able to grasp all that takes place in its surroundings:

Something moves
just beyond the mind's
clumsy fingers.

It has to do with seeds.
The earth's insomnia.
The garden going on
without us

needing no one
to watch it (123)

Evoking the spontaneity of the garden through its seeds, Crozier
suggests it is never restful; it holds the stored potential for present and
future growth: in other words, an unending cycle of life, decline, and
renewal. These natural processes are capable of operating "without us,"
beyond humans' perceptual reach or influence. Fittingly, the phrase
"The garden going on" occupies its own line, while "without us" is
separated through the enjambment. In this poem, Rose sees "a parallel
and companionate world to our own that generates and lives by its
own light, a world that human consciousness is sometimes privileged
to enter partially" (61).

Certainly, "In Moonlight" characterizes the human presence as
a "clumsy" mind: an imagination not certain how to access or sense
different ways of being in the world that are distinct from, yet proximate to, the world of "us." The fact remains, however, that as much
as Crozier is interested in this natural world, she is equally fascinated
by human perception and artistic re-vision: the need to move beyond
conventional or "naturalized" ways of seeing and interacting. Crozier
has admitted that many of the terrains or natural objects in her poems

are figurative in their inception: "In most of my poems I use the images that surround me ... but the poems are *about* something else ... [T]he outside is always filtered through my way of seeing things. I believe the landscape in my poems is more an internal landscape than an external one" (Meyer and O'Riordan 28). If we re-read "In Moonlight" in this way, the poem positions the human subject, whose work is a kind of mental toil, as attempting to use the "garden" in order to access or develop his or her own comprehension. This active mode of perception moves beyond what is most visible by operating "in moonlight," or trying to see into the dark, as the gardener works to extend him or herself beyond what is habitual, most apparent, or most easily grasped. The poem gestures towards, therefore, the purposeful tending of new awareness for areas of life and experience that have remained, for too long, unnoticed and undetected. With the "mind's / clumsy fingers," this gardener of perception resists closure and instead is motivated by the garden's suggestions of process, which in turn inspire creative attempts to gain a renewed and renewing understanding which, unfortunately, remains just out of reach.

Differentiating between Crozier's "nature poetry" and "garden poetry" means, then, that the receptive function of the human subject, as Rose outlines it, needs to be qualified to allow for an additional active and determining role. As much as a garden is a process (and not just of its own accord but also through human intervention), it is a product: an artistic expression and place created, in part, through human endeavour. A gardener is an artist, a comparison that Lane expands upon in his memoir, *There Is a Season* (2004): "Done well, a garden is a poem, and the old lesson of gardening is the same in poetry: what is not there is just as important as what is" (202). Because the garden is an artistic arrangement, Lane argues that one must pay attention to rhythm, space, and transition, all terms that can be equally applied to the poetic craft (202–3). In the context of Crozier's writing, the inverse of Lane's statement also holds true: a poem can be a "garden" through the purposeful design and arrangement of language. The "gardener-poet" manipulates through the use of aesthetic devices, initiating his or her own creative process with the aim of constructing an artistic product, or effect, which can in time enter into another creative process through continual re-vision. When we consider these two aspects of gardens – process and product – in Crozier's poetry, we see that her garden poetics involves not only receptiveness to process and changeability, but also conscious engagement with language and device in order to expose and to form alternative levels of significance. Ultimately then, one of the central aspects of Crozier's garden poems has very little to do with receptivity and what is "natural" and more to do with purposeful artistic intervention.

Crozier's appreciation of the garden as both a process and a product has been gradual and not without its challenges. Throughout her career, readers witness a steady embracing of paradox and an eventual adoption of the garden and gardening as models for her poetry and creative practice. In the early years, Crozier conceptualizes the garden as an instrument of power and a product of hegemonic culture. In her first collection, *Inside Is the Sky* (1976),[3] readers are affronted by gardens coerced into being, which can, in turn, be used to control a human subject, as Crozier demonstrates real distrust of, even disillusionment over, archetypal ideals. In the poem "Backyard Eden," the garden is neither a welcoming nor "natural" environment, as physical aggression and near-antiseptic perfection render it a lifeless, superficial place:

> All summer rubber-gloved
> she digs her fingers
> in the garden soil.

Her silver hoe
slashes every weed.
Rose lice she kills
with a quick swish of poison.
Plastic ribbons she ties on the wind
to frighten the robins (23)

Rubber-gloved, this gardener does not enjoy sensuality; her metal tools, poison, and plastic distance her from nature and from the nurturing qualities normally, or rather ideally, associated with a cultivator. Instead, she subjugates the terrain according to her desires and categorization of what life forms are deemed worthy of existence and inclusion. In this way, the poem's title creates and then fails to meet readers' expectations through an ironic refusal to reward the anticipation of paradise, as this "natural" beauty is sustained primarily through destruction. The poem enacts an aesthetic manipulation of its own through layered and doubled signification that allows for a disturbing transformation as to meaning and effect.

At one point in "Backyard Eden," the gardener seems to recreate the desired perfection with "well-ordered life" and "color creations / in the greys of the city" (23). In the monotone urban setting, she generates an otherworldly terrain where the magic of synesthesia sets "canterbury bells / tinkling mauves and pinks through the air" (23). The array of colours stimulates the senses, but this paradise is ultimately artificial and deathly. After presenting an aesthetic product controlled according to the gardener's strict vision, Crozier concludes her poem through the notion of process and its transforming potential, as this highly regulated garden meets its own demise. In Crozier's poem, this paradise is (already) lost to the past, signaled through the change in tense in the final lines of the poem: "Yesterday / there was a frost" (23).

The violence and disillusionment that take place in "Backyard Eden" find expression in other ways in such pieces as "The Fattening" (from *Inside Is the Sky*), in which a woman is led down the garden path by her predatory, manipulative male suitor, or "From the Garden I See Him" (from *Humans and Other Beasts*, 1980), in which the female speaker addresses how the romance of the garden shapes her evolving perspective on her relationship and her ambivalent feelings towards her far-from-perfect lover. In these poems, Crozier exposes the garden as a product of cultural codes linked to beauty, romance, and idyllic nature. In its capacity as a powerful cultural ideal, the garden is not only internalized to the point that it skews an individual's perceptions, but also used (frequently by men) to manipulate the female subjects of Crozier's poems. When Crozier reflects on the early stages of her career, she recognizes that she often expressed her emotions in palpable ways: "'The early books ... were very much a young person's work. They were very dark, angry, probably too strident. I married too young at 20, to a high school physics teacher'" (Adachi M3). In the television episode for the *Recreating Eden* HGTV series, Crozier admits the difficulties she faced as a young poet trying to find her voice and much-needed encouragement.[4] In an interview in 1989 (after having published seven books of poetry and having received awards and two Governor General's nominations for her work), Crozier reflects that while she "still [has] a lot of anger that has to come out," as a seasoned poet she expresses it in more subtle, experimental ways, having learned "a lot about diction and tone" over the course of her career: "I think that self-confidence allows you take more risks and to extend yourself, to try different things" (Meyer and O'Riordan 28). Even though the dark tone of her early collections results in a harsh critique of the archetype of the garden, Crozier appears, even at this early stage, to be searching for ways to revise her conceptualization of the garden by opening it up to change (such as the transforming frost of "Backyard Eden"). As her career progresses, Crozier increasingly embraces this space, recognizing the garden to be a model of re-vision: the particular creative process that increasingly informs her poetry.

### Unearthing Desire: "The Sex Lives of Vegetables"

In 1985, with the publication of *The Garden Going On Without Us* and its subsequent nomination for the Governor General's Award, Crozier achieved public recognition as the gardener-poet, and particularly as the "carrot lady" (Walker E3). Although she had composed numerous garden poems prior to this collection, the sequence "The Sex Lives of Vegetables" garnered Crozier the most attention and continues to do so. In 2008, the *Literary Review of Canada* nominated Crozier's poem "Carrots" (and the entire sequence) as one of Canada's most memorable poems not only because of "the startling rightness of the imagery" but also because of its daring at the time of publication: "During the 1970s and into the early '80s, the big voices in the poetry tent were male, still pegged down by names like Layton and Cohen. The League of Canadian Poets had gone through an acrimonious convulsion in the creation of a feminist caucus. 'Carrots' and its sister poems emerge from that period as a confident, witty, female take on sexuality, as frank as anything Irving Layton wrote. Neither strident nor defensive, it is embracingly human" ("Canada's Most Memorable Poems" 15). This sequence of seventeen poems marks a departure, as Crozier shifts from relating to the garden primarily as a product of hegemonic culture and an instrument of control and instead views it as a process of destabilization and a creative instrument of change. One factor that undoubtedly accounts for this development is Patrick Lane.

As artists who work with both words and plants, Crozier and Lane understand and share the garden as a site of mutual encouragement and creativity. This companionate vision persists in the media's characterizations of Crozier, particularly with respect to the development of her career. Elizabeth Philips' article "Crozier and Lane: The Sexologist of the Garden Meets the Carpenter of Words" from *Western Living* magazine implies that Crozier has been "cultivated" into the poet she is today through her relationship with her poet-husband. Philips describes Crozier as a "budding poet" when she left her first husband for Lane in her late twenties with only one "slim collection" to her name (147). In this regard, the article attributes both gardening (in a figurative sense) and carpentry to Lane and positions Crozier, the "Sexologist of the Garden," as a garden herself. Such gendered divisions of agency within the garden seem "second nature," and coincidently are precisely what interest Crozier. Once Crozier and Lane joined forces in pursuing a creative life together, there was no looking back: they co-authored *No Longer Two People* in 1979, Crozier earned her Master of Arts degree in 1980 from the University of Alberta, and she "decided 'to quit full-time work and 'become a poet'" (Kirchhoff C11). An interview from 1990 recounts Crozier and Lane's transient, yet productive existence as poets living in eight different cities in ten years as they accepted various writer-in-residence positions at universities and colleges across Canada. While Lane has undoubtedly supported Crozier's development as a poet (and she, his) throughout their relationship,[5] he has also provided inspiration in a real, or material, sense when it comes to the garden. Lane has usually been the primary gardener throughout their relationship, and Crozier admits that the idea for "The Sex Lives of Vegetables" actually came from "sitting in our back yard [in Regina] and contemplating Patrick's garden" ("A Western Poet's Journal" 6).

What is most evident in *The Garden Going On Without Us* is Crozier's growing commitment as a poet to her pluralist feminism and to Rich's concept of feminist re-vision. Crozier explicitly acknowledges Rich's influence in her interview with Carey in 1990, and it is reflected in her subsequent collections through the highly disruptive, changeable terrains she creates. In "The Sex Lives of Vegetables," Crozier populates the garden with vegetable-writers: the "Scarlet Runner Beans" are the "Lyricists and scribes" who "illuminate the vegetable / book of hours" (115). In contrast with her earlier poems where the garden is a site of human domination, "The Sex Lives of Vegetables" infuses it with expressive agency through multiple vegetable-subjects. Moreover, Crozier re-envisions the garden as an ongoing process of creativity by experimenting with the form of the poetic sequence. She admits that she "would never have written a poem in sequence in the early years" and that she has "become more and more interested in taking more than one look at something … from le[f]t and right and upside-down" (Meyer and O'Riordan 28). Crozier embraces this potentially subversive genre, particularly in terms of developing a strategy that works to question and to disrupt through alternative perspectives. In Elizabeth Philips' interview, "Seeing Distance," Crozier states that the appeal of the sequence is precisely its plurality: "That's why you see so many of my poems [are] written in parts. I love poetic sequences, like the ones I wrote on penises, vegetables, Icarus, etc. You can say, well, here's one way of doing it, one way of seeing it, and here's another, and another. And if you push and go a little deeper, you surprise yourself and find yet another version, the one buried deepest underground – and all of them are possible at the same time" (144). By accessing parts of the garden that are "buried deepest," Crozier intimates that she is looking to unearth repressed, multiple knowledges of the erotic. Moreover, because she transforms some of the vegetables into writers who record the sex lives of their fellow counterparts, she further suggests that this process of exposure is, in fact, the particular role of a poet attuned to the garden.

For some of the vegetables, primarily those depicted as female, the poems are dramatically curtailed, a distinction that implies these particular sex lives are controlled and delimited by what is taboo according to the societal norms and "natural" gender hierarchy of the garden. Just as Crozier sees gaps in the literary tradition that require feminist intervention, she reveals an imbalanced culture at work in the garden. Through their foreshortened entries (only four to six lines in length) and a narrow focus on appearance and dress, the female vegetables' desires remain the most concealed even as the unnatural containment of their sexuality is critically and humourously exposed. Dictated roles become apparent in "Lettuce," as the subservient courtesan is "Raised for one thing / and one thing only" with her body controlled and distorted to satisfy a particular ideal: "Under her fancy crinolines / her narrow feet are bound" (102). In "Tomatoes," the promiscuous seductresses go by the names "*Pixie. Pretty Patio. / Red Cushion.* No wonder / they all have round heels / and rouge their nipples" (105). At the other end of the spectrum are the virginal "Peas," who "never liked any of it" and remain resistant, tightly closed, "keeping their knees together" (111). Within the limitations of the virgin-whore dichotomy and its one-dimensional archetypes of female sexuality, individualized female desire remains repressed. Because of this predicament, Crozier devises strategies of re-vision that take full advantage of the garden trope, turning over this terrain for a critical third nature perspective.

Unearthing female desire for the "vegetable-subjects" of her poems is a process that Crozier appreciates must begin with a renewed engagement with language and with alternative approaches. In the essay "Changing into Fire," she observes that for too long female desire and sexuality have been kept in the dark, obscured by euphemisms – such as the phrase "down there," which fails to name the female body and its experience: "'Down there' was what my mother called it. The words made me tingle with excitement and fear. 'Down there' also meant the cellar with its earthen walls and floors, its shelves of canning, the bins of softening potatoes scabbed with mud, the smell of damp and darkness. Something was always just behind me as I ran up the wood stairs ... Down there was dangerous. Down there was where your hand shouldn't wander, and later, where a boy shouldn't touch you. A no man's land, my mother hoped, down there" (71). Crozier likens female sexual organs to an underground world: the cellar which is dark, mysterious, unappealing, and dirty. Venturing into this unknown space can be a difficult, even a forbidden task for a woman writer who must contend with internalized notions of social propriety and modesty, making the process of feminist re-vision far from straightforward. In her introduction to *Desire in Seven Voices*, a collection of women writers' thoughts on gendered experiences of desire, Crozier describes desire as something that is "subterranean" and extremely challenging to unearth through language: "The difficulty the seven of us had in finding words for what has been unspoken is surely a sign of tremendous force building to a breaking point just below the surface. When desire finds expression in the voices of such writers as these, its resistance to words, its own stubborn desire to remain subterranean creates a complexity and an energy that suffuses every sentence" (17). Desire that is "subterranean" holds the potential for ideological upheaval because if it works its way to the surface, it demands acknowledgment and disrupts sexual and gendered conventions. The challenge for the woman writer is to devise artistic strategies for re-visioning and voicing this desire, particularly when society's norms have perpetuated its unspoken condition.

In "The Sex Lives of Vegetables," Crozier unearths desire in a number of ways, the garden itself being one of the most effective vehicles for her process of feminist re-vision. Lane observes that "'Lorna has always had an erotic relationship to the landscape ... She has written poems about gardens ... and is a wonderfully sensitive, sensual woman so she has a palpable erotic relationship with everything in the world. The garden is just one aspect. She responds to it very viscerally'" (Litwin C4). This particular kind of engagement with the garden finds its way into the bodily and bawdy manner in which Crozier writes her vegetable-subjects. For instance, while female sexuality and the body have been obscured as the forbidden terrain "down there," Crozier re-visions the female vegetables through her explicit use of language, naming female genitalia when she describes the "clitoral" peas in the pod (111). The virginal peas may not (yet) engage in intercourse, but even so, Crozier exposes and identifies their potential bodily sources of pleasure. In this way, the sequence challenges readers to reflect upon how language shapes, contains, or alternatively denies certain experiences.

While an explicit use of language in her poetry is one means of unearthing desire, this process of re-visioning is also embodied in the vegetable-subjects themselves. Crozier's decorative vegetables dress up sexuality in unfamiliar ways, rendering that which is supposedly "natural" strange and disconcerting. The female vegetables may be kept under wraps and silenced, yet bodily knowledge counters the restrictive roles these vegetables are forced to fulfill when, like the lettuce, they are "Raised for one thing / and one thing only" (102). In her erotic vegetable patch, Crozier works to reveal alternative experiences derived from female pleasure and especially from plurality, as multiple layers of significance are accessed through language and the garden's growth in "Onions":

The onion loves the onion.
It hugs its many layers,
saying O, O, O,
each vowel smaller
than the last.
...
If Eve had bitten it
instead of the apple,
how different
Paradise. (104)

This "different / Paradise" undermines restrictions on the feminine and dramatically revises garden mythology.[6] With its multiple, orgasmic "O's," the onion offers Eve a different sensation and knowledge of both the world and herself. This alternative understanding is not singular but formed of the "many layers" of the onion, as Crozier locates desire in a bodily language, in the repeated yet changing vowel sounds. In this way, she signals language's facility for recreating the world by shifting away from male-centred knowledge (as symbolized by the patriarchal convention of the forbidden fruit of knowledge, or the apple) and imagining new forms and unconventional sources of knowing. Eve finds agency and delight in language and experiences she can bite into and enjoy for her own purposes. The result is not Adam and Eve's expulsion from the garden, but altogether different: the realization of an alternative "tasting" of language, pleasure, and the multilayered self.

While Crozier addresses female desire through a defamiliarized use of language, she also supplies an explicit, humourous vision when she grapples with paradigms of male sexual bravado. The poem "Carrots" features erotic male thrusting in an ineffectual attempt to penetrate the female underground of mother earth:

Carrots are fucking
the earth. A permanent
erection, they push deeper
into the damp and dark.
All summer long
they try so hard to please.
*Was it good for you,*
*was it good?* (99)

With their unrelenting drive, the carrots strive to gratify the "damp and dark" earth, which remains unresponsive to the carrots' questions regarding their sexual performance: "the earth won't answer" (99). The carrots' potency is diminished, then, as Crozier suggests that these ineffectual vegetables can only fulfill other appetites:

While you stroll through the garden
thinking *carrot cake,*
*carrots and onions in beef stew,*
*carrot pudding with caramel sauce,*
they are fucking their brains out
in the hottest part of the afternoon. (99)

The casual "stroll" of the "you" renders ridiculous the carrots' mindless sexual exertion. At the same time, the listing of possible desserts and main courses signals a role reversal, as the carrots are transformed from sexual subjects to objects of consumption, a shift in agency that unravels both their supposed supremacy over the feminized terrain and their endurance as "A permanent / erection."

Crozier's unabashed use of explicit, even vulgar, language, and her dismantling of myths of female containment and male sexual potency have made "The Sex Lives of Vegetables" highly controversial. On numerous occasions, she has reflected on the troubled reception of her garden sequence. In her essay "Speaking the Flesh" Crozier writes, "I heard from a teacher who was using McClelland & Stewart's *The New Canadian Poets* anthology in his Canadian literature course at a community college. He had been called to the principal's office because several students, men and women, had complained about my section in that book, particularly the poem, 'Carrots.' He didn't think he'd put the text on his course another year" (91). In an interview, Crozier also admits that people have walked out of her poetry readings in protest, and she has even received "the occasional 'hate letter' in the mail" (Meyer and O'Riordan 28). Cooke observes that the discomfort and anger with which Crozier's vegetable poems have been received derive from her addressing sexuality in a not only frank, but also humourous manner (93). Furthermore, Crozier's unconventional approach to a traditionally high art form raises eyebrows, in Cooke's view, as it "forces reviewers to come to terms with the relationship between humour, politics, and poetry" (93). For Crozier, humour is central to her strategy of feminist re-vision, as she describes it in "So Much Sorrow, and Then Pancakes After": "Treating our terrors as farce, mocking them, is a step towards recognizing our own power and the power of words ... In feminist poetry with a humourous twist, it is often anger, not laughter, that is the driving creative force producing poems both funny and deadly serious at the same time" (28–30). To laugh openly at sex within a poetic medium implicates Crozier in a kind of bawdiness not viewed as particularly feminine or even artistically respectable. In her interview with Barbara Carey, Crozier confirms this assessment of the gender politics at work in the troubled reception of the vegetable poems: "I think [people] don't expect a woman to be saying 'dirty words' out loud, in front of an audience," or, for that matter, in a poem (15).

Reviews of *The Garden Going On Without Us* often deem the vegetable poems a frivolous, ineffectual exercise, but the sheer notoriety of the sequence, as well as its 2008 nomination by *Literary Review of Canada* as one of the nation's most memorable poems, suggests it should not be so readily dismissed. When the poems first appeared, Shirley Neuman, for instance, called the work narrow-sighted in its preoccupation: "when the sequence asks the reader to play Peeping Tom on the entire garden in 17 poems that tell us about the joys of sex from artichoke to zucchini, she may long to put the pathetic phallacy behind her and to imagine what else might be going on in the garden without her" (32). Fraser Sutherland similarly describes the sequence as "clever but pointless" and considers it more of a parlor game than poetry; in other words, it is not to be taken seriously and the critical aspect of Crozier's humour is overlooked: "Okay everybody listen. The game is to imagine a vegetable as someone or something else. If turnips were politicians who would they be? Winner gets an extra helping of ratatouille" (D20). While some critics may see these poems as lacking, at the end of the day, the sequence has captured readers' imaginations and generated extreme, even hostile, reactions, including that of a politician, as Crozier relates in "Speaking the Flesh": "When the poems first came out in the Winnipeg-centred arts magazine *Border Crossings*, a Manitoba MLA took the issue to the legislature and demanded the government cease its funding of the publication. The poem he read [into Hansard] to demonstrate his accusation of pornography was 'Peas'" (91). Although Crozier uses an immodest female voice of sexual experience, she admits that this cannot be the sole reason behind the poems' troubled reception: "Call me naïve, but I thought the vegetable sequence was simply fun. Obviously, for many people it's more than that. Weird as it sounds, these common garden vegetables are threatening" (92). She struggles with this conclusion, however, and adds, "it can't be because they are doing it in the garden. There's more blatant sexuality on prime time TV than in these poems" (92). I believe that the dramatic response to the vegetable poems is in large part because the vegetables *are doing it* in the garden.

The absurd pairing of a seemingly asexual terrain with the display of sexuality forces readers to examine gender and sexuality without familiar, reassuring constructs. Ironically, through this pairing, both the garden and, most especially, human sexuality become denaturalized (or defamiliarized), as Crozier draws on the fantasy mode and renders the garden subversive, using its third nature role to great effect. In "When Fact Meets Fantasy," Caroline Heath argues that an "infusion of fantasy" has become present in recent years in prairie literature, and identifies Crozier as a poet who partakes in this mode of writing. In terms of Crozier's mandate of feminist re-vision, fantasy is particularly strategic because, as Rosemary Jackson reveals, "fantasy characteristically attempts to compensate for a sense of lack resulting from cultural constraints: it is a literature of desire, which seeks that which is experienced as absence and loss" (3). Fantasy is not necessarily about inventing another separate reality, but rather about "inverting elements of this world, re-combining its constitutive features in new relations to produce something strange, unfamiliar, and apparently 'new', absolutely 'other' and different" (8). Crozier states that the vegetable sequence is "political in the sense of being poems about very ordinary things" (Barbara Carey 15), and she has transformed the common kitchen garden in unusual and revealing ways. Part of the appeal of the fantasy mode is, according to Jackson's theory, that "natural" categories are challenged: "Gender differences of male and female are subverted and generic distinctions between animal, vegetable, and mineral are blurred in fantasy's attempt to 'turn over' 'normal' perceptions and undermine 'realistic' ways of seeing" (49).

"The Sex Lives of Vegetables" enacts, therefore, fantastical processes of contrast, inversion, and exposure. With the clitoral peas, the orgasmic onion, and the penile carrot, Crozier employs a seemingly benign and insignificant subject (vegetables) in order to access another decidedly more problematic subject (human sexuality) buried beneath patriarchal conventions, social propriety, and taboos.

By turning to the fantasy mode in her garden poetry, Crozier effectively brings together two expressive avenues that both have the potential to inform and transform our understanding of what, in Jackson's words, we "have taken to be real," or the norm, or "second nature" (22). As with the relational art of fantasy, the relational art of the garden has the capability to provide a new perspective on the human subject's way of being in, and ordering, the world. Whether formulated in plants or poetry, garden art is, to use John Dixon Hunt's words, "in large part defined by its response to the other natures and cultures that surround it (either literally or figuratively)" ("*Paragone*" 67). Crozier's aim to uncover sexual taboos by way of relationship and contrast counter the traditional understanding of gardening's and literature's cultivating, or refining, influence. While poetry from the eighteenth and nineteenth centuries was supposed to "dress and adorn Nature" as one of the three sister arts that tamed the unruly (Hunt and Willis 11), Crozier's post-modern poetry of re-vision both undresses and redresses the garden at the level of language, denaturalizing gender paradigms of sexuality in a paradoxically earthy nature. Crozier enacts this process of exposure in both literal and literary ways through a veritable striptease that flaunts human sexuality through common, yet tauntingly decorative, garden vegetables.

"The Sex Lives of Vegetables" introduces the notion of creative process through the unexpected procreative activity of the vegetable-subjects and vegetable-scribes. In subsequent collections, Crozier works to harness even further the creativity of the garden by transforming the human subject (in her poems) into a gardener-poet. The garden becomes not merely a topic or site of poetic exploration but rather a figurative model for her own artistic medium, with gardening aligning itself with the writing and re-writing (or re-visioning) process. This can be seen in such poems as "Gardens" from *Inventing the Hawk* (1992), where many gardens exist simultaneously: in the earth, in the imagination, and on the page through the lines (or garden "rows") of the poem and its poetic devices (117–18). Further to this point, in the chapbook of ghazals *Eye Witness* (1993), which is reproduced as a long poem in *Everything Arrives at the Light* (1995) under the new title "If I Call Stones Blue," Crozier makes an explicit connection between writing and gardening. Relating the experience of encountering a new second nature after moving from the prairies to British Columbia, Crozier emphasizes the poet-speaker's discordant vision in relation to a burgeoning west coast environment. Unsure how to "garden" in this new climate, the displaced poet is frustrated in her efforts to turn her infertile imagination into a creative process and product through the germination of a poetry journal that records the seasonal changes:

> Something doesn't bloom,
> doesn't blossom.
>
> Keep a weather journal.
> Write: first day of spring.
>
> Write: the naked gardens of my skin.
> Write: no buds on this tree. (88–9)

If poems are "gardens" and writing is "gardening," it follows, then, that

Crozier's own poetry must be open to an ongoing process. Thus Crozier has reworked some of her previously published poems and transformed them into new creations. For instance, the long poem "If I Call Stones Blue" in *Everything Arrives at the Light* provides some of the re-visioned lines for a new poem (in the same collection) entitled "A Good Day to Start a Journal," which follows the transplanted poet-speaker during her second spring on the west coast, still recording the weather but with a new perspective. "A Good Day to Start a Journal" finds a parallel to the gardener-poet's own writing in the work of her "lover in the garden" as he "turns and turns the earth" (135) until the previous image of "no buds on this tree" (from "If I Call Stones Blue" and, before that, *Eye Witness*) transforms into "one blossom" (135). By the conclusion of the poem, her understanding of the past, the seasons, her body, and her writing all "turn / a page" through this renewing vision (135).

"A Good Day to Start a Journal" demonstrates Crozier's delight in the fact that published works are potentially never finalized, and she adopts this same approach when she enters the literary "gardens" of others either as a source of inspiration, by seeing her poetry transformed in creative projects undertaken by various artists, or as a palimpsestic writer in her own right, creatively tending her intertextual poems. "The Sex Lives of Vegetables," in particular, has proven to be fertile ground for other artists, with Crozier collaborating in these projects to varying degrees. Between 1988 and 1990, she provided creative input to Lise Melhorn-Boe, an artist based in Ontario, who reproduced and manipulated "The Sex Lives of Vegetables" into one of her published projects. The biography on Melhorn-Boe's website identifies her as a "books and sculptural bookworks" artist and her online archive features photographs and descriptions of her bookworks, including *The Sex Lives of Vegetables: A Seed Catalogue* (1990): "The text is superimposed on colour-copies of these vegetables. The handmade paper pages are accordion-folded, cut in the shape of vegetables and enclosed in a handmade paper folding case with a garden-twine closure."[7] In a personal letter addressed to Crozier in 1990, Melhorn-Boe reveals the pastiche effect of her composition-in-progress: "I have written my own seed catalogue, and inserted among the various kinds of vegetables, you'll find your poems. I like the contrast between the straight-forward information and the humour and surprise of the poems." The letter outlines further the ways in which Melhorn-Boe manipulates Crozier's poetry into a palimpsest: breaking some of the original lines to fit the dimensions of her cut-out pages (the vegetable images and silhouettes); rearranging the poems into alphabetical order as "it made more sense seed-catalogue-wise"; reclassifying "Yams" under "Sweet Potatoes," since "[t]echnically, yams are not sweet potatoes"; and assigning revised titles since the vegetable poems are "varieties" in Melhorn-Boe's seed catalogue format. Mailing both a hand-drawn illustration and physical mock-up of her catalogue, Melhorn-Boe invites feedback, to which Crozier offers both praise for the new creation and a number of suggestions, including a title revision: "Hardy Nantes" in place of Melhorn-Boe's "Nantes Long Hard" (for the original poem "Carrots") in order to create "something that puns but not so excessively" (30 May 1990). From a distance, Crozier clearly enjoys participating in another artist's reworking of her poems as "The Sex Lives of Vegetables" is both textually and physically transformed into a book sculpture, a version of a seed catalogue that is reminiscent of Robert Kroetsch's suggestion that a young Canadian imagination (without established literary models) had to first encounter the material environment, often in the form of palimpsestic objects (Banting 95). In the case of Melhorn-Boe, her contemporary garden palimpsest, as both layered, sculptural object and text, operates in a somewhat different manner as she initially drew her creative inspiration not from the physical environment, but from a textual source (Crozier's poems), a literary garden tradition.[8]

As further evidence of the highly generative potential of Crozier's sequence, "The Sex Lives of Vegetables" was also transformed into a dramatic palimpsest in September 2007 when the University of Victoria's Student Alternative Theatre Company (SATCO) staged a production under the direction of Barb Hall at the Phoenix Theatre's McIntyre Studio.[9] As director, writer (of the adaptation), producer,

FIGURE 5.1 SATCO dramatic production of Lorna Crozier's *The Sex Lives of Vegetables*, 2007

and co-choreographer, Hall refers to the piece as a series of "veggie-vignettes" with the various characters dancing or "reciting the poems to music" (Letter to author). In a telephone interview, Hall described how during the play, Crozier's poems were projected onto a giant white projector screen, setting the stage for their embodied performances. "Lettuce" (the subservient courtesan) was brought to life with both a dancing actor dressed in a lettuce costume and a video in the background featuring a close-up of a mouth devouring romaine lettuce. As part of the poems' adaptation into this dramatic, multi-media garden "plot," Hall used the scarlet runner beans (the scribes) as hosts who took the audience on a garden tour throughout the course of the play, and also incorporated the story of a boy, who experiences puberty and eventually transforms into a zucchini. Similar to Melhorn-Boe's book-works palimpsest and her seed catalogue's re-titling of the poems into "varieties" of vegetables, Hall's dramatic palimpsest bestowed human names onto parts of the garden when the poem "Yams" was recreated through "video footage of a Yam named Neil in love."[10] This process of renaming (or effacement, in the case of Kroetsch's unnaming of Traill) is one strategy for making a garden palimpsest an artist's own, as Hall reflects that when she first read Crozier's sequence she "could see the characters" in both their beauty and darkness, and wanted to develop them further on stage (Interview). Hall envisioned the production as a "celebration of the poems" and how they enable readers "to look at veggies in a greater way."[11] Drawing upon the garden's critical third nature that illuminates not only what is "second nature" (or taken for granted and habitual), but also what we are uncomfortable in perceiving, the SATCO play purposely exposed some of the more troubling aspects of Crozier's sequence through scenes of violence and even pedophilia, or "pea-dophilia" in the case of the zucchini. Hall reflects that at the time of the play's production, she was especially interested in "experiment-ing with collective creation in theatre" and was grateful for Crozier's support and generosity in "giving away the poems" so that the stu-dents could interpret and perform the piece. She also remembers that Crozier participated in the final dress rehearsal by reading "The Sex Lives of Vegetables" to cast members to inspire their performance.

It is precisely in these kinds of ventures – opening up old texts to new creativity – where Crozier (as well as her fellow artists and admir-ers) encounters the paradox that is a garden: being both product and process. But nowhere is this creative interplay more exemplary than in her most sustained experimentation with literary palimpsest: *A Saving Grace: The Collected Poems of Mrs. Bentley* (1996).

## A Pioneer Garden Palimpsest: Crozier's Mrs Bentley

In *A Saving Grace: The Collected Poems of Mrs. Bentley* (1996), Crozier explores the intersection of gardening and re-writing through the genre of palimpsest when she responds to Sinclair Ross' 1941 novel *As for Me and My House*. In taking a seemingly finalized, published prod-uct and submitting it to a new creative process, Crozier participates in a Canadian tradition of pioneer garden palimpsests. As we saw in chapters one and two, Margaret Atwood and Robert Kroetsch rework the texts of Susanna Moodie and Catharine Parr Traill, respectively. The published works of these nineteenth-century writers plant seeds of future creativity for contemporary authors, with the garden serving as a model of this renewed growth. Cognizant of this tradition, Crozier pays tribute in the poem "Wilderness" when her poetic persona, Mrs Bentley, identifies herself as another pioneer figure in a different kind of landscape:

> Like Mrs. Moodie I could say
> the wilderness moved inside me
> but where there is no bush,
> the wilderness is different. (77)

Crozier likens her Mrs Bentley to Atwood's "Mrs. Moodie," yet she also acknowledges that she is toiling in an altogether different "wilderness": the prairie dust bowl and its imaginative tradition. As with Atwood's "The Bush Garden" and Kroestch's "Pumpkin: A Love Poem," Crozier's *A Saving Grace* reveals that a literary garden is both a product and a process, and an art of milieu. Atwood's and Kroetsch's recreations serve different purposes: for Atwood, Moodie captures thematic interpretations of Canadian literature popular during the 1970s, including the garrison mentality and survival, while Kroetsch explores the position of the post-colonial, post-modern poet attempting to carve out his own space and identity amidst his predecessors. Crozier brings her own interests – her pluralist feminism, practice of re-vision, and garden poetics – to bear on Ross' novel, a book she long ago credited, in an interview with Doris Hillis, with making her "head fl[y] open" as a young writer: "I think my education began then. It was the discovery of my own country" (6). In this line of palimpsestic poets – Kroetsch, Atwood, and Crozier – early nineteenth-century and twentieth-century texts are reworked, creating textual products that are very different from the originals.

In its capacity to respond to a previously existing text and alter the value scheme, a palimpsest has obvious gendered implications in terms of exposing or obscuring various ideologies, experiences, and perspectives operating within its composite discourse. Gérard Genette's foundational work *Palimpsests: Literature in the Second Degree* describes palimpsest as "any relationship uniting a text B (which I shall call *hypertext*) to·an earlier text A (I shall, of course, call it the *hypotext*), upon which it is grafted in a manner that is not that of commentary" (5).[12] A palimpsest "is a transformative process" (5), as a hypertext relates in some capacity to an original source text, expanding upon, condensing, or altering the hypotext through such devices as satire and parody (5). In her gendered model of the genre, Patricia J. Thompson argues that the alternative layers of the palimpsest are either subtle agents of suppression, or are suppressed in their own right: "The patriarchal palimpsest that 'lies beneath' feminist texts often influences the visible thoughts or ideas. I maintain there may be yet another palimpsest – a hestian palimpsest – that remains invisible beneath the surface of patriarchal texts" and masculine value systems (75). Thompson derives her notion of a "hestian palimpsest" from the Greek goddess Hestia, a "sedate guardian of the hestia, or hearthfire ... Hestia is thus associated with the Family and the systems of action necessary to sustain and nurture it" (xv). In other words, a hestian palimpsest can potentially bring to light feminine perspectives on the personal, familial, and private – those perspectives that, according to Thompson, have been subsumed by patriarchal discourse and its traditional valuing of the public domain.[13]

Thompson's model of a hestian palimpsest converges well with Crozier's own pluralist feminism and her conscious efforts to reveal what lies below the surface, particularly in regard to women's experiences and the domestic realm. In her feminist poetic re-writing of Ross' novel, Crozier has suggested that one of her objectives was to develop some of the silences, or muted aspects of the original character. In an interview at Simon Fraser University with Clea Ainsworth, Crozier states that she wanted "to give more body to ... Mrs. Bentley" (n.p.). Crozier does not consider this silence around the original Mrs Bentley's physical self and sexuality as "a fault in the novel," but rather that "it was just something [she] wanted to try" (n.p.). The primary departure from Ross' novel is Crozier's enabling of her Mrs Bentley to expose additional personal experiences and taboos through confessional poems, such as "Sins of Omission," "Confession," and "The Truth." The poem "Sins of Omission" provides an unabashed account of life's details, a list of things Mrs Bentley did not mention in her journal (in Ross' novel), such as "toiletries, relatives, bankers, / favorite books, hobos, yeast infections" (51).

Part of giving voice to Mrs Bentley's previously muted experiences as a woman involves Crozier's incorporation of other stories of the prairies during the 1930s. In the acknowledgments to *A Saving Grace,* Crozier identifies her many published and unpublished sources for her palimpsest: "Mrs. Bentley's journals, as well as numerous local histories, Barry Broadfoot's *Next-Year Country: Voices of Prairie People,* and Edward McCourt's *Saskatchewan* helped give me the flavour of the Depression era. As important were my mother's stories and the prodigious memory of my aunt, Gladys Hovde, who graciously tolerated my many questions" (93). At one point in the collection, in the poem "Mrs. Bentley," the names of Crozier's mother ("Peg") and aunt actually circulate as possible first names for the unnamed Mrs Bentley, suggesting that behind this persona lie countless other untold, personal stories of women whose histories have been muted or unwritten.[14] In his review of *A Saving Grace*, Michael Holmes argues that Crozier fails to make her persona "come alive like Atwood's poetic medium or [Michael] Ondaatje's romantic antihero" (66). He locates this failure precisely in the lack of a clearly defined identity, as exhibited in the poem "Mrs. Bentley" with its multiple suggestions of names: "And nowhere in these pages / can you find my name. / Gladys, Louise, Madeline?" (83–4). I read this poem differently in that the line breaks create ambiguity as both a negative statement and a question, with the inclusion of possible names revealing Crozier's interest in palimpsest and, especially, plurality. The names reflect her re-visioning: her desire, as she states in the Ainsworth interview, "to populate the town with more characters and stories than were available in [Ross'] text" (n.p.). The gesture is reminiscent of Gabrielle Roy's and Carol Shields' recuperative mandates, writing women's lives spent in, and expressed through, the garden, yet not necessarily recorded. Together, the evocation of multiple names, the inclusion of women's bodily and quotidian experiences, and the fact that the Mrs Bentley persona writes so creatively and self-assertively render Crozier's palimpsest a transformation of Ross' novel.

Crozier's most compelling re-working is that she makes Mrs Bentley a conscious artist through the subtitle of the work: "The Collected Poems of Mrs. Bentley." Traditionally, critics consider *As for Me and My House* a novel of failed artistry. In "Disunity as Unity," Kroetsch describes Ross' text as "a set of diary entries about an unwritten novel" (24). Ironically, just as the dejected minister, Philip Bentley, fails to paint or write, Mrs Bentley creates art in her journal "without recognizing it" (25). Pamela Banting sees this erasure of artistry working on numerous levels: "The artfulness of writing in *As for Me and My House* is hidden under at least four 'veils.' In the first place, generally speaking diaries are not considered to be art, and this is especially so of the diaries of housewives. Secondly, within the particular form the narrative takes in this novel, books disappear. That is, Sinclair Ross' writing is under erasure, Philip Bentley's has been erased, and what the reader is given instead is the diary of the failed writer's wife! And her attention is deflected away from herself and toward her husband" ("Miss A and Mrs. B" 31). In some respects, Crozier's palimpsest creates a slight erasure of Crozier as author through the subtitle that names Mrs Bentley as poet, an identification which clearly differs from Atwood's subtitle for her collection on Moodie: "Poems by Margaret Atwood." Where this contemporary reworking of Mrs Bentley truly departs from Ross' novel, however, is in its explicit presentation of its persona not just as a poet, but as a poet of palimpsest. This Mrs Bentley reworks Ross' original story (and other sources) as she consciously writes, erases, and rewrites, creating layers of meaning. In the poem "Sins of Omission," for instance, the divulgence of a miscarriage becomes a fragmented statement, itemized to the point of being buried not just within the garden "where nothing grows" but within the list itself:

> ... what came out
> of me that night, chinook arches, grasshopper
> plagues, the white enamel pan Philip
> carried to the garden, Bennett buggies,
> chokecherries, burying what was in it,
> box socials, potato moonshine,
> where nothing grows (51)

Mrs Bentley's confessional poem operates as a site of both composition, in her writing down of the details of her life, and decomposition, in her obscuring – her literal and figurative burying – of the "truth" in the strata of her garden and the progressive lines of her poem. Creating layers, only to work through them, this poet-persona undertakes a simultaneous exposure and concealment of herself. Especially central to this study's concerns is the fact that Crozier locates Mrs Bentley's project as a poet of palimpsest in the figurative space of the garden. While it is an appropriate choice (and a not altogether unexpected one) when one considers Crozier's abiding interest in the garden as a model of interplay between product and process, it is also a decidedly ironic choice when one reflects on the original Mrs Bentley's prairie garden.

# Sinclair Ross: Writing the Depression-Era Garden

Described by Ross as "bare, inert, impaled by the rays of the sun" (119), the garden in the novel is instrumental in symbolizing suppressed domestic desires and failed creativity. A site of a woman's work (and occasionally men's), the original garden is intimately related to Mrs Bentley's barrenness, her empty flirtation with Paul Kirby (the school-teacher), the emotional and sexual drought of her marriage to Philip (the town's minister), and the frustrated artistry that circulates in the novel. For Ross' Mrs Bentley, the fertile life that the garden is supposed to represent is but a distant dream and memory, painfully suppressed. She discloses this fact when she recalls her miscarriage: "I had a garden once. The bright seed packages on display in one of the stores this morning reminded me. It was the year after the baby was born" (59). Paul Denham notes that Mrs Bentley's subsequent attempt to garden in the drought-ridden town of Horizon becomes a reflection of her childlessness and marital ineptitude: "In [eleven years] Mrs Bentley has tried only once before to grow a garden, the summer after the baby died. In realistic terms this is remarkably slovenly housewifery; only in symbolic terms does it make sense, the single withered garden paralleling the single dead child" (121). Making another attempt during the drought of the Great Depression, Mrs. Bentley encounters mostly failure and death, as she rakes the dead plants and scatters the seeds of one surviving poppy as if, in Philip's words, "Casting the ashes to the wind" (138). Rather than revitalizing the marriage, the garden has almost the opposite effect. Just as Philip confines himself to his study, Mrs Bentley admits to enclosing herself in the space of her garden to maintain both emotional and physical distance from her husband: "If I don't have the garden he's going to hate the sight of me by fall" (58).

Unfortunately, this lack of intimacy is the inverse of what Mrs

Bentley's ideal garden would entail: a site of romantic union, a partnership of fecundity. Not surprisingly, it is from her garden that Mrs Bentley hears the music of the saxophone from the community dance hall and "imagin[es] the couples moving round the floor" (64). In contrast, she remains "shut away from life, too old, forgotten" and does not have the opportunity to dance with the "helpless, wooden" Philip who states halfheartedly, "I suppose if I knew how, we could dance just a little ourselves out here [in the garden]" (64). The Bentleys are a pathetic semblance of marital partnership, and when the couple temporarily adopts the young boy Steve, Mrs Bentley suggests that there is a dysfunctional, complicated "growth" at work underneath the appearance of this makeshift family: "Philip, Steve and I. It's such a trim efficient sign; it's such a tough, deep-rooted tangle that it hides" (81).

Unlike Mrs Bentley's lack of companionship with her husband, other more productive yet decidedly short-lived pairings take place in the "garden." She recalls, for instance, a time when she was a young, aspiring pianist, accompanying the talented violin player Percy Glenn. She played Debussy's *Gardens in the Rain* with Percy and he encouraged her musicianship (102). Now in drought-ridden Horizon, the only mutual garden work Mrs Bentley partakes in is with Paul, who helps her to widen her window sills for her geranium pots (92), and to clear away the dust from her bean plants (100). Responding to Ross' original character in the essay "The Fear of Women in Prairie Fiction," Kroetsch concludes, "Mrs. Bentley must come close to being the most incompetent gardener in all of fiction" (77). Although Crozier's Mrs Bentley maintains this dubious reputation in a literal sense (nothing grows in her garden), she nevertheless undergoes a significant transformation in her new role as a poet who reworks her textual terrain, enabling new meaning to circulate and develop. For this re-imagined Mrs Bentley, words, poetry, and in particular the palimpsest genre are her means of expressing this newfound fecundity.

## Mrs Bentley and Her Palimpsestic "Garden"

Ross' Mrs Bentley finds in Paul a sympathetic partner who temporarily shares the literal and imaginative space of her garden by reading below the surface of things. For example, during a scene in Mrs Bentley's dismal garden, Paul reveals that language hides alternative, forgotten meanings: "But while words socially come up in the world, most of them morally go down. Retaliate, for instance: once you could retaliate a favour or kindness ... but memories being short for benefits and long for grievances, its sense was gradually perverted" (101). According to the *Oxford English Dictionary*, the verb "pervert" means "[t]o turn aside (a process, action, text, etc.) from a correct state, course or aim," or in other words, to "turn upside down."[15] In the context of this study, it is also important to note that the root of "pervert" – "vert" – means "[t]o turn up, root up (the ground)" or "to turn or twist out of the normal position."[16] Paul's attention to perversion is about unearthing words' original meanings and highlighting society's corrupting influence on language. Drawing on etymology in his interactions with Mrs Bentley, he entertains her with the flirtatious innuendo of words like "garden," "cupidity," "erotic," "venereal," and "aphrodisiac" (100–1). While this linguistic foreplay between Paul and Mrs Bentley may be an attempt to break ground in this new relationship and reveals an underlying attraction, the flirtation remains unconsummated in the novel. Fittingly, Mrs Bentley's actual garden fails to thrive despite Paul's assistance, just as Paul also relinquishes transforming words into new possibilities of meaning, as many critics contend.[17]

It is this partnership, this shared interest in layers of meaning and significance, that Crozier develops in order to turn Mrs Bentley into a gardener-poet. In the poem "Garden," Crozier re-writes the scene in the novel when Paul uses his exposure of "perverted" etymology to flirt with Mrs Bentley. Her Mrs Bentley not only entertains Paul's verbal propositions while working in her garden, but also counters with her own sexual innuendo:

> Out of the blue
> while he helps me
> carry water to the garden,
> Paul says *breast*
> used to rhyme with *priest*.
> ...
> He claims two hundred years ago
> the pronunciation changed
> to the way we say it now.
> Another theory is that *breast*
> comes from *brustian*,
> *to bud or sprout*.
>
> I make a joke about the garden,
> say it's more like a priest,
> the rows of seedlings
> abstemious and thin. Paul
> smiles, but nervously.
> We've gone too far. (41)

In the novel, Ross' protagonist merely comments on Paul's interest in the roots of words. In contrast, Crozier's Mrs Bentley actively engages in sexual flirtation and verbal foreplay, choosing to thwart the origins of some of the words that Paul traces in order to serve her own purposes. In her joke, she disassociates her husband (the minister) from her own body (signified by the original rhyme between "priest" and "breast" that Paul identifies) and proceeds to undermine Philip's sexuality by associating him, rather than herself, with the inert garden and its ineffectual seedlings. Words are a powerful means of reshaping her world according to her own desires. Reveling in the transformative potential of the word made flesh, she later admits inside the house, "it only takes a word for me / to bud and moisten, brustian" (42). Here, Mrs Bentley is intent on working creatively and perversely despite her circumstances, as her sexual innuendo elicits her own arousal. She remains "Mrs. B in her celibate garden," yet her subtle renaming of herself with a single initial both elides her married identity (and possibly her vows), and suggestively recalls the "B" words of "breast" and "brustian" with their erotic associations.

Instead of maintaining Mrs Bentley as a figure of barrenness and unrealized (or unrecognized) creativity, Crozier transforms Ross' character into a poet of generative potential. This Mrs Bentley exhibits a consciousness previously curtailed in the novel as she re-imagines her garden as a textual palimpsest through which she provides subversive commentary on her marriage and communicates her emotions and desires. Whereas Ross' original character claims that she needs her garden and the (unproductive) work she undertakes within it to escape from her skewed world and to reassert her unfulfilled ideals ("And that's why I need the garden ... The house huddles me. I need a tussle with the wind to make me straight again"; Ross 58–9), Crozier's Mrs Bentley instead uses her textual garden as a highly critical, reflective third nature, revealing her dark vision through the artistic expression of the deficiencies in her life. She foregrounds not her "straight," but rather "bent" perspective as an artist of perversion: turning the world upside down and away from its "natural" purpose and original order.

The art of perversion that Crozier develops has its roots in Ross' novel. In one of the final diary entries in *As for Me and My House*, Mrs Bentley describes spreading dozens of drawings on the table and calling Philip to view her selection. It is her wish that Philip capture in his art a palimpsest layered with original desires and life's superimposed realities: "I'd like to see what he'd do with his own expression – if he'd catch it all, the dreams that are there, underneath, like the first writing of a palimpsest, and their paraphrase by life as well" (202). While Mrs Bentley yearns for the register of changing emotions brought about by experience and time, Philip argues for a more detached vision, focused purely on form. He instructs his wife to turn his artwork upside down in order to see it correctly, to judge through a process of defamiliarization as to whether or not the form of the work is effective and in proportion:

> "You can't be detached about your own work," he said presently. "You feel it too much – and the right way is only to see it. That's your trouble, too. These things all mean something to you because you've lived in these little Main Streets – with me while I was doing them. You're looking at them, but you're not really seeing them. You're only remembering something that happened to you there. But in art, memories and associations don't count. A good way to test a picture is to turn it upside down. That knocks all the sentiment out of it, leaves you with just the design and form." (202)

While Philip is self-assured in his detached assessment of art and its proper interpretation, Mrs Bentley appears unwilling to engage in this debate: "I gathered [the drawings] up then, and trying to laugh, said the exhibition was closing for lack of an appreciative public" (202). In his essay "'Turn It Upside Down': The Right Perspective on *As for Me and My House*," Wilfred Cude categorizes Philip's and Mrs Bentley's artistic visions according to gender, defining them as rational and emotional respectively, and ultimately discrediting Mrs Bentley. According to Cude, Mrs Bentley misuses art and her music as "sensual snares" for the people in her life (470). Alternatively, Philip offers the most valid aesthetic vision: "the one enduring response to art is intellectual: a work must be appraised strictly as a construct" (469). Cude censures Mrs Bentley, and because she is reticent to challenge her husband or assert her point of view, she gives herself an air of uncertainty when evaluating art, its purpose, and its effect.

In direct contrast to the novel's portrayal, Crozier's Mrs Bentley repudiates any argument for emotional detachment through her own artistic invention that is at once visceral and analytical. The original conversation between husband and wife occurs at the conclusion of Ross' novel, but Crozier recreates it near the beginning of her collection, changing the chronology of the original narrative as a way of framing the poems and promoting Mrs Bentley's perspective. In the poem "Confession," Mrs Bentley recounts Philip's instruction "to turn / his drawings upside down" (15), but she refuses to turn away from her own interpretation. Finally, she breaks her silence to the reader (but not to Philip) and speaks her opinion on her husband's artistic shortcomings:

> I've never said it
> but there's something missing,
> something about this place
> he hasn't caught. (15)

As a poet, Mrs Bentley objects to Philip's "upside down" vision of cool detachment. His focus on pure visual form and impersonality leaves her longing for the artistic process of an earth-bound creator: engaged, immediate, and sensual:

> His hand is connected
> only to his eye
> as if he were the god
> who's forsaken all his creatures
> …
> forgetting what his hands
> must have felt
> as he pulled them from the mud. (16)

Philip is "connected / only to his eye": a phrase suggestive of the visual, the aesthetic form, and the singular "I" perspective. He forgets the feel of mud, the sensations and emotions of past experience, but Mrs Bentley, in her self-titled poem, declares, "I've walked through this story / in housedresses and splay- / footed rubbers" (83). In her self-portrait, she is situated in her daily, material existence: in the places in which she lives, in her experiences and emotions, and in her composite use of multiple sources. This "splay-footed" gardener-poet traverses and spreads out across her textual gardens; unlike Philip, she is very much a part of her creations. While Ross' protagonist longs for a palimpsest of emotional variety in her husband's work, Crozier's Mrs Bentley consciously produces a layered art in words that directly counters her husband's position and ultimately results in a transformed representation of the Bentley marriage.

Superimposing her vision onto Philip's, Mrs Bentley in effect re-writes his "upside down" objectivity according to her own mandate. This rewriting results in what Genette refers to as "transvaluation": a shift in the value scheme of the original text (367). Indeed, Crozier's Mrs Bentley goes as far as to pervert Philips' intended notion of an "upside down" critique, using it instead as a highly personal and intertextual means of critical expression. The result is that these garden poems communicate the degenerative (or upside-down) growth of the Bentley marriage and her emotional devastation over Philip's adulterous affair. Mrs Bentley accomplishes this task by drawing upon the "Song of Songs" from the Old Testament to create a subversive, layered expression of her sexual desires, the failure of her marriage, and her visceral response to her husband's rejection of her.

According to Alicia Ostriker, the "Song of Songs" (also referred to as the "Song of Solomon" or "Canticles") has long been interpreted as an allegorical text praising the love and devotion "between God and Israel, love of Christ for Church, or for the individual Christian soul, or the mystical marriage of God and the Virgin Mary" (38). In addition to being a song of praise, the "Song of Songs" also functions as a "countertext" in that it is one of the most erotic passages of the Bible, celebrating sensual love between husband and wife, or even unwed lovers (43). The lush pastoral tropes that form the "Song of Songs" foster a sense of natural intimacy. The woman and her sexual purity are a "garden inclosed," a "spring shut up, a fountain sealed" (4.12). These property metaphors may seem to subordinate the woman, but biblical scholars, such as J. Cheryl Exum, note that the female speaker can be read as a non-conformist, autonomous subject active in the pursuit of her beloved: "[the Song of Songs] boldly celebrates female desire … A woman initiates sexual encounters; a woman roams the streets looking for the lover; a woman speaks openly about her desire" (24). As an intertextual layer of Mrs Bentley's poetic palimpsest, the "Song of Songs" resonates with her yearning for her husband and "a watered garden" of mutual love and desire in her aptly titled poem "I Feed on

Thistles" (48). Unfortunately, all that thrives in Mrs Bentley's world is this drought-tolerant plant, a Christian symbol of suffering.

Mrs Bentley uses scripture to infuse a tone of reverence in her appeal for love, yet she also contextualizes her own song of songs, entitled "Comfort Me," according to her particular setting and circumstances – the second nature landscape of the prairies. Instead of adhering solely to the biblical references to apples and "roe" (Eurasian deer), Mrs Bentley incorporates the flora and fauna of Saskatchewan:[18]

> *Comfort me with apples,*
> *for I am sick with love.*
> Comfort me with sweet grass,
> wound around your fingers
> for I am sick with love.
> Let me follow the antelope's
> trails into the pastures
> of your flesh, let me lie
> where the graceful one is sleeping. (43)

Imagining a figurative prairie pasture of her beloved's body, Mrs Bentley yearns to "lie / where the graceful one is sleeping," and both meanings of the word "lie" are possible because the poem quickly deteriorates from its pastoral foundation, ultimately failing to communicate mutual or honest love. In "Tips for Writers" Crozier has stated that one must "Lie, lie lie, to get to the truth" (12),[19] and here, Mrs Bentley constructs a tender palimpsest that paradoxically reveals the cold realities of her marriage and her spiteful sentiment towards her unfaithful husband. Later in "Comfort Me," the commanding phrase "suckle the bud that never blooms, / for I am sick with love" sparks a profusion of dark associations: her heartache that has developed into "sick" obsession, her unrealized maternity, and her thwarted passion. The poem continues with the sad acknowledgement, "Lo, winter is past, / the seeds have been scattered / and the rains do not come" (43). These images of infertility and drought are in keeping with Ross' original setting of the story during the Great Depression, and provide a direct contrast to the "Song of Songs'" recounting of seasonal renewal: "For, lo, the winter is past, the rain is over and gone; The flowers appear on the earth; the time of the singing of birds is come" (2.11–12). In this way, Mrs Bentley divulges her status as one who lives askew or "bent." Her "sick" love prohibits her from being "the upright [who] love thee" as the original "Song of Songs" describes (1.4); instead, she offers a perverted, "unnatural" perspective, overturning any straightforward declarations of love or desire.

After being denied any horticultural tropes through the cumulative failures of her marriage, her garden, and her barren body, Crozier's Mrs Bentley ultimately generates a textual, palimpsestic "garden" in the poem "Judith." In this poem, she lays claim to Philip's "upside down" vision in order to produce an alternative, subjective, and critical representation of her marriage. "Judith" begins in a dream-like state. This reflects both Ross' novel, in which Dr Bird prescribes Mrs Bentley sleeping powders that "stupefy" (161) her and induce her into a frightening reverie before she wakes to search for Philip, and the "Song of Songs," in which the female speaker rises from her sleep to search for her beloved: "By night on my bed I sought him whom my soul loveth: I sought him, but I found him not. I will rise now, and go about the city in the streets" (3.1–2). In arguing that the "Song of Songs" functions as the female speaker's inner discourse, Daphna V. Arbel comments that the nighttime images from the biblical verse are not from real events but rather from dreams: "Such a search by night is highly unrealistic, considering the accepted norms of the writer's patriarchal society.

Thus her introduction, 'upon my bed at night', is necessary. It characterizes this experience as a mental search in which she is not passive, as in a dream, but active, as in a personal process of imagination" (92). In a similarly altered state of consciousness that harkens back to both source texts, Crozier's Mrs Bentley awakens with a fever and leaves her bedroom in search of her husband, only to encounter his sexual betrayal:

> That night I moved through my fever
> as if it were a house; remember
> the game you played as a child?
> Lying on your back in bed you stared
> till the ceiling became the floor.
> You stepped over a ledge
> through the doorway, circled
> the lightbulb, stem tall as a tulip's.
>
> *The beams of our house are of cedar*
> *and our rafters of fir.*
>
> That's where I was, on the ceiling,
> looking down. They weren't in the woodshed. (57)

Mrs Bentley fully inhabits her fever-induced poetic reverie "as if it were a house," an image that highlights the unhealthy (or altered) state of both herself and the Bentley marriage. Although she views her world from the ceiling, she does not perceive as Philip does: as a detached god with his hand connected only to his eye/I. Instead, the upside-down appearance of her home is an embodiment of Mrs Bentley's thwarted desires and the reality of her husband's sexual betrayal.

Walking across the ceiling, Mrs Bentley notes the structural aspects of her home: the tulip lightbulb, wooden beams, and fir rafters. Her home has been turned into a third nature, a "garden" experienced and placed in an unnatural direction. Here, the italicized passages from the "Song of Songs" are reduced to mere description, as the original figurative meaning is displaced by Mrs Bentley's skewed vision of an even more skewed domestic circumstance: that is, the act of adultery she is about to witness below her. The biblical verse no longer functions as part of the female speaker's address to her beloved: "Behold, thou art fair, my beloved, yea, pleasant: also our bed is green. The beams of our house are cedar, and our rafters of fir" (1.16–17). Instead, Mrs Bentley's home is one that houses sexual corruption, its "green" growth perverted.

As Mrs Bentley's upside-down palimpsest progresses, her writing elides both Ross' novel and the "Song of Songs" as she transforms the meanings of these original texts to suit her own purposes. She witnesses Judith and Philip in the sexual act (as opposed to just hearing them as she does in the novel) and places them in the kitchen, not in the woodshed (as Ross does) in order to highlight the domestic betrayal and the selfish appeasing of sexual appetites:

… It made it worse somehow,
in my kitchen. He sat naked on a chair.
She straddled him.

*He feedeth among the lilies.*

I seemed to float above their heads
though I could clearly see
the swell and gleam of her buttocks
and hear him groan.

*I am my beloved's*
*and his desire is towards me.*

My whole body ached (58)

The italicized, offset passages from the "Song of Songs" create a visual effect of layered lines in this palimpsest, but it is the further manipulation of the biblical verse that reveals a corrupted garden vision. Mrs Bentley actually reverses the order of the lines in order to overturn and distort their meaning. In the "Song of Songs," verse 2.16 states, "My beloved is mine, and I am his: he feedeth among the lilies." The female speaker describes mutual rapture and concludes with the image of herself as her lover's garden of purity, suggested through the lilies. In Mrs Bentley's poem, however, the garden image opens (rather than concludes) the biblical passage. Furthermore, the "Song of Songs" becomes fragmented when Crozier inserts the account of adultery between the biblical lines that once communicated commitment and fidelity. After witnessing her husband and Judith having sexual intercourse, Mrs Bentley writes *"He feedeth among the lilies,"* to accentuate Philip's self-indulgent betrayal. The lily passage – severed from the opening words of the original verse and inverted from its original order – transforms into an upside-down, visceral expression of Mrs Bentley's devastation: "My whole body ached." When the words, *"I am my beloved's / and his desire is towards me"* are finally uttered in the poem, the voice is rendered ambiguous. Although the passage appears to come from the speaker of the poem, Mrs Bentley, as she desperately reasserts the partnership of her marriage, the voice also carries the threatening tone of an interloper, Judith, who provides the title of the poem and lays a present claim to an alternative pairing beyond the now-broken covenant of husband and wife.[20]

Layering and rewriting both the "Song of Songs" and Ross' novel within her own poems, Mrs Bentley not only revises the idyllic garden trope of mutual love, but also offers an alternative model of an upside-down creative vision when she asserts her personal sense of the world. She consciously rewrites her barren life, marriage, and identity by entering into a new creative process with perversion at its root. Being, as she describes herself in "Bag of Oranges," "a gourd with hard / and bitter seeds" (64), she germinates fictions and truths in all their uncertain, coexistent forms through her palimpsestic practice. As she ambiguously confesses in the poem "The Truth," "Truth is, the only ending / is the one you make up, the one you can't / live without, the sweet, impossible birth" (92). From "bitter seeds" springs this "sweet, impossible birth," an artistic labour Mrs Bentley refuses to deny herself as she exposes, conceals, and generates the story of her domestic world. The garden as a model of palimpsest becomes, therefore, in Crozier's reworking of Ross' novel, a layered paradigm for Mrs Bentley's newfound counter-creativity. Through this textual "garden," Crozier highlights Mrs Bentley's body, sexuality, marriage, and artistic expression – all of which feed her realization of (unnatural) fecundity previously curtailed within the scope of the novel. Indeed, in one of the final poems "Leaving," Mrs Bentley imagines herself in a dormant meadow as she gives birth to stories that nobody desires: stories reminiscent of long-decayed, sun-bleached bones.

Through *A Saving Grace*, Crozier demonstrates the paradox that lies at the center of her garden writing and her inter-related practice of re-vision: the interplay of both product and process. From the humourous vegetables of "The Sex Lives of Vegetables" to the degenerative garden of Mrs Bentley, the garden's many reformulations provide an illuminating lens, a third nature through which to perceive the evolving creative work of one writer. Turning over both old and new terrain,

Crozier is an exemplary gardener-poet in a long Canadian tradition. As with a garden brought to maturity, a published, canonical text such as *As for Me and My House* seemingly exists as a final product, the end-point of Ross' creative endeavour. Crozier reveals, however, that even such a text contains the seeds of new creativity, the potential for a process of growth and change. In the acknowledgements, Crozier writes that the "voice in [the original Mrs Bentley's] journals has been as hard to dispel from my imagination as a caragana rooted in soil" (93). Some texts take hold because of their richness, others because of the gaps they present. Like strong-willed plants in a garden, such stories will continue to propagate in the terrain of other writers' imaginations.

CONCLUSION

In this study, domestic gardens have provided a lens for seeing intersections between writing and gardening that are at once enduring and multifaceted, indicative both of the shifting contexts of Canadian literature and of women's overlooked past contributions. The works of the five women considered here are revelatory in light of Northrop Frye's predominantly wilderness-focused model and its dismissal of stories of the everyday. In her essay "The Postmodernization of Landscape," Dianne Harris argues that "landscape is both the product of cultural forces and a powerful agent in the production of culture (435). This is precisely why the writers in this study embrace the garden and its creative third nature: their garden "plots" are purposeful expressions and affirmations of change within their specific domestic and gendered frameworks. They reveal that female subjects and gender paradigms transform through a necessary, critical relationship with the second-nature world of established conventions and modes of living.

Ultimately, this study's focus – the different time periods, the distinctive textual formulations of garden processes and forms, and the array of genres – demonstrates that the reading of literary gardens should not be schematized. Gardens reflect both the writers who compose them and the contexts from and in which they take their shape. In the case of Susanna Moodie and Catharine Parr Traill, readers witness two female pioneers drawing upon alternative traditions in their creation of backwoods kitchen-garden "plots." Their material garden palimpsests directly inform their literary transplanting of the cultivated woman of nineteenth-century Canada through the spatial frame and language of the garden. Through re-contextualization, Moodie's and Traill's third-nature garden plots highlight the hardiness required of the female pioneer in unusual circumstances that have become the daily norm. Moving forward in time to the early half of the twentieth century, Gabriélle Roy explores the insecurities of a young artist setting out in the 1930s, and the isolation of diverse linguistic and ethnic groups in western Canada shape her innovative bower plots. Roy's third nature is a transformative, transitional space, underscoring that artistic agency and mobility are typically impeded by women's situated identities as homemakers. Rather than negotiating a move beyond the home and its traditional gender roles, as Roy does, Carol Shields celebrates domestic lives by infusing her fiction with the myth of paradise, thereby challenging the relevance of a national imagination (rooted in the wilderness) that minimizes the twentieth-century realities of her characters. Questioning both overly idealized and narrowly defined notions of the domestic, Shields uses the theatrical components of the third nature when she strategically places garden "scenes" throughout her novels in order to illuminate the acting out of possible configurations in the life plots of her characters. And finally, Lorna Crozier embraces the garden's interplay of process and product through poetry that models a feminist writing practice of re-vision. Through her palimpsestic experimentation, this gardener-poet disrupts and questions the "natural" at every turn, generating a third nature of the literary postmodern bent on deconstruction. Together, these five writers demonstrate that as with real gardens, their literary counterparts draw on an art of milieu, facilitating expression and insight on a number of fronts: on the larger issues and themes at work in the respective texts; on the socio-cultural and temporal contexts in which the literary gardens are originally created; on the changing literary traditions in which the gardens subsequently "reseed" themselves as palimpsests for other writers; and on writers' abiding artistic preoccupations as exhibited through sustained attention on gardens across numerous works.

Any study of the garden ultimately emulates its paradoxical nature: the play between the permanent and impermanent, the tended and the uncontrollable – those very notions of product and process that define a garden. In my own delineation, or plotting out, of the strategies of these writers, I also kept discovering unexpected points of intersection through a seemingly organic, and sometimes meandering, path of inquiry. While Moodie's and Traill's backwoods kitchen-garden plots of class-related gendered transgressions led to Crozier's more explicit interrogation of sexual norms and taboos in her erotic vegetable patch, in turn Crozier's pioneer palimpsest invited a return visit to the actual backwoods gardens as material palimpsests of composite terrain. Through these explorations, the pioneer garden palimpsest tradition (Atwood on Moodie, Kroetsch on Traill, Crozier on Ross), as well as the more recent creative undertakings (Melhorn-Boe and SATCO theatre on Crozier) began to emerge. In a similar manner, Roy's enclosed bower plots for the female artist took on a sustained form in Shields' paradisal life plots, her garden "scenes" staging pivotal moments in her characters' development. It is tempting to read Daisy Goodwill

Flett, the unemployed but much loved garden columnist of *The Stone Diaries*, as a woman artist denied, contained and despairing in her Ottawa "bower," longing for that formidable transformation into the writer's life she accidentally but only temporarily discovers. In contrast, Crozier's Mrs Bentley darkly revels in her new role as palimpsestic poet through the perverted textual garden she inhabits and creates, telling lies and truths through layered lines. For many of these writers (both the real authors and those figured in their texts), the garden is a means of purposely drawing attention to life's many plots and pre-scripted roles, and the testing of other formulations. Such intersections reveal the expressive capacity of gardens that are situated in the daily experiences of the domestic, a world that, for too long, remained unwritten or overlooked. To counter such erasure, these writers have facilitated imaginative regenerations through their literary accounts of ephemeral gardens of the past, where only in rare cases (such as those of famous pioneers) small remnants endure of women's expressive work through stored-away seeds and dried flowers.

Future examinations of Canadian writers and their literary gardens promise to reveal the continuing growth of this tradition. Harris believes that "gardens and landscapes have helped marginalized groups and individuals adapt to a range of settings shaped by the dominant culture" (438). Literary gardens most certainly have this same potential to elucidate the experiences of individuals and communities delineated by gender, race, language, sexual orientation, class, or other factors. Shani Mootoo, for example, has garnered critical praise for her exploration of post-colonial sexual identities in the haunting garden imagery of *Cereus Blooms at Night* (1996). Mootoo's short story "A Garden of Her Own" (1995) also merits attention for its portrayal of the balcony garden of a recently arrived immigrant whose brutal experience at the hands of her husband erodes her hope for her newly adopted country. With respect to contemporary Native literatures, Thomas King's humourous story "A Seat in the Garden" from *One Good Story, That One* (1993) imaginatively addresses the historical expropriation of Native lands through a vegetable patch. Likewise, Eden Robinson's *Monkey Beach* offers fertile ground for an examination of one character's (grandmother Ma-ma-oo's) traditional practices of harvesting indigenous foods in and around her Haisla community, as opposed to other family members' cultivation of monstrously sized gardens and consumption of industrially processed foods. Because literary gardens are so intrinsically tied to their temporal contexts, they provide a spectrum of both personal and social critiques. While on the one hand, readers may encounter an intimate, figurative space of healing and reflection in Patrick Lane's garden memoir, *There is a Season* (2004), on the other, they glimpse Canadian society's ongoing negotiations with the social environment through acts of gardening, such as Anne Shirley's participation in the Avonlea Improvement Society (a smaller version of the "City Beautiful" movement) in L.M. Montgomery's *Anne of the Island* (1915), or Helen Humphreys' depiction of the "Dig for Victory" campaign during the Second World War in *The Lost Garden* (2002). Not surprisingly, then, with present-day concerns over the impending environmental crises, we are seeing speculative garden "plots" take form, such as Margaret Atwood's *The Year of the Flood* (2009), which features the God's Gardeners, a roof-top gardening cult preaching the benefits of a sustainable lifestyle.

For Canadian writers, the garden as a critical third nature has been, and will likely continue to be, a strategic means of addressing society's changing relationship with the physical-cultural environment, that "second nature" world in which we live and negotiate our many paths.

From long-standing archetypal associations to more particular expressions and formal effects, literary gardens provide space for heightened contemplation and evoke imaginative experiences for readers, taking us beyond our habitual modes of perceiving. When exploring these literal and figurative terrains, readers must remember to tread not simply with pleasure, but with care.

# Notes

## Introduction

1 Frye initially proposed his "organic" model of the Canadian imagination in 1965, well before the publication of Atwood's poem, in *Literary History of Canada*; the original conclusion was later reprinted in *The Bush Garden*.

2 Bentley notes that the term "paradise" is applied either to the wilderness or to the pioneer settlement (the "hinterland" and "baseland" orientations according to Bentley's terms) depending on the writer's particular point of view: "Was [the European] presence positive or negative for the country's [N]ative peoples and natural environments? Were the British in Canada creating an Edenic realm or destroying one?" (163–4). Edward H. Dahl similarly contends that paradise metaphors are used by settler writers to justify an ideal rural state, as "wilderness plus industry yields a garden or paradise" through a religiously sanctioned reclaiming of the land (42). For an aesthetic-focused argument on the paradise trope, see W.H. New, who argues that "European visual codes" for the land as communicated by nineteenth-century writers further the colonial process of appropriation during the settlement period, as the process of "differentiating between a paradisal earthly garden and a savage earthly wilderness determines that there exists a 'natural right' to territorial expansion" (22).

3 One of the most renowned uses of a paradisal motif in modern Canadian poetry, for example, is A.M. Klein's "nth Adam taking a green inventory / in a world but scarcely uttered" in his poem "Portrait of the Poet as Landscape" (135–6). For other studies of the paradise archetype see Wanda Ruth Campbell's doctoral dissertation "The 'Bildungsgedicht' as Garden in Nineteenth- and Twentieth-Century Canadian Long Poems," which parallels the growth of the individual with the growth of the community through a garden topos and trope. Her central preoccupation is the paradise metaphor as applied to the Canadian landscape, yet she also addresses alternative readings of the garden by examining the transplanting of aesthetic and literary forms. For a regional perspective on this theme, Karen Clavelle's 2005 doctoral dissertation, "Imagine the Prairies: The Garden in Post-Depression Prairie Fiction," traces Edenic visions of the prairies in twentieth-century Canadian literature.

4 See also Dennis Duffy's *Gardens, Covenants, Exiles* for his investigation of Loyalist writers and their use of a troubled paradise motif to counter American imperialism.

5 See also Stephanie Ross' *What Gardens Mean* for her allusion to Walpole, promoting historical, eighteenth-century garden design as "high art" (xiii) over the daily gardening of contemporary America, which she dismisses as an amusing pastime: "[G]ardening today is not a full-fledged sister to painting and poetry" (192).

6 An example of an overtly legible garden is the emblematic garden, which was popular in England during the eighteenth century. As Ross explains in *What Gardens Mean*, emblematic gardens are a complex integration of landscape, sculpture, architecture, and written inscriptions: "A number of these gardens are laid out as a circuit. The visitor strolls along a path which brings him past a series of monuments, scenes, and vistas. The viewer's experience is carefully controlled. Benches and inscriptions indicate special points of interest – striking views or sculptural or architectural

ensembles with complex charged meanings" (51). Alexander Pope's Twickenham garden (begun in 1719) serves as an example, as the open terrain incorporated statues of Classical figures and inscribed quotations from his favourite ancient works in architectural features. In contrast, his grotto with its stream and decorated walls and ceilings (covered in mirrors and shells that Pope had gathered from his travels and from friends) implied a more personal, contemplative space (56–7).

7 Deciphering the gendered ideologies that operate through the socio-cultural product that is a garden and related discourse, (such as Walpole's figurative trope), Carole Fabricant argues in "Binding and Dressing Nature's Loose Tresses: The Ideology of Augustan Landscape Design" that the descriptions of landscape gardens during the eighteenth century that are composed by both garden designers and poets "are not merely commonplaces or figures of speech (though through repeated usage they may have come to be these as well) but statements about how power was conceived and wielded during this period. There is little doubt as to who was the master, who the obedient and submissive servant" (113).

8 Hunt quotes both from *La Villa* (published in 1559) in which Taegio writes, "'The industry of an accomplished gardener, incorporating art with nature, makes of the two together a third nature" (*Greater* 243n7), and from a letter dated 1541 in which Bonfadio describes the grounds of his country villa to a friend: "'For in the gardens … the industry of the local people has been such that nature incorporated with art is made an artificer and naturally equal with art, and from them both together is made a third nature, which I would not know how to name" (*Greater* 33).

9 Even though the wilderness is not my focus, it is important to reiterate here, as Hunt does in *Greater Perfections*, that first nature "is inevitably constructed by a given culture as a means of differentiating kinds of identity or behavior, or of protecting parcels of territory for special purposes" (51). While the wilderness could be "invoked by writers such as Cicero

as places to locate the mysterious and sometimes fearful presence of the gods" (51–3), other "societies have made wilderness the place where the wicked, the criminal, or other outcasts were banished to perish" (53), and still others see the wilderness as a "backyard" (54).

10 *OED Online*. June 2012. Oxford University Press, s.vv. "plot, n.," http:// dictionary.oed.com/view/Entry/145915 and "plot, v.1," http://dictionary. oed.com/view/Entry/145916 (accessed 1 July, 2012).

11 The garden has not necessarily been favoured as the ideal model for women's expression. Feminist scholars such as Elaine Showalter and even Hélène Cixous privilege the open, vast wilderness (or the first nature of the unknown and mysterious, as Hunt describes it) as an appropriate articulation of women's yet-unexpressed desires and experience outside of patriarchal culture. Showalter proposes a "wild zone" of female culture: "Spatially it stands as an area which is literally no-man's-land, a place forbidden to men ... Experientially it stands for aspects of the female life-style which are outside of and unlike those of men" (200). Resonating with this inarticulated female "zone" that exists beyond male-centred language and culture is Cixous' "dark continent" of feminine difference in her theory of *l'écriture féminine* (1096): "Now women return from afar, from always: from 'without,' from the heath where witches are kept alive; from below, from beyond 'culture'" (1092).

12 See feminist architectural historian Dolores Hayden's *The Grand Domestic Revolution* in which she contends that material feminists reformulated domestic designs during the nineteenth and twentieth centuries with the understanding that space is crucial to women's lives and self-direction. Hayden writes, "It requires a spatial imagination to understand that urban regions designed for inequality cannot be changed by new roles in the lives of individuals" (28). Through the development of kitchen-less houses and cooperative living, feminist designers believed women would have more options in terms of working outside the house. Although not

focused on gendered delineations of space, Hunt similarly theorizes in "*Paragone* in Paradise" that gardens are places that enable ideas to take on a material form: "The shaping of sites ... makes them 'privileged matrix[es] of symbolization through which patterns of belief, authority and social structure are realized (not merely reflected)'" (55–6).

## Chapter One

1 *The Canadian Settler's Guide* appears first in 1854 under the title *The Female Emigrant's Guide, and Hints on Canadian Housekeeping. The Canadian Settler's Guide* (2nd edition) is the most recognizable, as McClelland and Stewart reprinted this edition in 1969 for their New Canadian Library (NCL) series. All page references refer to the 1969 NCL edition, unless otherwise specified.

2 *The Canadian Settler's Guide* showcases gardening in the opening sections, but Traill's hand-written revisions (circa 1880) for a new edition of her book (which were never implemented or published) reveal that she intended to adjust the sequence. In a note to her publisher Traill writes, "I am inclined to think that the pages which were arranged at the beginning of the book on gardening would be better placed further on – I am so tired or I would have entirely rearranged the matter. I must leave it entirely to the discretion of your editor" (*Canadian Settler's* Revisions). Traill gives no reason for the suggested revision, yet it perhaps indicates a nation now more settled than when she first emigrated. She maintains the garden's importance, however, by outlining a new table of contents that contains the headings "The Vegetable Garden" and "On Gardening: the use and value of a garden" (*Canadian Settler's* Revisions).

3 Some notable studies on Moodie's and Traill's treatments of landscape include those by Margaret Atwood, Edward H. Dahl, Susan Glickman, W.H. New, Michael Peterman, Rosemary Sullivan, and Clara Thomas.

4 *OED Online*. March 2005. Oxford University Press, s.v. "palimpsest," accessed 28 November 2005, http://dictionary.oed.com/cgi/entry50169692.

5 Glickman derives her definition of the sublime from Edmond Burke's *A Philosophical Enquiry into the Origins of Our Ideas of the Sublime and the Beautiful* (1775) in which he attributes the sublime with causing feelings of pain, terror, awe, and astonishment. Objects of the sublime are "vast in their dimensions," "rugged and negligent," "dark and gloomy," and "solid and massive" (Burke 140). As for the picturesque, Glickman stresses the artistic aspect of this term: "The result, seen throughout eighteenth-century literature, was poetry organized according to techniques of painterly composition. For example, the poem is represented as seeing a 'prospect,' and describes it from foreground to middle ground to distance in an orderly progression of images" (9). In the context of gardening design, the definition of the picturesque, according to the *Oxford English Dictionary*, is slightly different in that it signals not only "the arrangement of a garden so as to make a pretty picture," but also the aesthetic features of "irregular and rugged beauty" (*OED Online*. 2003. Oxford University Press, s.v. "picturesque," accessed 12 January 2003, http://dictionary.oed.com/cgi/entry/00178776).

6 According to Edward Casey, the English landscape garden had its beginnings in the early 1700s and was prompted by a fashionable desire "to leave, or at least appear to leave, nature in an unenclosed and unaltered condition" with home and estate being oriented outward toward the environment (164). Lancelot "Capability" Brown (c. 1715–83) and his successor Humphrey Repton (1752–1818) showcased the features of the larger landscape within, and beyond, a landowner's immediate property, making the entire scene appear "natural," which meant designing stretches of lawn with groupings of trees, undulating paths, curve-shaped lakes, and the creation of numerous visual prospects. John Dixon Hunt and Peter Willis reveal in their study that Brown's nickname

derived from the fact that he "alerted his clients and their friends to the natural capabilities of the countryside" (31). In contrast to Brown, Repton encouraged formal ornamentation around the home through the creation of a pleasure ground of shrubs and flowers to accommodate human activity, as he believed that the "leading feature in the good taste of modern times is the just sense of general utility" (*The Art* 67). Despite alterations for convenience, Repton still maintained that "the flower-garden except where it is annexed to the house, should not be visible from the roads or general walks about the place" (*The Art* 144).

7 Repton's designs worked to confirm the social status and wealth of the male landowner, as made evident by his proposal for Blaise Castle (1795–96): "This is the first instance in which I have been consulted where all improvement must depend upon the axe, and tho' fully aware of the common objection to cutting down trees, yet, it is only by the bold use of that instrument that the wonders of Blaise Castle can be properly displayed" (362–3).

8 A vocal opponent of Brown, Richard Payne Knight (1750–1824) objected to sweeping, monotonous terrain, or "shaven lawns," as artificial in appearance (3; bk. 2). Promoting the use of additional greenery, his poetic treatise *The Landscape, A Didactic Poem* (1794) describes Brown as a figure of destruction, "whose innovating hand / First dealt thy curses o'er this fertile land" (301–2; bk. 1).

9 F.K. Stanzel makes a similar argument to that of Glickman when he suggests that Moodie and Traill do not have "innocent" eyes, but "predetermined" (97) visions, as their writing strives not only to compose the landscape, but also to convey "the cultivation of the appropriate feeling when confronted with sublime or picturesque nature" (106). His use of the term "cultivation" is key, as he creates a parallel between the composed landscape and the women themselves. Their trained eyes for nineteenth-century aesthetics suggest they are as capable of being

"cultivated" as the surrounding territory they view. The implications and gendered tensions of this figurative, land-related term need to be considered further, because Moodie and Traill did not only perceive and respond to large-scale scenery (in their "cultivated" status) but also directly shaped the small-scale terrain of their gardens (in their role as cultivators).

10 Buss argues that nineteenth-century women writers "react to the strange-ness of the Canadian landscape by merging their own identity, in some imaginative way, with the new land" (126). Annette Kolodny's *The Land before Her* presents gardening as the foremost example of American women pioneers' direct engagement with their wilderness surroundings.

11 I use the term "backwoods garden" in order to avoid conflation with Atwood's and Frye's "bush garden." Unlike the oppositional, gothic "bush garden" of animalistic plants that first appeared in Atwood's poem, the "backwoods garden" is an actual garden formed in and through the Upper Canadian surroundings and described in words.

12 Davidoff and Hall write that "[t]he main feature of the middle-class garden was the lawn. The eighteenth-century lawn had been a 'great plain in a Park adjoining a Noble seat' ... cropped by sheep or laboriously by hand scythe. In the nineteenth century, it evolved into the suburban green carpet kept in trim by the iron lawn mower, first manufactured in 1830 by the Ransomes of Ipswich. The lawn was bordered by shrubberies, flower beds, fruit trees and vegetable beds, if there was no separate kitchen garden" (370–1).

13 John Loudon believed that in addition to ornamental plants, fruit-bear-ing trees and flowers, the cottage garden should house "bees, poultry, rabbits (if only for the children), pigeons and a cat" (qtd. in Sayer 36). Incidentally, the Strickland children owned pet rabbits which lived in their garden at Reydon Hall.

14 The name "Roselands" holds obvious symbolic meaning. In terms of the

cottage garden, Sayer writes, "Roses are, of course, commonplace in these scenes, signifying both an English idyll and femininity, there being a commonplace equivalence between flowers and women at the time" (49).

15 When discussing the Scarlet Cup flower in *Studies of Plant Life in Canada*, Traill recalls having seen a similar plant in a cottage garden back in England. Her limited familiarity with the flower suggests that the lower classes grew varieties that were less popular with more genteel gardeners: "I do not know if our brave Scarlet Cup of Canada has any floral relationship to an herb known in the Old Country as 'Clary,' or by its local and descriptive name of 'Eye-bright.' It is an old-fashioned flower sometimes found in cottage gardens. I remember its curiously colored leaves and bracts attracted my notice when first I saw it in a neglected corner of a poor old woman's garden" (43).

16 See Brent Elliott's *The Royal Horticultural Society: A History 1804–2004* for an extensive discussion of the history of Chiswick gardens, which were leased by the Society from the Duke of Devonshire beginning in 1822 (13). The Society created a public garden at Chiswick and sold seeds and cuttings, but "there was to be no thought of competing with nurseries, only introducing new plants, and, by stimulating the public taste for horticulture, causing 'an increase of demand on the nurseries'" (13). With Traill's cabbage seeds coming from Chiswick, they were likely a less commonly known variety.

17 *Forest and Other Gleanings* is a compilation of Traill's articles that were published individually in nineteenth-century journals in Canada, the United States, and Britain. While the original manuscript was never published as a whole, editors Michael Peterman and Carl Ballstadt attempt, here, to recreate the collection.

18 Canadian garden historian Helen Ross Skinner points to Traill's hot-bed as an example of an island bed, a round or oval-shaped bed placed in front of the house and popular among nineteenth-century settlers for its

convenience. The small size "would have been easier to care for ... Close to the house too, the bed would have been freer from marauding farm animals and handy for cultivation and picking" (36).

19 English landscape designers worked to create continuity between the park and surrounding landscape. Rather than using fences or hedges as boundaries that would appear artificial by disturbing the flow of the terrain and signaling agricultural use, Capability Brown incorporated the ha-ha, as historian Roger Turner explains: "Brown's sunk fences are normally placed so that they lie at right-angles to the line of sight; in this way one looks straight over the ditch and not along it. Furthermore, these sunk fences always run along the contours; never against them which would look most awkward" (Turner 80). Laurence Fleming and Alan Gore further speculate the sunken fence "has become known to us as a HaHa, perhaps because those who observed it said 'Aha,' while those who did not caused their friends to say 'HaHa' when they fell into it. Horace Walpole said that the common people called them Ha!Ha's! 'to express their surprise at finding a sudden and unperceived check to their walk'" (89).

20 Tracing pioneer gardens of Upper Canada through writings and drawings from the nineteenth century, Skinner notes that characteristic features emerge: "The vegetable garden would be shown beside or behind the house; a shrub or two would be beside the doorway ... vines such as hop or trumpet creeper would be climbing on the pillars of the verandah; an island bed would be bright with flowers in front, some young shade trees placed about the lawn and a few shrubs growing along the fence which would completely surround the house and garden" (37). The garden features that Skinner lists as well as the blend of pragmatic and decorative gardening are central to the advice Traill bestows in *The Canadian Settler's Guide.*

21 In a letter to her daughter, Annie Atwood, Traill writes, "I will take up, and lay by ... Canadian creeper, and clematis to plant at the pillars, of the veranda and I have some nice white spruce and some shrubs for the garden if you come in time to get them. A plot of them planted together would be nice and grow better than solitary as they shelter each other and are less trouble to take care of" (*I Bless You in My Heart* 201). Alternatively, in a letter dated 1882 and addressed to her son William, who was living in what would later become the province of Saskatchewan, Traill focuses on the edible garden, with a quick final mention of flowers: "I enclose some pips of the Snow-apple from my garden – I do not know if apples will bear your winters – if the plants come up and thrive you might get grafts ... I am so glad that you can raise good vegetables – I make great use of mine especially in soups – with very little meat I can make good dinners ... Does Harriette love flowers? – If I send garden seeds soon, you will get them in the spring in time for sowing" (*I Bless You in My Heart* 223–4).

22 *Cot and Cradle Stories* (1895) makes reference to the tidy, well-kept paths of the Strickland family's garden at Reydon Hall. In "The Five Little Gardeners," the father gives the sisters "a piece of ground ... just outside the garden wall" to cultivate because, as Traill reports, "'the gardener was very cross at them when they plucked flowers out of the garden borders or made litters on the walks'" (54). The eldest sister, Agnes, aspires to a trim, well-kept garden when she creates a dividing path between her plot and that of her sister Sara, covering the ground with white sand to keep "the path neat and nice if it rained ever so hard" (55).

23 In her handwritten revisions to her *Canadian Settler's Guide*, Traill describes another way of incorporating stumps into the garden, indicating her ongoing, creative responsiveness to her circumstances. She recommends placing poles around the base of the stump and tying them together at the top. Large stones rolled around the stump "form a sort of

circular wall," which is then filled with "rubbish, turf, and clods of earth with a good deep topping up of mould" in order to plant wild clematis, grape vine, seeds of morning glory, dwarf phlox, or "any small flowery creeper" (*Canadian Settler's* Revisions).

## Chapter Two

1 Mary Agnes FitzGibbon was a granddaughter of Susanna and John Moodie, making Catharine Parr Traill her great-aunt. FitzGibbon assisted Traill in preparing the manuscript for *Cot and Cradle Stories* and wrote the introduction to *Pearls and Pebbles*.

2 Labbe refers mainly to More's *Essays on Various Subjects, Principally Designed for Young Ladies* (1777) and *Strictures on the Modern System of Female Education with a View of the Principles and Conduct Prevalent among Women of Rank and Fortune* (1799).

3 Forcing beds are specifically designed terrain (often enclosed to trap heat) that gardeners use "[t]o hasten by artificial means the maturity of (plants, fruit, etc.)" (*OED Online*. 2006. Oxford University Press, s.v. "force, v," accessed 8 August 2006, http://dictionary.oed.com/cgi/entry/50087777).

4 Harris warns that in reading manuals there is "a real need to exercise caution ... because the extent to which any manual advice is followed is unknown and there is no necessary relationship between manual advice and cultural acceptance of that advice. Women did not necessarily garden more or become feminists because they read these books, but they are evidence of conditions in English and American society that made the writing and publishing of these books acceptable" ("Cultivating Power" 13).

5 Related to this botanical re-naming is the fact that Traill refers to the ship she sailed aboard during her transatlantic crossing as the *Laurel*.

In Peterman's explanatory notes in the CEECT edition of Traill's *The Backwoods of Canada,* he writes, "The Traills actually sailed on the brig *Rowley*" (240). According to Anne Dumas' floral lexicon, laurel typically symbolizes victory or glory: "The Ancients made crowns from laurel leaves for their heroes and others famed for their wisdom or special talent. The laurel was seen as a symbol of victory, over others or oneself, and of the peace which resulted" (68). Laurel has long been associated with poets and writers by celebrating and crowning their artistic achievements. Traill's re-naming of the ship possibly communicates her optimism as a transplanted woman and writer hoping to extend her success in the colony.

6 *OED Online.* 2003. Oxford University Press, s.v. "transplant, v.," accessed 16 February 2003, http://dictionary.oed.com/cgi/entry/00256487.

7 *OED Online.* 2003. Oxford University Press, s.v. "harden, v.," accessed 16 February 2003, http://dictionary.oed.com/cgi/entry/00102548.

8 Although "Jeanie Burns" was not included in the original publication of *Roughing It in the Bush* in 1852, Carl Ballstadt explains his decision to incorporate this sketch in the critical edition because "'Jeanie Burns' was clearly meant by Susanna to be included" (an intention signaled by Moodie in a letter to her publisher, Richard Bentley; xlix).

9 Thompson credits Traill, in particular, with addressing gender in a tangible, public way, as she transforms the "English lady" into a pioneer "heroine": "Once this lady, the well-educated and cultivated gentlewoman … arrives in the backwoods, a process of redefinition begins … to suit the exigencies, realities, and demands of backwoods society" (58).

10 MacLulich's discussion of Traill's Crusoe-like resourcefulness in the wilderness speaks to Bentley's suggestion that female emigrants' departure from England, their crossing of the Atlantic Ocean, and their arrival in Upper Canada enable the dismantling of their original socio-cultural

apparatus: "Yet a form of Herculean heroism was achieved by several female emigrants to Canada, including ... Moodie herself – women who, by performing such traditionally masculine labours ... blurred the conventional distinctions between the sexes" ("Breaking the 'Cake of Custom'" 95–6). Similarly, Rouslin contends, "On the borders of the frontier, no-one really had the time or the patience for insisting upon the correct jobs for women ... Adapting was ... the prerequisite in such harsh circumstances" (329). For the most part, these critics applaud what they view as the liberation of female pioneers.

11 Dean's description of Traill's *Guide* resonates with Fowler's own textile metaphor, illustrating how female emigrants took cover under the embroidered tent of their "sheltering shawls" "cut from conventional patterns of female behaviour" (Fowler 7). Both critics' figurative models are in keeping with Atwood's *The Journals of Susanna Moodie* and her poetic motif of sewing. In the epigraph to the collection, Atwood's Moodie persona mentions cutting the photo of herself with her "sewing scissors" (n.p.) and begins the opening poem, "Disembarking at Quebec," by referring to her knitting and shawl.

12 In his article "'Splendid Anachronism': The Record of Catharine Parr Traill's Struggles as an Amateur Botanist in Nineteenth-Century Canada," Peterman laments the fact that Traill's naturalist work has only attracted a handful of scholars (Jean Cole, Elizabeth Collard, and Elizabeth MacCallum) who produced primarily descriptive articles during the 1970s (173).

13 According to Stefaniak, Traill works in the "amateur world of women's domestic botany" (238) and is fully aligned with this conservative, middle-class, gendered tradition. Through an interdisciplinary approach of biology and post-colonial theory, the Stefflers alternatively emphasize Traill's tensions as a naturalist cognizant of her own position, wanting both to protect and to settle the Upper Canadian wilderness environment:

"Closely intertwined, the plant of the garden and the plant of the text often describe a literal colonization of the landscape or environment that reflects the writer's own colonized condition and colonizing activities" (127). The Stefflers examine in detail Traill's botanical descriptions of both native and introduced species as being indicative of "her own evolution and adaptation" (140).

14 Traill's "A Garden Party" explores the same implications of class and social transgressions as Katherine Mansfield's similarly named short story, "The Garden Party" (1922). In Traill's story, the youngest sisters "[run] wild" during a lapse in supervision because of the absence of their eldest sister and mother, and their father's confinement to the sickroom. The girls take to playing with "a rustic lad" (63) named Jonathan Spilling because they "[have] no playmates of [their] own class" (62). The girls allow Jonathan to eat the fruit from Mr Strickland's prized gooseberry bush as payment for his entertainment and gifts, but eventually they are sent out of the garden by their angered father in punishment for taking the fruit and for associating with Jonathan.

15 "The Miss Greens" features two wealthy spinsters known as much for their fortune as for their unattractiveness. Residing in "an ugly, ill-proportioned old maidish-looking dwelling" (94), the Miss Greens enclose themselves in a suburban garden that reflects their unaccommodating, greedy dispositions: "Above this formidable fence, well guarded with broken glass bottles and spike-nails, luxuriant pear-trees waved their fruitful branches and apple-trees coquettishly displayed their crimson and golden treasures, defying the artful wiles of mischievous boys, who looked and longed in vain for the forbidden fruit" (94). The miserly sisters' material abundance is a temptation to outsiders, but theirs is a closed world that withholds. When John Andrews, a widower and father of three boys, proposes marriage to sister Polly, the financially advantageous union threatens the bonds of family. John heeds the ghostly pleas of his deceased wives, who

urge him to safeguard their children (as Miss Polly hates boys). When the wedding day arrives, John refuses to exchange vows, renouncing his greed and following his natural inclinations: "'I am sorry to disappoint a lady, but there's no forcing nature'" (146). In the end, England's class system and the financial status it represents pose a hindrance to the "natural" bonds of family and love.

16 In contrast to the amusing story of "The Miss Greens," the story of Noah Cotton in *Flora Lyndsay* offers a dark account of the trials of illegitimacy and class distinction. Noah is the secret son of the wealthy landowner Squire Carlos and Mrs Cotton, a humble "widow." Noah resents his lack of socio-economic status, and his tragic story operates through spatial frames that foreground his marginal yet trusted position with respect to Carlos' extensive park: Noah resides at the edge of the grounds in the porter's lodge, he opens and closes the gate regularly for the gentlemen to pass through, and he regulates illegal poaching. In the chapter "The Plot," Noah plans and executes the murder of Carlos, framing two other men for the crime. The landscape is sullied by Noah's dark deeds when he buries his disguise and the Squire's stolen pocket-book in a hot-bed in the garden (286), and a blood stain appears on the stone where he murdered his father (299). Originally tasked with protecting the landscape park, Noah commits the horrendous crime at the perimeter of the property, highlighting his transgressions against his morality, his trusted relationship with the Squire (his father), and his own station in life. The story represents a primarily masculine relationship to space in the form of the landscape park, rather than the more contained, modest-scaled, feminine "garden plot."

17 In *Flora Lyndsay*, Noah dreams of land and a "noble alias" that are seemingly for the taking in America, but not in England (277). The rigid class system fosters his resentment and the growth of his immoral nature: his "heart ... a blank moral desert – a spot in which every corrupt weed

had ample space to spread and grow without let or hindrance" (271). Similarly, in "The Miss Greens," Moodie outlines a corrupt English society that promotes marriage for money rather than for love. The story opens with a plea to young women to "marry for love, and emigrate with the husband of their choice to those British Colonies, where education gives rank, and independence is the reward of industry" (82). As for England, "as long as society retains its present organization, such evils must be. The young, the fair, the beautiful, the penniless scions of respectable families, must take the journey of life alone" (82). Here, England's skewed values lead inevitably to an unproductive, even infertile life as the young "scions" remain unwed (82).

18  In an interview in 1972 with Russell Brown, Kroetsch conceptualizes Canada as "a peculiar kind of border land – and a border land is often the place where things are really happening" (14). Pointing to this interview in his essay "Bordering On: Robert Kroetsch's Aesthetics," Lecker argues that in "Kroetsch's borderline world," a dialectic is always at play: "naming meets un-naming, creation meets de-creation; fabulation meets documentation; form meets anti-form. In each of these meetings Kroetsch concerns himself with that border point at which opposites unite and undergo a metamorphosis. The border is … always in the process of transformation" (125).

19  The original publication of the long poem *Seed Catalogue*, for instance, features Kroetsch's words superimposed in green ink on excerpts from a MacKenzie seed catalogue that he located in the Glenbow Museum archives in Alberta.

20  For a related discussion of Morag Gunn's rejection of Catharine Parr Traill in Margaret Laurence's *The Diviners*, see Eva-Marie Kröller's and Faye Hammill's essays on contemporary rewritings of the Strickland sisters. Kröller argues that in *The Diviners*, Morag is "haunted" by the voice of "C.P.T." "in the shape of a resolute matron and determined rationalist"

(42). While Laurence presents her protagonist, Morag, as "poetic" (42), she affords C.P.T. no such artistic capacity. Such a characterization of Traill yet again denies her artistic achievements and contributions working within and across a range of genres. Kröller concludes that this particular ancestor must be "abandoned" and "safely exorcised" at the end of Laurence's novel so that other, contemporary artists (fictional or otherwise) may use Traill "to formulate contradictions" in a move towards "feminine self-definition" (42). In "Margaret Atwood, Carol Shields, and 'That Moodie Bitch,'" Hammill similarly suggests, via the context of Harold Bloom's *The Anxiety of Influence: A Theory of Poetry* and Linda Hutcheon's *A Theory of Parody*, that Morag "gradually frees herself from the burden of Susanna Moodie's sister, Catharine Parr Traill. Morag constructs a parodic image of Traill, since parody is one method by which the strong poet may dethrone her predecessor" (76).

21 From this point on, "Moodie" refers to the author of the text, and "Susanna" refers to the character Moodie creates through her writing.

22 Tom Wilson is a friend of John and Susanna Moodie whom they meet upon their arrival in Upper Canada. Tom arrived in the colony months prior to them, but unfortunately he fails miserably in his efforts to establish himself and returns to England.

23 While Susanna is unpacking, a young girl enters her home and with "a forward, impudent carriage, and a pert, flippant voice, stand[s] upon one of the trunks, and survey[s] all [the] proceedings in the most impertinent manner" (86). Susanna appreciates neither the unannounced, intrusive nature of this visit, nor the transformation of her private domain into common property and spectacle. For the duration of Susanna's residence in this first home she must endure the young woman's family, who constantly borrow items from the Moodies which they either return in bad repair or not at all.

24 Sherrill Grace argues that the three earlier "dream" poems (including

"Dream 1: The Bush Garden" with its bloody plants) suggest "the internalizing of the wilderness and prepare the way for 'The Double Voice'" (39), a poem that concludes the second section of the book by "mark[ing] an important point in [Moodie's] discovery of land and self" (39). Judith McCombs similarly reads "The Double Voice" poem as Moodie "com[ing] to see herself … as the source of an interior Gothic wisdom that derives from the wilderness landscape: there are two voices inside her head, dividing reality between convention and horror. The truths she chooses are 'jubilant with maggots'" (46).

25 Grace similarly concedes that "[a]lthough the *Journals* follow the life of the historical Mrs. Moodie and reflect certain of her attitudes, they tell us primarily about Margaret Atwood's vision of the Canadian psyche (42).

26 According to Dean, *Flora Lyndsay* is an example of the "miracle of [Moodie's] distancing techniques" (37). Embedded within Moodie's novel is the fictional story of Noah Cotton, which the protagonist composes during her Atlantic crossing: "Susanna Moodie writes a story of Flora Lyndsay; partway through this story, Flora writes a story of Noah Cotton; partway through this story, the voice of Flora disappears as Noah Cotton tells his own story; and partway through this story, Cotton's mother takes over to tell her own story in the first person. Thus Moodie's life is relegated to forming a frame narrative to the book *Flora Lyndsay*; the voice of the writer and her narrator, Flora, completely disappear from a work which is seemingly autobiographical" (37). The embedded tale of Noah Cotton's predicament and the injustices of England's class system reflects on Flora's need to emigrate.

27 Carl F. Klinck, Carol Shields, and Michael Peterman discuss Moodie's use of secondary characters in general and Malcolm Ramsay in particular as a way for Moodie to foreground her own character. Klinck argues, "The amusing imperfect people around [Susanna] were 'touched up' to be foils, revealing the central figure who could bear comparison with impunity"

(475–6). In *This Great Epoch of Our Lives*, Peterman writes that Ramsay's confessions of murder and of squandering money make him an example of "gentility gone vicious" with the "New World merely provid[ing] a playground for his vices and indulgences" (95). Peterman believes that Moodie has a particular and troubling fascination with this man: "He remained both an unsolved mystery and a kind of insistent affront, an unsettled account in her psyche that was intimately connected with her personal testing in the backwoods" (97). These critics point to physical description and behaviour as key components of Moodie's approach to characterization, but do not consider Moodie's use of space and framing. Shields touches on spatial relations with respect to Ramsay when she contends that Moodie's "self-contradicting" description "suggests sexuality, and this impression is strengthened as Mrs. Moodie circles around Malcolm, drawing sometimes closer, sometimes further away" (29).

28 In the explanatory notes, Ballstadt quotes Irving Sablovsky's *American Music* and explains that Ramsay's reference to "Jim Crow" is an allusion to one of America's first international hit songs from the late 1820s. The actor and singer Thomas Dartmouth "Daddy" Rice observed an elderly, lame Negro man working in a field singing and dancing a jig, which Rice later adapted (593).

## Chapter Three

1 From this point on, the first name "Gabrielle" refers to the fully developed character who Roy (the author) creates in order to tell her life's story in *Enchantment and Sorrow*.

2 *The Cashier* serves as an example of men's imprisonment and alienation in the modern city. In his job at the bank, Alexandre is a nameless "little man in cage number two" (28). He lacks words to express his "captive soul" (21) in this mechanical, anonymous world (25, 38).

3 This pattern of containment is not restricted to Roy's urban novels; rural settings also isolate and delimit women. See Phyllis Grosskurth's discussion of *Where Nests the Water Hen* and especially the chapter entitled "Luzina takes a Holiday," which suggests an irony about women's lack of enjoyment and freedom as the purpose of Luzina's annual vacation to Sainte Rose du Lac is to give birth (10).

4 In a typically feminine way, the convent garden in *The Hidden Mountain* is diminutive, enclosed, and decorative in nature: "Then, from the miniature convent behind the flowers, there emerged a nun in her spreading gray habit, her white headdress flapping against her face. At a sort of half trot she was on her way to the garden" (20–1). Gardens of this sort have an infamous reputation for facilitating the submissive, chaste withdrawal of feminine subjects. Pointing to the Medieval garden or *hortus conclusus*, where walls secure a virginal female inhabitant, Eleanor Perényi argues that historically, the garden has contained women's freedom and bodies, operating as a kind of green and growing "chastity belt" (263). Inside this "flower-filled feminine ghetto" (263), women are aestheticized, their agency minimized.

5 In her article "Feminism and Traditionalism in the Early Short Stories of Gabrielle Roy," Lewis does not explicitly define "feminine humanist" but suggests that the term refers to Roy's "deep preoccupation with female characters [and] her sensitivity to their problems" coupled with "more of a general humanism, a deep sensitivity for women, men, and children, and all of nature" (29).

6 Whitfield points to a number of indicators of a feminist politics, including Roy's interest in particular genres such as "the more personal, autobiographical, in short, more feminine type of writing which she, herself, most wanted to explore" (27); her thematic interest in spectacle and the appearance of the "other" (27); her depiction of men and their oftentimes "inferior status" (25); and her concern for women's sexual equality (22).

7 McPherson's reading of Roy's "innocent" gardens is a persistent interpretation carried forward by more recent scholars. In *Le cycle manitoban de Gabrielle Roy,* Carol J. Harvey describes Roy's gardens as special
domains of childhood: "Le jardin de l'enfance est présenté comme le
cadre spatio-temporel par excellence de l'âge de l'innocence, où même
les mauvaises expériences se font vite oublier" (The childhood garden is
presented as the exemplary spatial-temporal terrain of innocence, where
even bad experiences are quickly forgotten; 179).

8 Men make brief appearances in Roy's fiction as pragmatic gardeners, but
their plots do not usually serve, as the women's typically do, as havens
of creative expression. In *The Hidden Mountain,* both Gédéon, the gold
miner, and Pierre Cadorai, the painter-protagonist, cultivate vegetables.
On his quest into the north Pierre tends an abandoned plot by an isolated cabin, but his actions are for practical purposes (to alleviate his
hunger) and he views his labour as part of an economic exchange: "The
vegetables tempted him. So he took the liberty of gathering some ... In
repayment he spaded a small area along the edge of the dwarfed and
bushy forest; he spent half a day weeding the almost smothered patch.
And, fearing this was not enough return for a few lettuces and one cabbage, he made a quick sketch of the place ... He pinned it to the door"
(65). In *Street of Riches,* Christine's father tends a mixed terrain of vegetables and flowers: he discusses "rosebushes, apple trees, and asparagus" with the neighbour (2), and acquaints himself with each individual
strawberry (113). Even so, he does not fully appreciate the importance
of flower gardening for the female settlers of the Russian colony of
Dunrea, Saskatchewan. He laughs at the "excess of adornment" when
the women's flowers line the paths from the houses to the privies: "Papa
... was a serious man, and his first concern was to look after the crops"
(76). Christine's father views cultivation primarily in terms of economic
benefit; the steadfastness of the women's desire points instead to the

centrality of gardening to their expression of a sense of home.

9 *OED Online*. 2004. Oxford University Press, s.v. "bower, n," accessed 6 April 2004, http://dictionary.oed.com/cgi/entry/00026108.

10 Mermin points to Elizabeth Barrett Browning's poem "The Lost Bower" in which the speaker fails to locate her bower as an example of this gendered exclusion: "It is the loss of a poetic world and a poetic subject, lost because she can't fill both roles that the story requires" (66).

11 In contrast, Marvell's speaker's imagination uniformly reflects the very fecundity of his surroundings, as he forms "a green thought in a green shade" (48).

12 Pierre paints his native country, but its wilderness landscape is ultimately unknowable to him, as his obsession leads to self-destruction. Almost capturing his vision of the northern mountain on his canvas at the conclusion of the novel, Pierre suffers an apparent heart attack and all his "[f]orms, beloved images, dreams, the witchery, and the colors" along with the hidden mountain "fad[e] away" (186).

13 In the biography, Ricard notes that at least four unpublished pre-texts to "Garden in the Wind" exist, including the short story "La lune des moissons" ("The Harvest Moon"; 1947), the screenplay "Le plus beau blé du monde" ("The Most Beautiful Wheat in the World"; 1950s), an unfinished novel about "Madame Lund" ("Mrs Lund"; 1950s), and the short story "Le printemps revint à Volhyn," which was revised and re-titled as "Un jardin au bout du monde" (448).

14 In "Un jardin au bout du monde," the names of Roy's protagonist and her husband are "Martha and Stépan Yaramko." In his English translation, Alan Brown changes the names to "Marta and Stepan Yaramko." Critics dealing with the French and English texts shift between the variant spellings; I use "Marta" and "Stepan" to be consistent with the published translation.

15 In a related article, "Gabrielle Roy: The Mother's Voice, The Daughter's

Text," Saint-Martin notes, "Throughout her works, Gabrielle Roy revalorizes traditional female crafts such as making paper flowers, sewing, decorating, and embroidery" (318).

16 Montreuil observes that the story entitled "Le printemps revint à Volhyn" focuses on the main character Madame Lund (this name later becomes "Martha Yaramko"), beginning with a springtime trip to Edmonton for medical care and a sojourn of "quelques jours dans la ville de Codessa, logé par diverses connaissances" (a few days in the village of Codessa, lodged by various acquaintances; 370). Madame Lund is a sociable person and lacks the quiet mood of introspection that comes from Marta's complete isolation in "Un jardin au bout du monde." Madame Lund interacts with various peoples, such as the Natives and trappers who visit the general store with their furs (370). According to Roy's original manuscript of "Le printemps revint à Volhyn," Madame Lund also places an order for "des graines de fleurs" (flower seeds) and "quelques bulbes" (a few bulbs) when the young boy Dimitri passes by her home, an opportunity that Marta of "Garden in the Wind" no longer has available to her (6). In the published story, Marta is the sole source of regeneration for her garden as any social encounters and exchanges of plants occurred long ago in the past. For an alternative, positive interpretation of the title, see Montreuil, who argues that the inclusion of "jardin" in the final version reveals that the garden triumphs over other spaces and thematic preoccupations: "l'élément qui donne son titre au texte final, le jardin, ainsi que le thème qui lui est lié, la création, sont absents de la nouvelle de 1947 et du scénario" (the element that gives its title to the final text, the garden, as well as the theme that connects to it, creation, are absent from the short story of 1947 and from the screenplay; 366).

17 The title of the published English translation ("Garden in the Wind") expresses neither the same degree of geographical isolation nor the out-of-time feeling; it maintains, however, a position within time, and especially

conveys the passing of time. The other-worldly or ephemeral quality of Marta's garden operates, in Mikhail Bakhtin's term, as a kind of "historical inversion" (147) in that mythological and artistic modes of thinking situate notions of perfection in the past: "In order to endow any ideal with authenticity, one need only conceive of its once having existed in its 'natural state' in some Golden Age, or perhaps existing in the present but somewhere at the other end of the world, east of the sun and west of the moon" (147–8).

18 In the *Inventaire des archives personnelles de Gabrielle Roy*, Ricard does not identify the revisions in this particular typescript; however, in two other drafts of the translation, hand-written changes are identified as those of the editor, the translator (Alan Brown), and Gabrielle Roy (42).

19 Roy's conceptualization of the female artist is closely aligned with the "relational" model of art as proposed by Adrienne Rich in her essay "When We Dead Awaken: Writing as Re-vision": "I want to make it clear that I am not saying in order to write well, or think well, it is necessary to become unavailable to others, or to become a devouring ego. This has been the myth of the masculine artist and thinker; and I do not accept it. But to be a female human being trying to fulfill traditional female functions in a traditional way is in direct conflict with the subversive function of the imagination ... There must be ways ... in which the energy of creation and the energy of relation can be united" (43).

20 In "Gabrielle Roy: The Mother's Voice, The Daughter's Text," Saint-Martin actually refers to the mother figure in Roy's texts as a storyteller, "an authentic artist" who "practices a subtle and suggestive art that relies on the power of images" (316).

## Chapter Four

1 *OED Online*. 2006. Oxford University Press, s.v. "paradise, n," accessed 5 October 2006, http://dictionary.oed.com/cgi/entry/50170966.

2 "Paradise" signifies a range of places and experiences: the Garden of Eden, heaven, a locale of extraordinary beauty, or a state of supreme pleasure and happiness. While the noun "Eden" and particularly its adjectival form "edenic" also suggest a "delightful abode or resting place, a paradise; a state of supreme happiness," the distinction between "paradise" and "Eden" lies in "Eden's" specific application as the name of the original "abode of Adam and Eve at their Creation" (*OED Online*. 2006. Oxford University Press, s.v. "eden," accessed 5 October 2006, http://dictionary.oed.com/cgi/entry/50072104).

3 In an interview with Eleanor Wachtel, Shields credits the work of Friedan with her own feminist awakening in the 1960s: "I didn't quite ever doze off quite the same again" (20). Shields also makes an explicit connection between how she conceived of *The Stone Diaries* and the argument behind *The Feminine Mystique* in an interview with Joan Thomas: "[Daisy] settled for exactly what she was offered, without ever forming the sentence parts for 'I want ...' She believed what the women's magazine said about women's work ... If only one person had said to her: Your life is your own and there is work you can do. (A lot of women never heard this articulated before *The Feminine Mystique* was published)" (81).

4 Shields portrays a number of her female characters as avid consumers of the magazine *Better Homes and Gardens*, illustrating Friedan's argument that the creativity of homemaking can be replaced with the unimaginative and the banal. In *Happenstance*, Brenda Bowman reads "'How to Put the Essential You in Your Home'" (27), an article that reappears in *The Stone Diaries* when Daisy Flett follows religiously the advice given in "'Putting the Essential You into Your Décor'" (194). Wendy Roy notes the lack of originality in Daisy's use of the decorating ideas taken from this same article (from *Canadian Homes and Gardens* magazine) when Daisy makes a display of family photographs for her coffee table (136).

5 Writing about Shields' successful career as a novelist, Eleanor Wachtel

reflects in her article "Telling It Slant" that "[the second novel] suffered from [Shields'] susceptibility to her editor's advice. *Small Ceremonies*, she was told, didn't have a lot happening. So Shields added [a climactic] plot, a pseudo-kidnapping and police, to *The Box Garden*" (13).

6 Judith, the writer-protagonist involved in the academic world in *Small Ceremonies*, feels that Canadian literature is at risk of becoming derivative, a compilation of "hackneyed tropes" that are easily reproduced by writers who either lack talent, or ironically know very little about Canadian society (91). She undermines the American writer Furlong Eberhardt by exposing his quintessentially western prairie identity as well as his critically lauded novel as fraudulent. Attacking the formulaic quality of Eberhardt's work, Judith states, "He opens, Chapter One, to waving wheat. Admit it ... Saskatchewan in powder form. Mix with honest rain water for native genre" (27). Hammill argues that Shields uses Eberhardt as a way to undermine the nationalist impulse that promotes "the myth that the spirit of Canada will only emerge in the writing of Canadian-born citizens" ("Carol Shields's 'Native Genre'" 97). The inherent irony of Eberhardt is that Shields herself grew up in Chicago, "yet her work," Hammill notes, "could be said to fit rather neatly into the category which her novels seek to dismantle" (97).

7 Hammill observes, for example, that *Small Ceremonies* "stops short of a full-scale rejection of the concept of Canadian literature" ("Carol Shields's 'Native Genre'" 93) because Judith values the notion of thinking in a "'thicket,'" an image reminiscent of the Canadian "wilderness" theme that highlights "the necessary role played in the production of a text by the geographical and historical positioning of its author" (94). Dee Goertz concurs with Hammill's conclusion, noting that "Shields was thinking about issues of symbolism and its viability in the postmodern era even at the beginning of her career" (231).

8 When it was first published, *The Box Garden* received harsh reviews partly

for its domestic subject matter. In a 1977 issue of *Maclean's*, Barbara Amiel deems (perhaps not surprisingly) the commonplace lives of Shields' characters as uninspiring: "For the past 15 years most Canadian ... writers have worked very hard to convince the public that small, grey, pinched characters have significance and, ugh, relevance to our lives – simply by virtue of their ordinariness. Carol [S]hields, an Ottawa writer of some ability ... gives us the latest example of this literary fallacy" (54).

9 Strong-Boag quotes one mother who, in an interview with *Star Weekly* in 1957, applauded living in Toronto's Iondale Heights precisely because of the natural surroundings, but not for the dearth of culture: "'We moved to the suburbs because of the children. We wanted to give them room to romp, where they wouldn't have to worry about street cars and fiend-driven automobiles. True, we have no museums or art galleries. But the children can go outside and see nature as it is'" (489). Suburbia's idyllic associations continue to have a tangible impact on how these environments are constructed and understood within contemporary Canadian society. Architectural scholars Nik Luka and Leo Trottier argue in "In the Burbs: It's Time To Recognize That Suburbia Is a Real Place Too" that the positive attributes most associated with the suburbs are its predictable buildings, space, privacy, and greenery (37).

10 Ironically, while this love of private green-space attracted people to the suburbs, Bumstead notes that untouched nature was not always part of Canadians' suburban experience, as farmland was appropriated for urban expansion and existing trees were removed by developers. Even so, marketers exploited buyers' aspirations "by giving fantasy names to the developments themselves ... or to street names (Shady Lane, Sanctuary Drive, Paradise Crescent)" (n.p.). A similar environmental impact has been noted in the context of late nineteenth-century England. Both Judy Giles and John Carey reveal that many writers blamed London's suburbs for irreparable damage to the English countryside, which was previously

enjoyed by a privileged few. Giles writes, "Suburbia's critics have frequently cast their condemnations in a form that espouses nostalgia for a lost Eden, imagined as a pre-industrial community under threat from the forces of modernisation" (30). Carey also notes, "The ruined childhood paradise [became] a familiar refrain in writers' biographies and autobiographies" (47). In contrast, Lynne Hapgood explores idyllic depictions of London's suburbs for the lower classes through the rising popularity of the garden romance genre and garden writing in general in her book *Margins of Desire: The Suburbs in Fiction and Culture 1880–1925*. Aristocratic garden ideals "filtered down through the diminishing plots of the middle class and of aspirants to the middle class, to the tiniest of terraces ... Where there was no garden at all, there were window boxes" (94–5).

11  The "Whole World Retreat" can be placed within a larger North American history of communal settlements conceived as "paradises." In "Communal Idealism and the American Landscape," Dolores Hayden reveals that while most "nineteenth century communards [such as the Shakers] were relatively poor people – farmers and artisans," "contemporary communards come from comfortable, suburban, middle-class backgrounds, which they explicitly reject in favor of a more 'natural' or a more 'responsible' lifestyle" (30). Watson's rural community is in keeping with these back-to-nature groups of the 1960s and 1970s in which a typical commune, according to Hayden's "Communal Idealism and the American Landscape," is "isolated from the larger society, which [its members] perceive to be collapsing and therefore irrelevant" (30).

12  Williamson suggests that Shields' interest in pairing – either through the linking of separate works through shared characters, or through a dual narrative perspective in a single novel – stems in part from Shields' graduate research, as *Susanna Moodie: Voice and Vision* pays particular attention to various kinds of pairs, particularly in terms of characters and gender (172). Williamson pairs *Swann* with *The Stone Diaries* because of

their focus on deceased characters, art of biography, and multiple points of view (173).

13 Reflecting on her mother's fiction, Anne Giardini states that "*The Box Garden* [is] a less domestic novel" (11) because in her view, Shields' literary "home ground" is what readers encounter in *Happenstance* and *A Fairly Conventional Woman*: "a comfortably married couple, two awkward children, an academic interest" (11). The comment betrays an underlying assumption behind what constitutes the domestic in Shields' fiction. Peculiarly, Stephen Henighan, an overtly harsh critic of Shields, echoes some of Giardini's observations by arguing that the novels exhibit "bedrock family values" (183).

14 For studies of the flower motif or a combination of stones and flowers see such critics as Chiara Briganti, Leona Gom, Naomi Guttman, Lisa Johnson, and Marie-Louise Wasmeier. A popular line of inquiry focuses on the flower imagery as characterizing different aspects of Daisy's life, with the merging of stones and flowers representing a united family legacy by the conclusion of the novel.

15 In a letter addressed to Blanche Howard in 1993, Shields reveals that stone imagery was central to her conceptualization of Daisy's story as the working title (at that time) was *Monument* (274). Critics (see Susan Grove Hall and Winifred Mellor as examples) often view Cuyler's stonework as Shields' model for both the pieced-together form of her text and the character of Daisy, who is, in Mellor's words, a "mute hollow structure" (99). Although another character's artistry becomes the focus in this line of inquiry, Gordon Slethaug concedes (in a footnote) that Daisy's cooking and gardening "are perhaps even more critical to her development than her father's imaginative sculpturing of stone" (79).

16 Johnson argues that in the play *Departures and Arrivals*, which takes place in the "theatre" of the airport, Shields creates a kind of social drama or spectacle "made of fragments, glimpses of many lives" (252).

17 In her psychoanalytical reading of Daisy's garden, Guttman argues that "we might see [Daisy] as plagued by her mother's death and her father's mourning, and conclude that Shields is portraying a character who has never developed the care of herself – the ego – that is said to be a natural part of growing from babyhood to independence. The garden, then, is both the baby she never was, merging with the mother, and her 'dearest child'" (103).

18 Barbara Sibbald's article in which she interviewed Shields is no longer available online (originally accessed in 2007). For further discussion of Shields' correspondence with her publisher and agent in which she refers to her original Ottawa home (582 Queen Elizabeth Driveway, where she lived from 1968–78) in the context of the fictionalized address of 583 The Driveway, see Catherine Hobbs' "Voice and Re-vision: The Carol Shields Archival Fonds" (49).

19 Ramon references Dickinson's *Here is Queer: Nationalisms, Sexualities and the Literatures of Canada* (University of Toronto Press, 1999).

20 Lisa Johnson similarly notes that "Daisy is effaced by the patriarchal custom of taking one's husband's name" (Barker was the original "Mr. Green Thumb"), yet Shields still "celebrates the real and worthy work of Daisy's hands" (206).

21 Important to note here is the fact that, as Wendy Roy reminds us, Daisy's early married life, as portrayed in the kitchen scene, is far from idyllic: "Daisy's culinary enterprises are described using the language of hell and damnation: her kitchen is 'hot as Hades' (157), and she says 'Damn it' five times under her breath" (136). The tragic isolation of Barker and Daisy's marriage is further echoed in a posthumous note Barker writes to his wife, acknowledging their lack of a shared garden of companionship: "The memory of our 'lady's-slippers' discussion has ... led me into wondering whether you perhaps viewed our marriage in a similar way, as a trap ... Between us we have almost never mentioned the word love ... I would

like to have danced with you through the back door, out into the garden"
(198–9). As for the previous generation, a realization of a less-than-satis-
fying union also occurs when a dying Cuyler revises his perceptions of
Mercy: "She is always in his recollections, standing at the doorway, waiting for him ... In fact, she had never once waited for him at the doorway,
being occupied at this hour with supper preparations. He must, however
clumsily, get that part right, that he had not been awaited" (275).

22 In an interview with *The Atlantic* in 1999, Shields commented that she
wrote *The Stone Diaries* as a "filter ... through Daisy's consciousness.
Every narrative is either what she hears people saying or what she imagines people are saying ... It's her interpretation of her own life. We're just
a bundle of impressions of other people, after all" (n.p.). During Daisy's
professional life, these voices dominate in the form of written correspondence, with Daisy paradoxically becoming more elided at this moment
(when she is supposedly coming into her own) than in the earlier chapters
of her life, where her consciousness often narrates her filtered impressions.

23 The fact that the retirement complex is called Bayside "Towers" is in keeping with Daisy's contained life and delimited roles. Commenting on how
the age difference between her parents sheltered her mother from change,
Alice reflects: "being a young wife to an older husband – it kept her girlish,
made her a kind of tenant in the tower of girlhood. There she remained,
safe, looked after" (235–6). Slethaug similarly makes note of this crystal-
lized image of Daisy's life, a life which progresses through all its phases in
a predictable manner: "the equivalent of a fairy-tale princess locked in a
tower" (61).

## Chapter Five

1 More recently, in an interview with Jay Ruzesky following the 2009 publication of her memoir, *Small Beneath the Sky*, which she wrote in prose,

Crozier also compares the essay genre to poetry: "Writing an essay feels a lot like writing a poem. There is an unfolding, a discovery for both the writer and the reader. I go into an essay not knowing where I'm going to end or even the direction I'm going to take to get there. That feels like entering the space of a poem" (51). This process of discovery that occurs within the "space" of Crozier's poems resonates with the concept of a garden "plot" being both a story and a contained space in which that story takes place.

2 Gingell sees in Crozier's collections a critical reworking of socio-cultural myths that stem from a variety of sources: religious narratives of the Judeo-Christian tradition to canonical myths of prairie literature. Gingell observes, "the prairie garden ... is the context of much of Crozier's poetry" (76), and in particular, "the sexual energy" of Crozier's garden poems is another way of "sabotag[ing] the idea of the prairie as the realm of the puritanical" (79). When it comes to identifying Crozier as a prairie writer, Dennis Cooley, in his short article "Correspondences: Two Saskatchewan Poets," links her preoccupation to a western, agrarian vision: "I know they grow vegetables elsewhere, but I like to think only a prairie poet could have written so rambunctiously, so affectionately, of the secrets their lives hold" (4).

3 Crozier's first three books of poetry, *Inside Is the Sky* (1976), *Crow's Black Joy* (1979), *Humans and Other Beasts* (1980), and her collaboration with Lane (*No Longer Two People*, 1981) were published using the last name Uher. With the publication of *The Weather* in 1983, Crozier resumed using her maiden name.

4 In the episode "Reflections of the Soul," Crozier reflects on her first marriage and her former husband's lack of understanding with regard to her craft: "My first husband was not a poet and he didn't understand half the time why I was so obsessed with language and with words ... And you know, he'd actually say, 'Why do you waste your time on this.'"

5 In an interview with Ruzesky that took place in 2009, Lane speaks to the creative exchange and support that continues to play a central part in the couple's long-term relationship: "We do show each other our work, particularly if one of us has a manuscript ready to go to the publisher. But our criticism of each other's work is not as often or intense as it was when we were younger. Still, we respond to the work and are honest in our assessments. Remember, we work out of the same house, our offices next to each other … I can tell just by looking at Lorna when she's in a state of writing. I wouldn't dream of interrupting her" (43). In her interview with Carey, Crozier similarly notes, "We're each other's best editors … So I think we give each other the little nudge you sometimes need as a writer to keep going" (16).

6 For a more recent re-vision of the Eden myth, see the poem "Original Sin" in *Apocrypha of Light* (2002). Crozier explores Lilith's (Adam's first wife) banishment from the Garden of Eden and the limitations of a pre-defined, demarcated terrain: Eve "walked to where the garden stopped / and everything Adam couldn't name / fell into poetry and silence" (22). Adam has already named the contents of the world, but Eve intuits an alternative form of expression and experience: "Beside the hawthorn hedge, the forbidden / tart on my tongue, I said *Lilith*" (22). Crozier's Eve bites not from the proverbial apple, but from the "forbidden / tart," creating another garden through the fruit, the word on her tongue, and the potentially erotic taste of Lilith.

7 Particularly interesting in terms of this study's exploration of a Canadian tradition of literary gardens is Melhorn-Boe's multi-media reworking of Crozier's poems; her experimentation with both text and physical form suggests another kind of border-crossing, to use Kroetsch's conceptualization of Canada and the work of its artists (Brown 14). In her reading of some of the other bookworks, Tara Hyland argues, "Melhorn-Boe crosses the boundaries of bookmaker, writer, and sculptor, causing, in the words

of one reviewer, a categorical crisis for the cataloguers at the National Library of Canada" (n.p.).

8  After revising the sculptural form of her bookwork for Crozier's poems (at first she had envisioned a pop-up book), Melhorn-Boe mentions in her letter that she eventually decided to use the genre of a seed catalogue after listening to gardeners, who were featured on an episode of CBC's radio program *Morning Side*, talk about catalogues and their plans for gardening.

9  In 2007 when Hall directed, produced, and wrote the play, she was majoring in theatre at the University of Victoria. After completing her Bachelor of Fine Arts (2010), followed by her Bachelor of Education in (2012), Hall began her career as a drama teacher in Victoria.

10  Letter to the author, 25 June 2012.

11  Much of what follows was conveyed in a telephone interview which took place on 26 June 2012. Hall also mentioned that she read Crozier's poem "Delight in the Small, The Silent" (which is not part of "The Sex Lives of Vegetables" but directly follows the sequence in *The Garden Going On Without Us*) as a kind of companion piece that informed her dramatic interpretation. This poem invites readers to see, hear, and take pleasure in that which normally escapes their notice both in the physical world and in language itself.

12  Genette's diction, here, subtly evokes the language of the garden in his conceptualization of the palimpsest genre. According to the *Oxford English Dictionary*, in a gardening context, the verb "to graft" means "To insert (a shoot from one tree) as a graft ... into another tree" (*OED Online*. 2012. Oxford University Press, s.v. "graft, v.1," accessed 30 June 2012, http://www.oed.com/view/Entry/80481). This shoot or scion is "inserted ... so as to allow the sap of the latter to circulate through the former" (*OED Online*. 2012. Oxford University Press, s.v. "graft, n.1," accessed 30 June 2012, http://www.oed.com/view/Entry/80476). The inter-relationship of

grafts is essential, as the old growth gives life to the new, which is not necessarily an identical replication. Quite the contrary, different species of trees may be grafted together. This definition reflects Canadian writers' creative reinterpretations of older texts, extending their combined reach, so to speak, by grafting on and branching out into new and varied formulations.

13 Thompson's gendered conceptualization of palimpsest speaks to other foundational scholarship on the topic. In the context of the Romantic and Victorian periods, Sandra Gilbert and Susan Gubar argue that women writers "produced literary works that are in some sense palimpsestic, works whose surface designs conceal or obscure deeper, less accessible (and less socially acceptable) levels of meaning" (73). The result of this suppression of a subversive feminine subtext within women's writing under patriarchy is the expression of psychological schism and monstrosity (77–8). Charlotte Perkins Gilman's short story "The Yellow Wallpaper" (1892) provides an example of this, a veritable "madwoman in the attic" fascinated with her suppressed self after being told not to write about her innermost thoughts by male family members.

14 Tellingly, Crozier dedicates *A Saving Grace* both to the memory of Sinclair Ross, and to her mother, Peggy Crozier, "who tells me her stories" (n.p.).

15 *OED Online*. 2006. Oxford University Press, s.v. "pervert, v," accessed 24 June 2006, http://dictionary.oed.com/cgi/entry/50176460.

16 *OED Online*. 2006. Oxford University Press, s.v. "vert, v," accessed 24 June 2006, http://dictionary.oed.com/cgi/entry/50276714.

17 Critics have differing opinions of Paul, yet they mostly agree he is fixated on the origins of words and their meaning as opposed to forming creative alternatives. In "An Awful Stumbling towards Names," Dennis Cooley argues that Paul's interest in etymology does not make him a poet, as Paul fails to demonstrate "any desire to use words in new ways. He does not ... advance into a dominion where the word is made flesh. Paul's names are

determined and confirming. His names, in other words, are for the most part confined to what once was" (112). Barbara Mitchell argues, on the other hand, that Paul is a kind of fool and poet in that, while his "preference is for the natural and original meaning of words and, by extension, of human values, he shows his knowledge of the laws of change and convertibility" (49).

18 In the original "Song of Songs," the female speaker states, "My beloved is like a roe or a young hart" (2.9).

19 For further details on Crozier's conceptualization of both lying and truth in poetry, see the interview with Hillis where Crozier subtly evokes the notion of layers: "One *invents* things, distorts the truth to find the real truth, the *poetic truth*, which is so much more important than the surface detail that started the poem" (9, original italics).

20 Further to this point is the fact that Mrs Bentley remembers the betrayal in the past tense, while the biblical verse is composed in the present. The difference in tense as well as the use of italicization suggest two voices, one sounding the experience of having lost a marital partnership, and the other, the new growth of an adulterous relationship. Carmen Leñero's discussion of Crozier's use of voice is especially relevant to Mrs Bentley's biblical garden palimpsest: "Lorna Crozier also knows how to listen to the voices that breathe within other poems ... That is why, rather than talking about intertextuality, I am referring to an intense 'intervocality' in Crozier's writing. Compelled by the musical expression that echoes in a particular passage, Crozier's poetic voice alters the original meaning, to enter instead into a new and personal dialogue with the passage" (119–20).

# Bibliography

## Archival Materials

Crozier, Lorna. Letter to Lise Melhorn-Boe. 30 May 1990. MS. 90-103 Lorna
Crozier. Box 6, File: Professional Activities "Sex Lives of Vegetables"
Project with Lise Melhorn-Boe 1988–90. University of Regina Library,
Regina.

Melhorn-Boe, Lise. Letter to Lorna Crozier. 21 January 1990. MS. 90-
103 Lorna Crozier. Box 6, File: Professional Activities "Sex Lives of
Vegetables" Project with Lise Melhorn-Boe 1988–90. University of
Regina Library, Regina.

Roy, Gabrielle. "Exiles." Translated by Alan Brown. Fonds Gabrielle Roy
Papiers 1936–1983. Box 58, File 4, Chapter 6. Library and Archives
Canada, Ottawa.

– "Le printemps revint à Volhyn." ts. Fonds Gabrielle Roy Papiers 1936–
1983. Box 56, File 3, Chapter 6. Library and Archives Canada, Ottawa.

Strickland, Agnes. Letter to Susanna Moodie. 23 May 1852. Patrick
Hamilton Ewing Collection of Moodie-Strickland-Vickers-Ewing
Family Papers/LMS-0139. Series 1, No. 130. Library and Archives Canada,
Ottawa.

Traill, Catharine Parr. *The Canadian Settler's Guide* Revisions, ms.

Traill Family Collection/MG 29, D81. Container 4, File 19-20. Library and Archives Canada, Ottawa.

– Memorabilia: Dried Flowers and Seeds. Traill Family Collection. Container 8, File 22. Library and Archives Canada, Ottawa.

Traill, Thomas. Letter to Frances Stewart, 5 June 1855. Traill Family Collection/MG 29, D81. Container 2, File 23. Page 2441-4. Library and Archives Canada, Ottawa.

## Books, Articles, and Internet Resources

Abrams, M.H. *A Glossary of Literary Terms*. 7th ed. Boston: Thomson Learning, 1999.

– et al., eds. *The Norton Anthology of English Literature*. 7th ed. Vol. 2. New York: W.W. Norton, 2000.

Adachi, Ken. "Discovering the Magic in Everyday Situations." *Toronto Star*, 24 December 1988, M3.

Ainsworth, Clea. "Defying Canonical Isolation: Poets Lorna Crozier and Patrick Lane." *The Peak* 96, no. 10 (7 July 1997). The Peak Publications Society. Simon Fraser University. Accessed 13 January 2006. http://www.the-peak.ca/1997/07/defying-canonical-isolationpoets-lorna-crozier-and-patrick-lane/.

Alexander, Catherine. "The Garden as Occasional Domestic Space." *Signs* 27, no. 3 (Spring 2002): 857–71.

Amiel, Barbara. "Look Back in Stupor." *Maclean's*, 5 September 1977, 54–6.

Andron, Marie-Pierre. "Parcs, squares et jardins dans *La montagne secrète de Gabrielle Roy*." In *Parcs, places, jardins: Representations québécoises et canadiennes anglophones*, edited by Marie Lyne Piccione and Bernadette Rigal-Cellard, 83–91. Talence: La maison des sciences de l'homme d'Aquitaine, 1998.

Arbel, Daphna V. "'My Vineyard, My Very Own, Is for Myself.'" In *The Song of*

*Songs: A Feminist Companion to the Bible,* edited by Athalya Brenner and
Carole R. Fontaine, 90–101. Second Series. Sheffield: Sheffield Academic,
2000.

Armstrong, John. *The Paradise Myth.* London: Oxford University Press,
1969.

Atwood, Margaret. *The Journals of Susanna Moodie.* Toronto: Oxford
University Press, 1970.

– *Survival: A Thematic Guide to Canadian Literature.* Toronto: Anansi,
1972.

– *The Year of the Flood.* Toronto: McClelland and Stewart, 2009.

Bailey, Geoff. "Time Perspectives, Palimpsests and the Archeaology of
Time." *Journal of Anthropological Archaeology* 26, no. 2 (2007): 198–223.
*Science Direct.* doi: 10.1016/j.jaa.2006.08.002.

Bakhtin, Mikhail. *The Dialogic Imagination: Four Essays.* 1975. Edited by
Michael Holquist. Translated by Caryl Emerson and Michael Holquist.
Austin: University of Texas Press, 1981.

Bal, Mieke. *Narratology: Introduction to the Theory of Narrative.* Toronto:
University of Toronto Press, 1985.

Ballstadt, Carl. Introduction to *Roughing It in the Bush or Life in Canada,*
by Susanna Moodie, xvii–lx. Edited by Carl Ballstadt. Ottawa: Carleton
University Press, 1988.

Banting, Pamela. "Miss A and Mrs. B: The Letter of Pleasure in *The Scarlet
Letter* and *As for Me and My House." North Dakota Quarterly* 54, no. 2
(Spring 1986): 30–40.

– "Robert Kroetsch's Translation Poetics: Questions of Composition in the
(Rosetta) 'Stone Hammer Poem' and *Seed Catalogue." West Coast Line*
27, no. 1 (1993): 92–107.

Bell, Susan Groag. "Women·Create Gardens in Male Landscapes." *Feminist
Studies* 16, no. 3 (1990): 471–91.

Bennett, Jennifer. *Lilies of the Hearth: The Historical Relationship between*

*Women and Plants.* Camden East: Camden House, 1991.

Bentley, D.M.R. "Breaking the 'Cake of Custom': The Atlantic Crossing as a Rubicon for Female Emigrants to Canada?" In *Re(Dis)covering Our Foremothers: Nineteenth-Century Canadian Women Writers,* edited by Lorraine McMullen, 91–122. Ottawa: University of Ottawa Press, 1990.

– *The Gay]Grey Moose: Essays on the Ecologies and Mythologies of Canadian Poetry, 1690–1990.* Ottawa: University of Ottawa Press, 1992.

Besner, Neil K., ed. *Carol Shields: The Arts of a Writing Life.* Winnipeg: Prairie Fire, 2003.

Blodgett, E.D. "Gardens at the World's End or Gone West in French." *Essays on Canadian Writing* 17 (Spring 1980): 113–26.

Bourbonnais, Nicole. "La symbolique de l'espace dans les récits de Gabrielle Roy." *Voix et images* 7, no. 2 (Hiver 1982): 367–84.

Brenner, Athalya, and Carole R. Fontaine, eds. *The Song of Songs: A Feminist Companion to the Bible.* Second Series. Sheffield: Sheffield Academic, 2000.

Briganti, Chiara. "Fat, Nail Clippings, Body Parts, or the Story of Where I Have Been: Carol Shields and Auto/Biography." In *Carol Shields, Narrative Hunger, and the Possibilities of Fiction,* edited by Edward Eden and Dee Goertz, 175–200. Toronto: University of Toronto Press, 2003.

Brown, Russell. "An Interview with Robert Kroetsch." *University of Windsor Review* 7, no. 2 (1972): 1–18.

– Donna Bennett, and Nathalie Cooke, eds. *An Anthology of Canadian Literature.* Rev. and abr. ed. Toronto: Oxford University Press, 1990.

Bumstead, J.M. "Home Sweet Suburb." *Beaver* 72, no. 5 (October 1992): 26+. *Academic Search Premier* (accessed 6 April 2011).

Burke, Edmond. *A Philosophical Enquiry into the Origins of Our Ideas of the Sublime and the Beautiful.* 1775. Edited by Adam Philips. Oxford: Oxford University Press, 1990.

Buss, Helen. "Women and the Garrison Mentality: Pioneer Women Autobiographers and Their Relation to the Land." In *Re(Dis)covering Our Foremothers: Nineteenth-Century Canadian Women Writers,* edited by Lorraine McMullen, 123–36. Ottawa: University of Ottawa Press, 1990.

Butler, Judith. *Gender Trouble: Feminism and the Subversion of Identity.* New York: Routledge, 1990.

Campbell, Wanda Ruth. "The 'Bildungsgedicht' as Garden in Nineteenth- and Twentieth-Century Canadian Long Poems." PhD diss., University of Western Ontario, 1991.

"Canada's Most Memorable Poems: The LRC Contributors' List." *Literary Review of Canada* 16, no. 3 (2008): 14–15.

Carey, Barbara. "Against the Grain: An Interview with Lorna Crozier." *Books in Canada* 22, no. 3 (April 1993): 14–17.

Carey, John. *The Intellectuals and the Masses: Pride and Prejudice among the Literary Intelligentsia, 1880–1939.* London: Faber, 1992.

Casey, Edward. *Getting Back into Place: Toward a Renewed Understanding of the Place World.* Bloomington: Indiana University Press, 1993.

Cicero. *The Nature of the Gods.* Translated by P.G. Walsh. Oxford: Clarendon, 1997.

Cixous, Hélène. "The Laugh of the Medusa." 1975. Translated by Keith Cohen and Paula Cohen. In *The Critical Tradition: Classic Texts and Contemporary Trends,* edited by David H. Richter, 1090–1102. New York: St Martin's, 1989.

Clavelle, Karen Anne. "Imagine the Prairies. The Garden in Post-Depression Prairie Fiction." PhD diss., University of Manitoba, 2005.

Coleridge, Samuel Taylor. "This Lime-Tree Bower My Prison." In *The Norton Anthology of English Literature.* 7th ed. Vol. 2. Edited by M.H. Abrams et al., 420–2. New York: W.W. Norton, 2000.

Cooke, Nathalie. "Lorna Crozier (1948– )." In *Canadian Writers and Their Works.* Poetry Series 11, edited by Robert Lecker, Jack David, and Ellen Quigley, 77–151. Toronto: ECW, 1995.

Cooley, Dennis. "An Awful Stumbling towards Names: Ross and the (Un) Common Noun." In *From the Heart of the Heartland: The Fiction of Sinclair Ross,* edited by John Moss, 103–24. Ottawa: University of Ottawa Press, 1992.

– "Correspondences: Two Saskatchewan Poets." *Border Crossings* 12, no. 1 (1993): 4–5.

Costantino, Vincenza. "Gabrielle Roy: Ses racines et son imaginaire." In *Colloque international "Gabrielle Roy": Actes du colloque soulignant le cinquantième anniversaire de Bonheur d'occasion,* edited by André Fauchon, 381–94. Winnipeg: Presses universitaires de Saint-Boniface, 1996.

Crawford, Rachel. *Poetry, Enclosure, and the Vernacular Landscape, 1700–1830.* Cambridge: Cambridge University Press, 2002.

– "Troping the Subject: Behn, Smith, Hemans and the Poetics of the Bower." *Studies in Romanticism* 38, no. 2 (1999): 249–79.

Crozier, Lorna. *Apocrypha of Light.* Toronto: McClelland and Stewart, 2002.

– "Changing into Fire." In *Desire in Seven Voices,* edited by Lorna Crozier, 63–85. Vancouver: Douglas and McIntyre, 1999.

– "Comic Books, Dead Dogs, Cheerleading: One Poet's Beginnings." *In 2 Print* (Fall 1998): 8–10. *Canadian Periodicals Index Quarterly.* doi: A30195092.

– *Everything Arrives at the Light.* Toronto: McClelland and Stewart, 1995.

– *Eye Witness: Variations for the Spring Equinox.* Victoria: Reference West, 1993.

– *The Garden Going On Without Us.* Toronto: McClelland and Stewart, 1985.

– Introduction to *Desire in Seven Voices,* edited by Lorna Crozier, 15–18. Vancouver: Douglas and McIntyre, 1999.

- *Inventing the Hawk.* Toronto: McClelland and Stewart, 1992.
- *A Saving Grace: The Collected Poems of Mrs. Bentley.* Toronto: McClelland and Stewart, 1996.
- "So Much Sorrow, and Then Pancakes After." *Contemporary Verse* 18, no. 4 (1996): 27–30.
- "Speaking the Flesh." In *Language in Her Eye: Views on Writing and Gender by Canadian Women Writing in English,* edited by Libby Scheier, Sarah Sheard, and Eleanor Wachtel, 91–4. Toronto: Coach House, 1990.
- "Tips for Writers." *In 2 Print (*Fall 1998): 12. *Canadian Periodicals Index Quarterly.* doi: A30197150.
- "A Western Poet's Journal." *Prairie Fire* 9, no. 1 (Spring 1988): 5–12.
- "Who's Listening?" *NeWest Review* 14, no. 3 (February–March 1989): 22–5.
Cude, Wilfred. "'Turn It Upside Down': The Right Perspective on *As for Me and My House.*" *English Studies in Canada* 5, no. 4 (1979): 469–88.
Cuthbertson, Yvonne. *Women Gardeners: A History.* Denver: Arden Press, 1998.
Dahl, Edward H. *Mid Forests Wild: A Study of the Concept of Wilderness in the Writings of Susanna Moodie, J.W.D. Moodie, Catharine Parr Traill and Samuel Strickland, c1830–1855.* Ottawa: National Museum of Man, 1973.
Davey, Frank. "Surviving the Paraphrase." In *Surviving the Paraphrase: Eleven Essays on Canadian Literature,* 1–12. Winnipeg: Turnstone, 1983.
Davidoff, Leonore, and Catherine Hall. *Family Fortunes: Men and Women of the English Middle Class, 1780–1850.* London: Hutchinson, 1987.
Dean, Misao. *Practising Femininity: Domestic Realism and the Performance of Gender in Early Canadian Fiction.* Toronto: University of Toronto Press, 1998.
Denham, Paul. "Narrative Technique in Sinclair Ross's *As for Me and My House.*" *Studies in Canadian Literature/ Études en littérature canadienne* 5, no. 1 (1980): 116–24.

D'Souza, Irene. "On Becoming a Writer: An Interview with Pulitzer Prize-Winning Author Carol Shields." *Herizons* 15, no. 3 (Winter 2002): 14–17.

Duffy, Dennis. *Gardens, Covenants, Exiles: Loyalism in the Literature of Upper Canada/Ontario.* Toronto: University of Toronto Press, 1982.

Dumas, Anne. *Book of Plants and Symbols.* London: Hachette, 2004.

Eden, Edward and Dee Goertz, eds. *Carol Shields, Narrative Hunger, and the Possibilities of Fiction.* Toronto: University of Toronto Press, 2003.

Elliott, Brent. *The Royal Horticultural Society: A History 1804–2004.* Shopwyke Manor Barn, Chichester, West Sussex: Phillimore, 2004.

Elliott, Charles, ed. *The Quotable Gardener.* Guildford: Lions Press, 1999.

Exum, J. Cheryl. "Ten Things Every Feminist Should Know about the Song of Songs." In *The Song of Songs: A Feminist Companion to the Bible,* edited by Athalya Brenner and Carole R. Fontaine, 24–35. Second Series. Sheffield: Sheffield Academic, 2000.

Fabricant, Carole. "Binding and Dressing Nature's Loose Tresses: The Ideology of Augustan Landscape Design." In *Studies in Eighteenth-Century Culture,* edited by Roseann Runte. Vol. 8, 109–35. Madison: University of Wisconsin Press, 1979.

Fauchon, André, ed. *Colloque international "Gabrielle Roy": Actes du colloque soulignant le cinquantième anniversaire de Bonheur d'occasion.* Winnipeg: Presses universitaires de Saint-Boniface, 1996.

Finlay, Mary Lou. *As It Happens.* 17 July 2003. Canadian Broadcasting Corporation. Accessed 1 June 2006. http://www.cbc.ca/news/obit/shields_carol/.

Fleming, Laurence. *The English Garden,* edited by Alan Gore. London: Michael Joseph, 1979.

Foster, Clarise. "An Interview with Lorna Crozier." *Contemporary Verse 2* 25, no. 3 (Winter 2003): 9–19.

Fowler, Marian. *The Embroidered Tent: Five Gentlewomen in Early Canada: Elizabeth Simcoe, Catharine Parr Traill, Susanna Moodie, Anna*

*Jameson, Lady Dufferin.* Toronto: Anansi, 1982.

Francis, Mark, and Randolph T. Hester, eds. *The Meaning of Gardens: Idea, Place, and Action.* Cambridge: MIT Press, 1990.

Friedan, Betty. *The Feminine Mystique.* 1963. New York: W.W. Norton, 1964.

Frye, Northrop. *The Bush Garden: Essays on the Canadian Imagination.* Toronto: Anansi, 1971.

Genette, Gérard. *Palimpsests: Literature in the Second Degree.* 1982. Translated by Channa Newman and Claude Doubinsky. Lincoln: University of Nebraska Press, 1997.

Giardini, Anne. "Reading My Mother." *Prairie Fire* 16, no. 1 (Spring 1995): 6–12.

Gilbert, Sandra M., and Susan Gubar. *The Madwoman in the Attic: The Woman Writer and the Nineteenth-Century Literary Imagination.* 2nd ed. New Haven: Yale University Press, 2000.

Giles, Judy. *The Parlour and the Suburb: Domestic Identities, Class, Femininity and Modernity.* Oxford: Berg, 2004.

Gilman, Charlotte Perkins. "The Yellow Wallpaper." 1892. In *The Harbrace Anthology of Literature.* 2nd ed. Edited by Jon C. Stott, Raymond E. Jones, and Rick Bowers, 946–57. Toronto: Harcourt, 1998.

Gingell, Susan. "Let Us Revise Mythologies: The Poetry of Lorna Crozier." *Essays on Canadian Writing* 43 (1991): 67–82.

Glickman, Susan. *The Picturesque and the Sublime: A Poetics of the Canadian Landscape.* Montreal and Kingston: McGill-Queen's University Press, 1998.

Goertz, Dee. "Treading the Maze of Larry's Party." In *Carol Shields, Narrative Hunger, and the Possibilities of Fiction,* edited by Edward Eden and Dee Goertz, 230–54. Toronto: University of Toronto Press, 2003.

Gom, Leona. "Stones and Flowers." *Prairie Fire* 16, no. 1 (Spring 1995): 22–7.

Grace, Sherrill. *Violent Duality: A Study of Margaret Atwood.* Montreal: Véhicule Press, 1980.

Graeber, Laurel. "Inside Daisy Flett." *The New York Times Book Review*, 27 March 1994, 3.

Groening, Laura. "Still in the Kitchen: The Art of Carol Shields." *Canadian Forum* (January–February 1991): 14–17.

Grosskurth, Phyllis. "Gabrielle Roy and the Silken Noose." *Canadian Literature* 42 (Autumn 1969): 6–13.

Guttman, Naomi Ellen. "Women Writing Gardens: Nature, Spirituality and Politics in Women's Garden Writing." PhD diss., University of Southern California, 1999.

Hall, Susan Grove. "The Duality of the Artist/Crafter in Carol Shields's Novels." *Kentucky Philological Review* 12 (March 1997): 42–7.

Hammill, Faye. "Carol Shields's 'Native Genre' and the Figure of the Canadian Author." *Journal of Commonwealth Literature* 31, no. 2 (1996): 87–99.

– "Margaret Atwood, Carol Shields, and 'That Moodie Bitch.'" *The American Review of Canadian Studies* 29, no. 1 (Spring 1999): 67–91.

Hapgood, Lynne. *Margins of Desire: The Suburbs in Fiction and Culture 1880–1925*. Manchester: Manchester University Press, 2005.

Harris, Dianne. "Cultivating Power: The Language of Feminism in Women's Garden Literature, 1870–1920." *Landscape Journal* 13, no. 2 (Fall 1994): 113–23.

– "The Postmodernization of Landscape: A Critical Historiography." *JSAH* 58, no. 3 (1999): 434–43.

Harvey, Carol J. *Le cycle manitoban de Gabrielle Roy*. Saint-Boniface: Plaines, 1993.

Hayden, Dolores. "Communal Idealism and the American Landscape." *Landscape* 20, no. 2 (1976): 20–32.

– *The Grand Domestic Revolution: A History of Feminist Designs for American Homes, Neighborhoods, and Cities*. Cambridge: MIT Press, 1981.

Heath, Caroline. "When Fact Meets Fantasy." In *Trace: Prairie Writers on Writing,* edited by Birk Sproxton, 193–8. Winnipeg: Turnstone, 1986.

Henighan, Stephen. *When Words Deny the World: The Reshaping of Canadian Writing.* Erin, ON: Porcupine's Quill, 2002.

Hillis, Doris. "The Real Truth, the Poetic Truth: An Interview with Lorna Crozier." *Prairie Fire* 6, no. 3 (Summer 1985): 4–15.

Hobbs, Catherine. "Voice and Re-vision: The Carol Shields Archival Fonds." In *Carol Shields and the Extra-Ordinary,* edited by Marta Dvořák and Manina Jones, 33–58. Montreal and Kingston: McGill-Queen's University Press, 2007.

Holmes, Michael. "Tight, Lyrical Reinterpretations." *Quill and Quire* 62, no. 9 (September 1996): 66.

Holy Bible. King James ed. Cambridge: Cambridge University Press, n.d.

Horace. "The Art of Poetry." In *The Critical Tradition: Classic Texts and Contemporary Trends,* edited by David H. Richter, 68–77. New York: St Martin's, 1989.

Humphreys, Helen. *The Lost Garden.* Toronto: HarperCollins, 2002.

Hunt, John Dixon. *Gardens and the Picturesque.* Cambridge: MIT Press, 1992.

– *Greater Perfections: The Practice of Garden Theory.* Philadelphia: University of Pennsylvania Press, 2000.

– *"Paragone* in Paradise: Translating the Garden." *Comparative Criticism* 18 (1996): 55–69.

– and Peter Willis, eds. *The Genius of the Place: The English Landscape Garden 1620–1820.* London: Elek, 1975.

Hyland, Tara. "Creative Meaning-Making: Reading the Bookworks of Lise Melhorn-Boe." *The Journal of Artists' Books* no. 11 (15 April 1999): 11–15. *Art Full Text (H.W. Wilson)* (accessed 28 June 2012).

Jackson, Rosemary. *Fantasy: The Literature of Subversion.* London: Routledge, 1986.

Johnson, Chris. "Ordinary Pleasures (and Terrors): The Plays of Carol Shields." In *Carol Shields: The Arts of a Writing Life*, edited by Neil K. Besner, 251–9. Winnipeg: Prairie Fire, 2003.

Johnson, Lisa. "'She Enlarges on the Available Materials': A Postmodernism of Resistance in *The Stone Diaries*." In *Carol Shields, Narrative Hunger, and the Possibilities of Fiction*, edited by Edward Eden and Dee Goertz, 201–29. Toronto: University of Toronto Press, 2003.

Johnston, Susan. "Reconstructing the Wilderness: Margaret Atwood's Reading of Susanna Moodie." *Canadian Poetry* 31 (Fall–Winter 1992): 28–54.

Jones, D.G. *Butterfly on Rock: A Study of Themes and Images in Canadian Literature*. Toronto: University of Toronto Press, 1970.

Keefer, Janice Kulyk. Review of *The Garden Going On Without Us*, by Lorna Crozier. *The Antigonish Review* 65 (Spring 1986): 59–68.

King, Thomas. "A Seat in the Garden." In *One Good Story, That One*, 81–94. Toronto: Harper Collins, 1993,

Kirchhoff, H.J. "In Person: Writers in an Ever-changing Residence U of T's Patrick Lane and Lorna Crozier have Lived in 8 Cities in the Past 10 Years; Now These Prairie Poets Are Ready to Go Home to Saskatoon and Put Their Feet Up." *Globe and Mail*, 31 March 1990, Arts and Entertainment: C11. *Canadian Periodicals Index Quarterly*. doi: A164500364.

Klein, A.M. "Portrait of the Poet as Landscape." In *An Anthology of Canadian Literature*. Rev. and abr. ed. Edited by Russell Brown, Donna Bennett, and Nathalie Cooke, 316–21. Toronto: Oxford University Press, 1990.

Klinck, Carl F. "Introduction to *Roughing It in the Bush*," in *Roughing It in the Bush; or, Life in Canada*, by Susanna Moodie. Edited by Elizabeth Thompson, 471–6. Ottawa: Tecumseh, 1997.

Knight, Richard Payne. *The Landscape, A Didactic Poem in Three Books.* 1794. 2nd ed. London: Bulmer, 1795.

Kolodny, Annette. *The Land before Her: Fantasy and Experience of the American Frontiers, 1630–1860.* Chapel Hill: University of North Carolina Press, 1984.

Kroetsch, Robert. "Disunity as Unity." In *The Lovely Treachery of Words,* 21–33. Toronto: Oxford University Press, 1989.

– "The Fear of Women in Prairie Fiction: An Erotics of Space." In *The Lovely Treachery of Words,* 73–83. Toronto: Oxford University Press, 1989.

– *The Lovely Treachery of Words: Essays Selected and New.* Toronto: Oxford University Press, 1989.

– "No Name Is My Name." In *The Lovely Treachery of Words,* 41–52. Toronto: Oxford University Press, 1989.

– "Pumpkin: A Love Poem." In *The Stone Hammer Poems, 1960–1975,* 26–7. Lantzville: Oolichan Books, 1976.

– *Seed Catalogue.* Winnipeg: Turnstone, 1977.

Kröller, Eva-Marie. "Resurrections: Susanna Moodie, Catharine Parr Traill and Emily Carr in Contemporary Canadian Literature." *Journal of Popular Culture* 15, no. 3 (Winter 1981): 39–46.

Labbe, Jacqueline M. "Cultivating One's Understanding of the Female Romantic Garden." *Women's Writing* 4, no. 1 (1997): 39–56.

Lane, Patrick. "Journey into Mystery." *Canadian Gardening,* August/September 2006, 52–5.

– *There is a Season: A Memoir in a Garden.* Toronto: McClelland and Stewart, 2004.

– and Lorna Uher. (Lorna Crozier) *No Longer Two People.* Winnipeg: Turnstone, 1979.

Laurence, Margaret. *The Diviners.* 1974. Toronto: McClelland and Stewart, 1992.

Lecker, Robert. "Bordering On: Robert Kroetsch's Aesthetic." *Journal of Canadian Studies* 17, no. 3 (1982): 124–33.

– *Robert Kroetsch*. Boston: Twayne Publishers, 1986.

Leñero, Carmen. "A Word with Wings." Translated by Janice Shewey. *The Malahat Review* 170 (Spring 2010): 115–24.

Lennox, John. "'Metaphors of Self': *La détresse et l'enchantement*." In *Reflections: Autobiography and Canadian Literature*, edited by K.P. Stich, 69–78. Ottawa: University of Ottawa Press, 1988.

Lewis, Paula Gilbert. "Female Spirals and Male Cages: The Urban Sphere in the Novels of Gabrielle Roy." In *Traditionalism, Nationalism and Feminism: Women Writers of Quebec*, 71–81. Westport: Greenwood, 1985.

– "Feminism and Traditionalism in the Early Short Stories of Gabrielle Roy." In *Traditionalism, Nationalism and Feminism: Women Writers of Quebec*, 27–35. Westport: Greenwood, 1985.

– *The Literary Vision of Gabrielle Roy: An Analysis of Her Works*. Birmingham: Summa, 1993.

– ed. *Traditionalism, Nationalism and Feminism: Women Writers of Quebec*. Westport: Greenwood, 1985.

Litwin, Grania. "Exploring Edens: Island Gardens Star in an Intimate Portrait of Gardeners on HGTV." *Times–Colonist* (Victoria), 10 April 2003, Life: C4. *Canadian Periodicals Index Quarterly*. doi: 325223091.

Lord, Marie-Linda. "Dans *La détresse et l'enchantement* de Gabrielle Roy, la chambre est un espace d'intégration psychique." *Francophonies d'Amérique* 4 (1994): 97–105.

Loudon, Jane. *Instructions in Gardening for Ladies*. London: John Murray, 1840.

Luka, Nik, and Leo Trottier. "In the Burbs: It's Time to Recognize That Suburbia Is a Real Place Too." *Alternatives Journal* 28, no. 3 (2002): 37–8.

Macey, J. David. "'Where the World May Ne'er Invade'? Green Retreats and Garden Theatre in *La Princesse de Clèves*, *The History of Miss Betsy*

*Thoughtless,* and *Cecilia.*" *Eighteenth-Century Fiction* 12, no.1 (1999): 75–100.

MacLulich, T.D. "Crusoe in the Backwoods: A Canadian Fable?" *Mosaic* 9, no. 2 (1976): 115–26.

Madigan, M. Kathleen. "Uncommon Ground in Gabrielle Roy's 'Un jardin au bout du monde.'" *Women in French Studies* 5 (Winter 1997): 69–76.

Maharaj, Robyn. "'The Arc of a Whole Life': A Telephone Interview with Carol Shields from Her Home in Victoria, BC, May 4, 2002." *Prairie Fire* 23, no. 4 (Winter 2002–03): 8–11.

Mansfield, Katherine. "The Garden Party." *The Garden Party,* 59–82. New York: Random House, 1922.

Marcus, Clare Cooper. "The Garden as Metaphor." In *The Meaning of Gardens: Idea, Place, and Action,* edited by Mark Francis, and Randolph T. Hester, 26–33. Cambridge: MIT Press, 1990.

Martin, Carol. *A History of Canadian Gardening.* Toronto: McArthur, 2000.

Martin, Sandra. "The Perils of Charleen." *Books in Canada* 6, no. 10 (December 1977): 15–16.

Marvell, Andrew. "The Garden." 1681. In *The Norton Anthology of Poetry.* Shorter 4th ed. Edited by Margaret Ferguson, Mary Jo Salter, and Jon Stallworthy, 274–6. New York: W.W. Norton, 1996.

McCarthy, Dermot. "Ego in a Green Prison: Confession and Repression in *Roughing It in the Bush.*" *Wascana Review* 14 (1979): 3–16.

McClung, William Alexander. *The Architecture of Paradise: Survivals of Eden and Jerusalem.* Berkeley: University of California Press, 1983.

McCombs, Judith. "Atwood's Haunted Sequences: *The Circle Game, The Journals of Susanna Moodie,* and *Power Politics.*" In *The Art of Margaret Atwood: Essays in Criticism,* edited by Arnold E. Davidson and Cathy N. Davidson, 35–54. Toronto: Anansi, 1981.

McGregor, Gaile. *The Wacousta Syndrome: Explorations in the Canadian Langscape.* Toronto: University of Toronto Press, 1985.

McHarg, Ian L. "Nature is More Than a Garden." In *The Meaning of Gardens: Idea, Place, and Action,* edited by Mark Francis and Randolph T. Hester, 34–7. Cambridge: MIT Press, 1990.

McMullen, Lorraine, ed. *Re(Dis)covering Our Foremothers: Nineteenth-Century Canadian Women Writers.* Ottawa: University of Ottawa Press, 1990.

McPherson, Hugo. "The Garden and the Cage." *Canadian Literature* 1 (1959): 46–57.

Melhorn-Boe, Lise. "About Lise." *Lise Melhorn-Boe.* Accessed 1 June 2011. http://www.lisemelhornboe.ca/lise.html.

– "Sex Lives of Vegetables: A Seed Catalogue," in "Gender Issues Bookworks for Sale." *Lise Melhorn-Boe.* Accessed 1 June 2011. http://www.lisemelhornboe.ca/list-gender.html#Sex-Lives.

Mellor, Winifred M. "'The Simple Container of Our Existence': Narrative Ambiguity in Carol Shields's *The Stone Diaries.*" *Studies in Canadian Literature* 20, no. 2 (1995): 96–110.

Mermin, Dorothy. "The Damsel, the Knight, and the Victorian Woman Poet." *Critical Inquiry* 13, no. 1 (Autumn 1986): 64–80.

Meyer, Bruce, and Brian O'Riordan. "Nothing Better Than Poetry? An Interview with Lorna Crozier." *Poetry Canada Review* 10, no. 1 (Spring 1989): 1, 3, 28–9.

Miller, Mara. *The Garden as an Art.* Albany: State University of New York Press, 1993.

Milton, John. *Paradise Lost.* 1674. 2nd ed. Edited by Scott Elledge. New York: W.W. Norton, 1993.

Mitchell, Barbara. "Paul: The Answer to the Riddle of *As For Me and My House.*" *Studies in Canadian Literature* 13, no. 1 (1988): 47–63.

Montgomery, L.M. *Anne of the Island.* 1915. New York: Seal, 1981.

Montreuil, Sophie. "Petite histoire de la nouvelle 'Un jardin au bout du monde' de Gabrielle Roy." *Voix et images* 23, no. 2 (Hiver 1998): 360–84.

Moodie, Susanna. *Flora Lyndsay; or, Passages in an Eventful Life*. New York: De Witt, 1854.

– *Letters of Love and Duty: The Correspondence of Susanna and John Moodie*. Edited by Carl Ballstadt, Elizabeth Hopkins, and Michael Peterman. Toronto: University of Toronto Press, 1993.

– *Life in the Clearings versus the Bush*. 1853. Toronto: McClelland and Stewart, 1989.

– *Matrimonial Speculations*. London: Richard Bentley, 1854.

– *Roughing It in the Bush or Life in Canada*. 1852. Edited by Carl Ballstadt. Centre for Editing Early Canadian Texts Series. Ottawa: Carleton University Press, 1988.

– *Susanna Moodie: Letters of a Lifetime*. Edited by Carl Ballstadt, Elizabeth Hopkins, and Michael Peterman. Toronto: University of Toronto Press, 1985.

– *Voyages: Short Narratives of Susanna Moodie*. Edited by John Thurston. Canadian Short Story Library Series 2. Ottawa: University of Ottawa Press, 1991.

Moore, Charles W., William J. Mitchell, and William Turnbull. *The Poetics of Gardens*. Cambridge: MIT Press, 1993.

Mootoo, Shani. *Cereus Blooms at Night*. Toronto: McClelland and Stewart, 1996.

– "A Garden of Her Own." In *The Other Woman: Women of Colour in Contemporary Canadian Literature*, edited by Makeda Silvera, 157–69. Toronto: Sister Vision, 1995.

Moss, John. "Bushed in the Sacred Wood." *The Paradox of Meaning: Cultural Poetics and Critical Fictions*, 13–28. Winnipeg: Turnstone, 1999.

Murray, Heather. "Women in the Wilderness." In *A Mazing Space: Writing Canadian Women Writing*, edited by Shirley Neuman and Smaro Kamboureli, 74–83. Edmonton: Longspoon-NeWest, 1986.

Neuman, Shirley. Review of *The Garden Going On Without Us*, by Lorna Crozier. *Journal of Canadian Poetry* 2 (1987): 28–33.

New, W.H. *Land Sliding: Imagining Space, Presence, and Power in Canadian Writing.* Toronto: University of Toronto Press, 1997.

O'Malley, Andrew. "Island Homemaking: Catharine Parr Traill's *Canadian Crusoes* and the Robinsonade Tradition." In *Home Words: Discourses of Children's Literature in Canada,* edited by Mavis Reimer, 67–86. Waterloo: Wilfred Laurier University Press, 2008.

Ostriker, Alicia. "A Holy of Holies: The Song of Songs as Countertext." In *The Song of Songs: A Feminist Companion to the Bible,* edited by Athalya Brenner and Carole R. Fontaine, 36–54. Second Series. Sheffield: Sheffield Academic, 2000.

Parker, Patricia. "The Progress of Phaedria's Bower: Spenser to Coleridge." *ELH* 40, no. 3 (1973): 372–97.

Perényi, Eleanor. *Green Thoughts: A Writer in the Garden.* New York: Modern, 2002.

Peterman, Michael. *This Great Epoch of Our Lives: Susanna Moodie's Roughing It in the Bush.* Toronto: ECW, 1996.

– "'Splendid Anachronism': The Record of Catharine Parr Traill's Struggles as an Amateur Botanist in Nineteenth-Century Canada." In *Re(Dis)covering Our Foremothers: Nineteenth-Century Canadian Women Writers,* edited by Lorraine McMullen, 173–85. Ottawa: University of Ottawa Press, 1990.

– *Susanna Moodie: A Life.* Toronto: ECW Press, 1999.

Philips, Elizabeth. "Crozier and Lane: The Sexologist of the Garden Meets the Carpenter of Words." *Western Living,* November 1991, 147–8.

– "Seeing Distance: Lorna Crozier's Art of Paradox." In *Where the Words Come From: Canadian Poets in Conversation,* edited by Tim Bowling, 139–58. Roberts Creek: Nightwood, 2002.

Potteiger, Matthew, and Jamie Purinton. *Landscape Narratives: Design Practices for Telling Stories.* New York: John Wiley, 1998.

Raiger, Michael. "The Poetics of Liberation in Imaginative Power:

Coleridge's 'This Lime-Tree Bower My Prison.'" *European Romantic Review* 3, no. 1 (1992): 65–78.

Ramon, Alex. *Liminal Spaces: The Double Art of Carol Shields.* Newcastle upon Tyne: Cambridge Scholars Publishing, 2008.

"Reflections of the Soul." *Recreating Eden.* Home and Garden Television. Picture Box, 2002. Videocassette (VHS), 22 min.

Repton, Humphrey. *The Art of Landscape Gardening; Including His Sketches and Hints on Landscape Gardening and Theory and Practice of Landscape Gardening.* Edited by John Nolen. Boston and New York: Houghton, Mifflin, 1907.

– "From the 'Red Book' for Blaise Castle (1795–6)." In *The Genius of the Place: The English Landscape Garden, 1620–1820,* edited by John Dixon Hunt and Peter Willis, 359–65. London: Elek, 1975.

Ricard, François. *Gabrielle Roy: A Life.* 1996. Translated by Patricia Claxton. Toronto: McClelland and Stewart, 1999.

– *Inventaire des archives personnelles de Gabrielle Roy.* Montreal: Les Éditions du Boréal, 1992.

Rich, Adrienne. "When We Dead Awaken: Writing as Re-vision." In *On Lies, Secrets, and Silence: Selected Prose 1966–1978,* 33–49. New York: W.W. Norton, 1979.

Richter, David H., ed. *The Critical Tradition: Classic Texts and Contemporary Trends.* New York: St Martin's, 1989.

Robinson, Christine. "Étude génétique du 'Printemps revint à Volhyn.'" In *Gabrielle Roy réécrite,* edited by Jane Everett and François Ricard, 55–74. n.p.: Nota Bene, 2003.

Robinson, Eden. *Monkey Beach.* Toronto: Random House, 2000.

Rose, Marilyn. "'Bones Made of Light': Nature in the Poetry of Lorna Crozier." *Canadian Poetry* 55 (Fall–Winter 2004): 53–64.

Ross, Sinclair. *As for Me and My House.* 1941. Toronto: McClelland and Stewart, 1989.

Ross, Stephanie. *What Gardens Mean*. Chicago: University of Chicago Press, 1998.

Rouslin, Virginia Watson. "The Intelligent Woman's Guide to Pioneering in Canada." *Dalhousie Review* 56 (Summer 1976): 319–35.

Roy, Gabrielle. *The Cashier*. 1954. Translated by Harry Binsse. Toronto: McClelland and Stewart, 1990.

– *La détresse et l'enchantement*. Montreal: Les Éditions du Boréal, 1984.

– *Enchantment and Sorrow*. 1984. Translated by Patricia Claxton. Toronto: Lester and Orpen Dennys, 1987.

– *The Fragile Lights of Earth*. 1978. Translated by Alan Brown. Toronto: McClelland and Stewart, 1982.

– *Garden in the Wind*. 1975. Translated by Alan Brown. Toronto: McClelland and Stewart, 1989.

– *The Hidden Mountain*. 1961. Translated by Harry Binsse. Toronto: McClelland and Stewart, 1962.

– *Un jardin au bout du monde*. Montreal: Beauchemin, 1975.

– *Letters to Bernadette*. 1988. Edited by François Ricard. Translated by Patricia Claxton. Toronto: Lester and Orpen Dennys, 1990.

– *The Road Past Altamont*. 1966. Translated by Joyce Marshall. Toronto: McClelland and Stewart, 1989.

– *Street of Riches*. 1955. Translated by Harry L. Binsse. Toronto: McClelland and Stewart, 1991.

– *The Tin Flute*. 1945. Translated by Alan Brown. Toronto: McClelland and Stewart, 1989.

– *Where Nests the Water Hen*. 1950. Translated by Harry L. Binsse. Toronto: McClelland and Stewart, 1989.

Roy, Wendy. "Autobiography as Critical Practice in *The Stone Diaries*." In *Carol Shields, Narrative Hunger, and the Possibilities of Fiction*, edited by Edward Eden and Dee Goertz, 113–46. Toronto: University of Toronto Press, 2003.

Rubinger, Catherine. "Actualité de deux contes-témoins: *Le torrent* d'Anne Hébert et *Un jardin au bout du monde* de Gabrielle Roy." *Présence francophone* 20 (Printemps 1980): 121–6.

Ruskin, John. "Of Queens' Gardens." 1865. *Sesame and Lilies*. 1865. Edited by Deborah Epstein Nord, 68–93. New Haven: Yale University Press, 2002.

Ruzesky, Jay. "Dancing on Neruda's Table: An Interview with Patrick Lane and Lorna Crozier." *The Malahat Review* 170 (Spring 2010): 39–53.

Saint-Martin, Lori. "Gabrielle Roy: The Mother's Voice, The Daughter's Text." *American Review of Canadian Studies* (Autumn 1990): 303–25.

– "Portrait de l'artiste en (vieille) femme." In *Colloque international "Gabrielle Roy": Actes du colloque soulignant le cinquantième anniversaire de Bonheur d'occasion,* edited by André Fauchon, 513–23. Winnipeg: Presses universitaires de Saint-Boniface, 1996.

– *La voyageuse et la prisonnière: Gabrielle Roy et la question des femmes.* Montreal: Les Éditions du Boréal, 2002.

Sayer, Karen. "The Labourer's Welcome: Border Crossings in the English Country Garden." In *Gender and Landscape: Renegotiating Morality and Space,* edited by Lorraine Dowler, Josephine Carubia, and Bonj Szczygiel, 34–54. London: Routledge, 2005.

Schein, Richard H. "The Place of Landscape: A Conceptual Framework for Interpreting an American Scene." *Annals of the Association of American Geographers* 87, no. 4 (1997): 660–80.

Shands, Kerstin W. *Embracing Space: Spatial Metaphors in Feminist Discourse.* Westport: Greenwood, 1999.

Shields, Carol. "About Writing." In *Carol Shields: The Arts of a Writing Life,* edited by Neil K. Besner, 261–2. Winnipeg: Prairie Fire, 2003.

– *The Box Garden.* Toronto: McGraw-Hill Ryerson, 1977.

– *Happenstance.* Toronto: McGraw-Hill Ryerson, 1980.

– *Larry's Party.* Toronto: Random House, 1997.

- "A Likely Story: A Conversation with Carol Shields." *The Atlantic Online*, 14 January 1999. The Atlantic Monthly Company. http://www. theatlantic.com/past/docs/unbound/factfict/ff9901.htm.
- *A Memoir of Friendship: The Letters between Carol Shields and Blanche Howard*. Edited by Blanche Howard and Allison Howard, 273–5. Toronto: Viking, 2007.
- "Narrative Hunger and the Overflowing Cupboard." In *Carol Shields, Narrative Hunger, and the Possibilities of Fiction*, edited by Edward Eden and Dee Goertz, 19–36. Toronto: University of Toronto Press, 2003.
- *Small Ceremonies: A Novel*. Toronto: McGraw-Hill Ryerson, 1976.
- *The Stone Diaries*. Toronto: Random House, 1993.
- *Susanna Moodie: Voice and Vision*. Ottawa: Borealis, 1977.

Showalter, Elaine. "Feminist Criticism in the Wilderness." *Critical Inquiry* 8, no. 2 (1981): 179–206.

Sibbald, Barbara. "Ottawa's Literary Environment: Part 2." *National Capital Letters: Ottawa's Literary Environment* 4 (Summer 2004). Ottawa Literary Heritage Society. Accessed 28 May 2007. <http://capletters.ncf. ca/capletters/4/index.htm#ottawa>.

Simo, Melanie Louise. *Loudon and the Landscape: From Country Seat to Metropolis 1783–1843*. New Haven: Yale University Press, 1988.

Skinner, Helen Ross. "With a Lilac by the Door: Some Research into Early Gardens in Ontario." *Bulletin of the Association for Preservation Technologies*. 15, no. 4 (1983): 35–7.

Slethaug, Gordon E. "'The Coded Dots of Life': Carol Shields's Diaries and Stones." *Canadian Literature* 156 (Spring 1998): 59–81.

Sparrow, Fiona. "'This place is some kind of a garden': Clearings in the Bush in the Works of Susanna Moodie and Catharine Parr Traill, Margaret Atwood and Margaret Laurence." *Journal of Commonwealth Literature* 25, no. 1 (1990): 25–41.

Spenser, Edmund. "The Faerie Queene." In *Spenser Poetical Works*, edited by J.C. Smith and E. De Selincourt, 1–406. Oxford: Oxford University Press, 1991.

Stanzel, F.K. "Innocent Eyes? Canadian Landscape as Seen by Frances Brooke, Susanna Moodie and Others." *International Journal of Canadian Studies* 4 (Fall 1991): 97–109.

Stefaniak, Lisa. "Botanical Gleanings: Susan Fenimore Cooper, Catharine Parr Traill, and Representations of Flora." In *Susan Fenimore Cooper: New Essays on Rural Hours and Other Works*, edited by Rochelle Johnson and Daniel Patterson, 232–48. Athens: University of Georgia Press, 2001.

Steffler, Margaret, and Neil Steffler. "'If We Would Read It Aright': Traill's 'Ladder to Heaven.'" *Journal of Canadian Studies* 38, no. 3 (Fall 2004): 123–52.

Strong-Boag, Veronica. "Home Dreams: Women and the Suburban Experiment in Canada, 1945–60." *Canadian Historical Review* 72, no. 4 (1991): 471–504.

Sullivan, Rosemary. "The Forest and the Trees." In *Ambivalence: Studies in Canadian Literature,* edited by Om P. Juneja and Chandra Mohan, 39–47. New Delhi: Allied, 1990.

Sutherland, Fraser. "Poets to Watch, If They Watch Themselves." *Globe and Mail*, 1 March 1986: D20. *Canadian Newsstand.* http://search.proquest.com/docview/386173341?accountid=35875.

Thomas, Clara. "Happily Ever After: Canadian Women in Fiction and Fact." *Canadian Literature* 34 (1967): 43–53.

Thomas, Joan. "'… writing must come out of what passionately interests us. Nothing else will do': An Epistolary Interview with Carol Shields." In *Carol Shields: The Arts of a Writing Life*, edited by Neil K. Besner, 73–85. Winnipeg: Prairie Fire, 2003.

Thompson, Elizabeth. *The Pioneer Woman: A Canadian Character Type.* Montreal and Kingston: McGill-Queen's University Press, 1991.

Thompson, Patricia J. *Fatal Abstractions: The Parallogics of Everyday Life*.
New York: Lang, 2004.

Thurston, John. Introduction to *Voyages: Short Narratives of Susanna
Moodie*, by Susanna Moodie, vii–xxix. Canadian Short Story Library
Series. Edited by John Thurston. Ottawa: University of Ottawa Press, 1991.

Traill, Catharine Parr. *The Backwoods of Canada*. 1836. Edited by Michael A.
Peterman. Ottawa: Carleton University Press, 1997.

– *Canadian Crusoes: A Tale of the Rice Lake Plains*. 1852. Edited by Rupert
Schieder. Centre for Editing Early Canadian Texts Series. Carleton:
Carleton University Press, 1986.

– *The Canadian Settler's Guide*. 1855. Toronto: McClelland and Stewart, 1969.

– *Cot and Cradle Stories*. Edited by Mary Agnes Fitzgibbon. Toronto:
William Briggs, 1895.

– *The Female Emigrant's Guide, and Hints on Canadian Housekeeping*.
Toronto: Maclear, 1854.

– *Forest and Other Gleanings: The Fugitive Writings of Catharine Parr Traill*.
Edited by Michael A. Peterman and Carl Ballstadt. Ottawa: University of
Ottawa Press, 1994.

– *I Bless You in My Heart: Selected Correspondence of Catharine Parr Traill*.
Edited by Carl Ballstadt, Elizabeth Hopkins, and Michael A. Peterman.
Toronto: University of Toronto Press, 1996.

– *Little Downy; or, The History of a Field-Mouse: A Moral Tale*. London:
Dean, 1822.

– *Narratives of Nature, and History Book for Young Naturalists*. London:
Lacey, 1831.

– *Pearls and Pebbles*. 1894. Edited by Elizabeth Thompson. Toronto: Natural
Heritage, 1999.

– *Sketches from Nature; or, Hints to Juvenile Naturalists*. London: Harvey,
1830.

- *Studies of Plant Life in Canada*. 1885. New and rev. ed. Toronto: William Briggs, 1906.
- *The Young Emigrants; or, Pictures of Canada Calculated to Amuse and Instruct the Minds of Youth*. London: Harvey and Dalton, 1826.

Turner, Roger. *Capability Brown: And the Eighteenth-Century English Landscape*. New York: Rizzoli, 1985.

Tymieniecka, Anna-Teresa. "*De Patria Mea*: The Passion for Place as the Thread Leading out of the Labyrinth of Life." *Analecta Husserliana* 44 (1995): 3–20.

Uher, Lorna. (Lorna Crozier) *Humans and Other Beasts*. Winnipeg: Turnstone, 1980.

- *Inside Is the Sky*. Saskatoon: Thistledown, 1976.

von Baeyer, Edwinna. *Rhetoric and Roses: A History of Canadian Gardening, 1900–1930*. Markham: Fitzhenry and Whiteside, 1984.

Vroom, Meto J. *Lexicon of Garden and Landscape Architecture*. Basel, Switzerland: Birkhäuser, 2006.

Wachtel, Eleanor. "Interview with Carol Shields." *Room of One's Own* 13, no. 1 (July 1989): 5–45.

- "Telling it Slant." *Books in Canada* 18, no. 4 (May 1989): 9–14.

Walker, Susan. "'Carrot Lady' Poet Pulls up Roots." *Toronto Star,* 13 April 1990, E3.

Wasmeier, Marie-Louise. "Fictional Fossils: Life and Death Writing in Carol Shields's *The Stone Diaries*." *Forum of Modern Language Studies* 41, no. 4 (2005): 439–48.

Waterman, Catharine H. *Flora's Lexicon: The Language of Flowers*. 1860. Classic Reprint Series. Ottawa: Algrove, 2001.

Waters, Michael. *The Garden in Victorian Literature*. Aldershot: Scholar, 1988.

Webb, Phyllis. "Marvell's Garden." 1956. In *An Anthology of Canadian*

*Literature.* Rev. and abr. ed. Edited by Russell Brown, Donna Bennett, and Nathalie Cooke, 443–5. Toronto: Oxford University Press, 1990.

Whitfield, Agnes. "Gabrielle Roy as Feminist: Re-reading the Critical Myths." *Canadian Literature* 126 (Autumn 1990): 20–31.

Whitlock, Gillian. "The Bush, the Barrack-Yard and the Clearing: 'Colonial Realism' in the Sketches and Stories of Susanna Moodie, C.L.R James and Henry Lawson." *Journal of Commonwealth Literature* 20, no. 1 (1985): 36–48.

Whitman, Walt. "Song of Myself." In *Walt Whitman, Emily Dickinson: Selections from the Norton Anthology of American Literature.* 4th ed. Edited by Hershel Parker, 22–64. New York: W.W. Norton, 1994.

Williamson, Dave. "Seven Steps to Point-of-View Perfection." In *Carol Shields: The Arts of a Writing Life,* edited by Neil K. Besner, 169–81. Winnipeg: Prairie Fire, 2003.

Woodhead, Eileen. *Early Canadian Gardening: An 1827 Nursery Catalogue.* Montreal and Kingston: McGill-Queen's University Press, 1998.

Wordsworth, Dorothy. *The Grasmere Journals.* Edited by Pamela Woof. Oxford: Clarendon, 1991.

Wordsworth, William. "Nutting." 1800. In *The Norton Anthology of English Literature.* 7th ed. Vol. 2. Edited by M.H. Abrams et al., 258–9. New York: W.W. Norton, 2000.

Ying, Kong. "'This Arc of Human Life': An Interview with Carol Shields." *Prairie Fire* 20, no. 1 (Spring 1999): 8–15.

# Index

Abrams, M.H., 15

Adachi, Ken, 213, 223

Ainsworth, Clea, 243, 245

Alexander, Catherine, 41

Amiel, Barbara, 295n8

Andron, Marie-Pierre, 143–4

apples: and C. Shields, 178; and G. Roy, 290; and J. Milton, 174; and L. Crozier, 230, 256, 302n6; and M. Laurence, 54; and pips mailed by C.P. Traill, 53, 279n21; and S. Moodie, 283n15

Arbel, Daphna V., 257–8

Armstrong, John, 173

Atwood, Annie, 53, 279n21

Atwood, Margaret, 98, 244, 246, 273n3, 287n25; and bush garden archetype, 3–4, 6, 26, 61, 177–8, 269n1, 276n11; on gardens, 4, 55; gothic vision of, 25–6, 105; and N. Frye, 3, 269n1; and pioneer garden palimpsest, 20, 25–6, 54, 95, 102–5, 114, 241–2, 265; and wilderness, 25–6, 98, 103–5, 273n3, 287n25

Atwood, Margaret, works of: "Alternate Thoughts from Underground," 104; "Disembarking at Quebec," 282n11; "The Double Voice," 103–4; "Dream 1: The Bush Garden," 3, 26, 61, 104, 177, 286n4, 276n11; *The Journals of Susanna Moodie*, 3, 25–6, 54, 95, 103–5, 282n11, 287n25; "The Planters," 61; *Survival*, 4, 55; *The Year of the Flood*, 267

backwoods kitchen gardens, 12, 277n18, 278n20; and aesthetics, 44–5, 48–9; and domestic economy, 40–1; and family involvement, 41–2; and female pioneers, 44–5, 48–50; and

Elliott, Brent, 277n16

English landscape parks, 28, 31–2, 64, 274n6; and ha-ha fence, 43; and H. Repton, 32, 274n6, 275n7; and L. "Capability" Brown, 32, 274n6, 275n8, 278n19; and male ownership, 28, 271n7, 284n16; and the picturesque, 28–9, 274n5; and R.P. Knight, 29, 275n8

Exum, J. Cheryl, 255

Fabricant, Carole, 271n7

feminism: and architecture, 272n12; first wave of, 123; and garden manuals, 75; and humanism, 120, 289n5; and pluralism, 215; second wave of, 123; and spatial metaphors, 123; and wilderness, 272n11

fences: and cottage gardens, 32; in disrepair, 90, 106–7; and ha-ha fence, 43, 278n19; hedgerows, 60; "Mrs. Traill's fence," 57, 60; of osiers, 35; and pioneer gardens, 55, 278n20; of pumpkins, 90–1; snake fences, 50, 111; as spatial frame, 90–1, 283n15; 284n16; of spike nails, 283n15; of split-rails, 38, 50, 57; of stone, 56; wattled fence, 57

Finlay, Mary Lou, 214

first nature, 10, 12, 16, 271n9; and

C. Shields, 177–8; and feminism, 272n11; and M. Atwood, 104; and S. Moodie and C.P. Traill, 31. *See also* wilderness

FitzGibbon, Mary Agnes, 62–3, 75, 280n1

Fleming, Laurence, 278n19

flower gardening, 6; and backwoods kitchen gardens, 38, 42, 44–5, 49, 51, 60, 278n20; and Canadian wild flowers, 34, 69, 154, 277n15; and English cottage gardens, 32–3, 36, 62, 71, 73–4, 126, 136, 276nn12–14, 279n22; and English landscape parks, 28, 274n6; and Flora, 76; and G. Roy's flower garden, 149–50; and *hortus conclusus*, 289n4; and male gardeners, 159, 290n8; and M. Atwood, 103; and nineteenth-century femininity, 68–70; as symbolic of women's virtue, 48, 70; as women's work, 29, 35, 66, 89, 119, 124–5, 132, 152–3, 162, 199–200, 214

Foster, Clarise, 217–18

four stages theory of settlement, 38–9

Fowler, Marian, 27–8, 60, 83, 113, 282n11

Francis, Mark, and Randolph T.

Hester, 11, 18

Friedan, Betty, 21, 123, 175, 294nn3–4

Frye, Northrop, 3–4, 263, 269n1, 276n11; *The Bush Garden,* 3; and the garrison mentality, 26, 28, 30, 177, 184, 242; influence of, 4, 27, 61; and *Literary History of Canada,* 269n1

gardens: and American literature, 5, 75, 276n10, 280n4; as art of milieu, 11, 37, 44–5, 113–14, 242, 265; as boundary, 12, 18, 57, 60, 179; and the bush garden archetype, 3–4, 6, 26, 61, 177–8, 276n11; and Canadian literature, 3–6, 14, 16, 18, 172, 263–4, 269n2, 270nn3–4; domestic, 6–7, 18, 21, 40, 263; and material nature, 12–13, 15, 19; as mimetic art, 11; as miniature models, 11, 179; and relationship with writing, 7–8, 12–15; as rhetorical landscape, 8–9, 270n6; text-as-garden, 14–15, 220–1, 236–7; as theatre, 197–8; and translation, 37; as woman, 9, 17–18, 271n7. *See also* third nature

garden rhetoric. *See* horticultural terms (figurative)

garden tools: box, 52, 177–8, 185, 187, 296n10; gloves, 65, 221–2; hand-sleigh, 68; hoe, 50, 68, 111, 221–2; Indian basket, 68; Indian rubber shoes, 21; kitchen utensils, 71; lady's spade, 65; lever, 56; newspaper cones, 159; plastic ribbons, 222; poison, 222; rubbers, 254; tramp, 65; tree-stump trellis, 55; trowel, 63; trug, 207–8; wardian case, 68–9; wire, 94

garrison mentality, the. *See under* Frye, N.

Genette, Gérard, 242–3, 254–5, 303n12

geraniums: and G. Roy, 124, 153; and S. Ross, 248; slips of, 52

Giardini, Anne, 211, 298n13

Gilbert, Sandra M., and Susan Gubar, 304n13

Giles, Judy, 296n10

Gilman, Charlotte Perkins, 304n13

Gingell, Susan, 216, 301n2

Glickman, Susan, 27, 30, 273n3, 274n5, 275n9

Goertz, Dee, 295n7

Gom, Leona, 191, 195–6, 199, 201, 298n14

Grace, Sherrill, 104–5, 286n24, 287n25

Graeber, Laurel, 190

grass: in backwoods gardens, 35, 45; in box gardens of C. Shields, 177–9, 185, 187; in English landscape gardens, 32; from grave of A. Strickland, 51, 53; Indian grass and C.P. Traill, 45, 69; sweet grass and L. Crozier, 256; and W. Whitman, 185–6. *See also* lawn

Great Depression, the, 247, 257

Groening, Laura, 212

Grosskurth, Phyllis, 120, 289n3

grottos: and C.P. Traill, 71; at Twickenham garden of A. Pope, 270n6

Guttman, Naomi Ellen, 200, 206, 298n14, 299n17

Hall, Barb, 239–41, 303n9, 303n11

Hall, Susan Grove, 298n15

Hammill, Faye, 177, 285n20, 295nn6–7

Hapgood, Lynne, 296n10

Harris, Dianne, 6–7, 17, 75, 263, 266, 280n4

Harvey, Carol J., 118–19, 290n7

Hayden, Dolores, 272n12, 297n11

Heath, Caroline, 234

Henighan, Stephen, 298n13

herbs, 74; in backwoods kitchen gardens, 39–40; in Century

Cottage garden, 136; in English cottage gardens, 29, 36; in Reydon Hall garden, 33

Hillis, Doris, 242, 305n19

Hobbs, Catherine, 299n18

Holmes, Michael, 244

Horace: *Ars Poetica*, 8

horticultural terms (figurative), 16, 63–4; bloom, 81, 129, 236–7, 256; budding, 195, 225, 251, 256; compost, 139; cultivated, 13, 19, 65–6, 68–71, 75–8, 99–100, 117, 225, 235, 264, 275n9, 281n9; digging, 63; exotic, 80; flower, 70, 81, 119; forcing-bed (hot-bed), 73–4, 82; gourd, 261; grafting, 184, 303n12; growth, 84; hardening-off, 78–82, 89; naturalize, 34, 74–5, 125, 197; pervert, 249–50, 255, 257, 259, 266; rooted, 27, 61, 110, 138, 248, 262; scion, 284n17; seedlings, 250–1; seeds, 3, 61, 73, 91–4, 154–5, 219, 247, 257, 261; transplanting, 4–5, 19, 78–82, 139, 270n3; turning, 237; uproot, 139, 174; wither, 80–1, 139. *See also* plot; weeds

horticultural terms (literal): bower, 77, 126; brustian, 250; composting, 41; cultivate, 30, 56; digging, 27, 42, 65; exotics, 34; forcing bed (hot-bed), 41, 78, 277n18, 280n3, 284n16; graft, 279n21, 303n12; hardening-off, 78; naturalize, 34; parterre, 35; plot, 15; root-house, 33; scion, 303n12; seedlings, 33, 44; transplanting, 33, 44, 56–7, 60, 78–9; vert, 249. *See also* seeds; weeds

*hortus conclusus*, 127, 129, 173, 289n4

Humphreys, Helen, 267

Hunt, John Dixon: on garden as art of milieu, 37, 45; on garden as theatre, 197, 199–200; on gardening and writing, 7–8, 15, 217, 235, 272n12; on L. "Capability" Brown, 274n6; on theory of three natures, 9–12, 40, 271n8, 271n9, 272n11

Hyde Park: and G. Roy, 166; photograph of workers digging trenches, 167

Hyland, Tara, 302n7

Jackson, Rosemary, 234–5

Johnson, Chris, 197, 298n16

Johnson, Lisa, 197; 298n14; 299n20

Johnston, Susan, 26, 98

Jones, D.G., 5

Keefer, Janice Kulyk, 215

Klein, A.M.: "Portrait of the Poet as Landscape," 270n3

Klinck, Carl F., 287n27

Knight, Richard Payne, 29, 275n8

Kolodny, Annette, 5, 276n10

Kroetsch, Robert: on border-crossings, 93–4, 96, 113, 285n18, 302n7; and bower genre, 120, 131; on C.P. Traill, 13, 91, 93, 95–7, 265; on environment, 95, 238; on naming, 5–6, 184, 240; and palimpsestic objects, 94–5, 238; on paradise myth in Canadian literature, 5–6, 184; and pioneer garden palimpsest, 20, 114, 131, 241–2, 265; and post-colonialism, 94, 96, 242; on S. Ross, 245, 248; on unnaming, 96, 285n18

Kroetsch, Robert, works of: "Disunity as Unity," 245; "The Fear of Women in Prairie Fiction," 248; "No Name Is My Name," 5–6, 184; "Pumpkin: A Love Poem," 91–7, 129, 131; *Seed Catalogue*, 285n19

Kröller Eva-Marie, 285n20

Labbe, Jacquelline M., 70, 280n2

Lane, Patrick: and *Canadian Gardening* magazine, 214; on garden as poem, 220–1; as

mock orange shrub: and C. Shields, 188

Montgomery, L.M., 267

Montreuil, Sophie, 158–9, 292n16

Moodie, John, 23, 60, 82, 106–7, 111–13, 280n1; and farming, 110

Moodie, Susanna: and backwoods kitchen gardens, 37–9, 41, 49–50, 60–1, 276n11; on dandelions, 56–8; and English cottage gardens, 29, 31–2, 276n13; and English landscape aesthetics, 27, 273n3, 275n9; and floral painting, 29, 57–8, 69; and flower gardening, 29, 45–7; and gardening as education, 73; and gardens as material palimpsests, 24–5, 31, 61; and garden plots in backwoods, 19–20, 86–7, 89, 97–114, 264; and garden plots in England, 87–8, 283n15, 284nn16–17; and garden rhetoric, 63–4, 70, 80–2, *see also* horticultural terms (figurative); on gardening as writing, 63–6, 86–9; gendered responses to wilderness of, 30–1, 276n10; and manual labour, 50, 110–11; and M. Atwood, 25–6, 54, 61, 95, 102–5; and N. Frye, 26–7; and vegetable gardening, 31, 49–51; and women

pioneers, 83–5, 113

Moodie, Susanna, works of: "The Fire," 100–3; *Flora Lyndsay*, 76–7, 88, 284nn16-17; 287n26; *Letters of Love and Duty*, 23; *Life in the Clearings versus the Bush*, 73-4; "The Little Stumpy Man," 100, 105–13; *Matrimonial Speculations*, 88, 283n15, 284n17; "The Miss Greens," 88, 283n15, 284n16; "Rachel Wilde," 71, 73; *Roughing It in the Bush*, 26, 41, 49–50; 56, 65, 68–70, 80–3, 97–103, 105–13, 198, 281n8; *Susanna Moodie: Letters of a Lifetime*, 29; *Voyages: Short Narratives of Susanna Moodie*, 73

Moore, Charles W., 8

Mootoo, Shani, 266

Moss, John, 4

Murray, Heather, 30–1

naming: and botany, 86, 277n15; and Canadian literature, 5–6, 184, 270n3, 302n6; of C.P. Traill's garden fence, 60; of female characters after flowers, 69, 76, 195, 209–10; of female desire by L. Crozier, 228–9; of female vegetables, 227; of L. "Capability" Brown, 274n6; of the *Laurel* ship

by C.P. Traill, 280n5; of male
characters in terms of nature,
106, 113, 176, 183–4, 188, 205; of M.
Atwood as author of *The Journals
of Susanna Moodie*, 245–6; of
Mrs Bentley by L. Crozier, 95,
244–6, 251; of pioneer settlements,
60, 276n14; as recording
women's lives, 160–1, 171, 245;
and R. Kroetsch, 5–6, 285n18;
of suburban neighbourhoods,
296n10; of S. Moodie by M.
Atwood, 95; of "Yams" by SATCO
dramatic production, 240. *See
also* unnaming

Neuman, Shirley, 233

New, W.H., 269n2, 273n3

O'Malley, Andrew, 78

Ostriker, Alicia, 255

palimpsest, 24–6, 303n12; as
landscape, 19, 24–5, 27, 31, 38–9,
44, 51, 54–6, 60–1, 84, 264–5; and
L. Melhorn-Boe, 237–8; literary
theories of, 242–3, 303n12, 304n13;
and L. Crozier, 21, 241–2, 244–6,
249–62, 264–6, 305n20; and M.
Atwood, 20, 25–6, 54, 61, 95, 98,
102–5, 114, 241–2, 244–6, 265,

282n11, 285n20, 287n25; and M.
Laurence, 54, 285n20; as material
object, 26, 94–5, 238–9, 285n19;
pioneer garden palimpsests,
20–1, 91, 95, 241–2, 265; and R.
Kroetsch, 13, 20, 91–7, 103, 114, 131,
240–2, 265; and SATCO dramatic
production, 239–41

pansies: and C. Shields, 208–9;
floral lexicon, 208

paradise, 173, 294n2; and Adam
figure in Canadian literature, 5–6,
176, 178, 183–8, 190, 214, 270n3; as
archetype of new world, 4–5, 172,
268n2, 270n3, 270n4; as bower,
129, 131; and C. Shields, 174–6,
178–9, 185, 187–90, 192–6, 200–2,
204–6, 209–11; as communal
settlement, 184, 297n11; domestic,
172–3, 184, 188, 190, 193–4; Eden,
172–4, 294n2, 302n6; and Eve
figure in Canadian literature, 5–6,
129, 174, 183–4, 190, 193–5, 214, 230,
302n6; and G. Roy, 142, 165–6; and
L. Crozier, 221–2, 230; as myth,
20, 172–4, 178, 183, 187–8, 212, 264;
as suburbia, 180–2, 196, 296n10.
*See also* Milton, J.

Parker, Patricia, 128

peas: and backwoods kitchen

influence on L. Crozier, 242, 262, 304n14; Mrs Bentley's garden, 247–8, 251; and palimpsest, 252–4; R. Kroetsch on Mrs Bentley, 248; and use of diary genre, 245

Ross, Stephanie, 13, 270nn5–6

Rouslin, Virginia Watson, 83–4, 281n10

Roy, Gabrielle: biography, 117, 133, 148–9, 151, 291n13; and bower as boudoir, 146–8; and Century Cottage (Upshire bower), 126–7, 132–4, 136–7, 141, 145–9, 163–5; on domestic work as artistry, 157–8, 291n15, 293n20; and domestication of bower, 125, 131–2, 137–8, 146–9, 151; early travels of, 117, 133–6, 138–9, 144–5; and fairytales, 136–7, 152–3; and female artists, 117, 120, 122–5, 131–2, 138, 146–9, 152–4; on female artists as maternal figures, 120, 155–9, 161–5, 291n15, 293nn19–20; and female muse, 146–7, 156–7, 160; and feminism, 120–1, 289nn5–6; on flower gardening, 124–5, 152–3, 290n8; on gardens and children, 118–19, 122, 290n7; on gardens and convent, 289n4; on garden of grandmother in Manitoba, 164–5, 169; and garden at Petite-Rivière-Saint-François, 148–51; and garden on Rue Dèschambault, 139–40; and gender politics of space, 117–20, 122–4, 127, 146, 288n2; 289n3; and heritage of exile, 115–16, 138–9, 153–5, 161, 164; on Hyde Park, 166; journalism career of, 121, 139, 152, 168; on male artists and journeys, 141–4, 163, 291n12; and male gardeners, 159–60, 290n8; and marriage plot, 120; and Montreal, 118, 141, 167–8; and narrator and framing technique, 161–2; and naturalization of the female artist, 125; and the north, 119, 143, 151, 291n12; and pastoral tradition, 121–2; pre-texts for "Garden in the Wind," 158–9, 291n13, 292n16; on public gardens and squares, 133, 135, 143–5; and relationship with mother, 163–4, 168; and Second World War, 166; and theatre, 133, 144–6; translations of her works, 161, 291n14, 292n17, 293n18

Roy, Gabrielle, works of: *The Cashier*, 118, 141–3, 288n2; *La détresse et l'enchantement*, 139–41, 168; *Enchantment and Sorrow*, 20, 116, 124, 126–7, 131–9, 144–9,

plots in England, 88, 283n14; garden rhetoric of, 63–4, *see also* horticultural terms (figurative); on gardening and feminine roles, 74, 77; on gardening and imperialism, 35, 39, 43, 45; on gardening as leisure, 41–2; on gardening pragmatics, 39–40; on gardening as writing, 62–3; gendered responses to pioneer landscapes, 30–1, 276n10; on ha-ha fence, 43; and herb-gardening, 39–40; on horticultural magazines, 23–4, 43; on Indian rice, 43; on manual labour, 42, 49, 81, 89; and models of female pioneers, 83–5, 281nn9–10, 282n11; on native Canadian plants, 34, 45; and N. Frye, 26–7; Reydon Hall, 32–3, 36, 279n22; on seed imports, 40, 43, 277n16; on seeds as payment, 24; on seed and plant exchanges, 51–3, 279n21; on trade with Chippewa Natives, 40–1; translation of gardening traditions, 37–8, 42–3, 55, 60–1; vegetables, 35, 38–40, 41–2, 279n21; weeds, 55

Traill, Catharine Parr, works of: *The Backwoods of Canada*, 34, 43–4, 54–5, 57, 86, 280n5; *Canadian Crusoes*, 77–8; *The Canadian Settler's Guide*, 23, 39–45, 48–50, 55–7, 60, 75, 78–9, 84, 89–91, 95, 106, 273nn1–2, 278n20, 279n23; *The Canadian Settler's Guide Revisions*, 44, 273n2, 279n23; *Cot and Cradle Stories*, 62, 88, 279n22, 280n1; *The Female Emigrant's Guide*, 273n1; "Female Trials in the Bush," 79–81; *Forest and Other Gleanings*, 40, 277n17; *I Bless You in My Heart: Selected Correspondence of Catharine Parr Traill*, 24, 279n21; *Little Downy*, 70–2; *Narratives of Nature*, 33–4, 71; *Pearls and Pebbles*, 71, 280n1; *Sketches from Nature*, 32–3; *Studies of Plant Life in Canada*, 45, 277n15; *The Young Emigrants*, 35–6

Traill, Thomas, 51, 60; and gardening, 42

Traill, William, 24, 53, 279n21

tree stumps, 55, 279n23; and relationship to "Little Stumpy Man," 106–7

Turnbull, William, 8

Turner, Roger, 278n19

Tymieniecka, Anna-Teresa, 15

Uher, Lorna (L. Crozier), 301n3

unnaming: and Canadian literature, 96; of C.P. Traill by R. Kroetsch, 91, 94–6, 105, 240; of Daisy as Mrs Green Thumb, 299n20; and R. Kroetsch, 96, 285n18; of S. Ross as author, 245. *See also* naming

von Baeyer, Edwinna, 8–9
Vroom, Meto J., 24–5

Wachtel, Eleanor, 294n3, 294n5,
Walker, Susan, 224
Walpole, Horace, 8–9, 270n5, 278n19
Wasmeier, Marie-Louise, 196, 298n14
Waterman, Catharine H., 188
Waters, Michael, 74
Webb, Phyllis: "Marvell's Garden," 130–1
weeds, 41, 54, 77, 204;  C.P. Traill's watercolour of, 59; as plant category, 55–7, 188; as symbol of moral corruption, 284n17; and weeding, 33, 49, 54, 65–6, 214, 222, 290n8; women as weeds, 70
Whitfield, Agnes, 121–3, 137, 289n6
Whitlock, Gillian, 97
Whitman, Walt: *Leaves of Grass*, 185–6
wilderness, 271n9; and Canadian

thematic criticism, 3–4, 16, 20, 26, 172, 177–8, 263, 295n7; domestication of, 27–8, 35, 39; and female pioneers, 30–1, 276n10; and feminism, 272n11; as inspiration for male artists, 141, 143, 145, 291n12; as paradise, 269n2; as prairie, 241–2; in relationship to gardens, 12, 27, 61, 104–5. *See also* Atwood, M.; first nature
Williamson, Dave, 190, 297n12
women: domestic roles of, 21, 31, 74, 79–80, 83–4, 117, 125, 175, 198–200, 214, 229, 272n12; as nature, 9, 17–18, 30, 68, 255, 271n7, 272n1;
Woodhead, Eileen, 7
Woolf, Virginia, 123
Wordsworth, Dorothy, 28–9, 66, 68
Wordsworth, William: "Nutting," 129

Ying, Kong, 170, 176